Fiona Kidman has written more than 20 books, mainly novels and short story collections. Her novel *The Book of Secrets* won the Fiction category of the New Zealand Book Awards, and several others — including her most recent novel *The Captive Wife* — have been short-listed. She has been awarded a number of prizes and fellowships, including the Mobil Short Story Award, the Victoria Writers Fellowship, and the OBE for services to literature. She is a Dame Commander of the New Zealand Order of Merit. Fiona Kidman lives in Wellington.

THE BEST NEW ZEALAND FICTION

VOLUME 3

EDITED BY
FIONA KIDMAN

VINTAGE

A catalogue record for this book is available from the National Library of New Zealand.

A VINTAGE BOOK
published by
Random House New Zealand
18 Poland Road, Glenfield, Auckland, New Zealand
www.randomhouse.co.nz

First published 2006

Introduction and this selection © 2006 Fiona Kidman
For copyright details of individual stories see page 7

The moral rights of the author have been asserted

ISBN-10: 1 86941 797 6
ISBN-13: 978 1 86941 797 0

Text design: Katy Yiakmis
Cover design: Dexter Fry
Cover photograph: PhotoNewZealand.com/Andy Reisinger
Printed in Australia by Griffin Press

'Stories Bodies Tell' © 2006 Maxine Alterio

'Three Stories' © 2005 Geoff Cochrane

'Conan' © 2006 Siân Daly

'The Weakness of Women' © 2006 Sue Emms

'Surface Tension' © 2006 Tracy Farr

'Figures in Ice' © 2006 James George

'Thin Earth' © 2006 Charlotte Grimshaw

'The Thing that Distresses Me the Most' © 2006 Lloyd Jones

'Patrick and the Killer' © 2006 Owen Marshall

'Disconnections' © 2006 Sue McCauley

'Rocking Horse Road' © 2006 Carl Nixon

'Mrs Bennett and the Bears' © 2006 Vincent O'Sullivan

'The Sheep, the Shepherd' © 2006 Jo Randerson

'Julia' © 2006 Tina Shaw

'Something Will Change' © 2006 Alice Tawhai

'Exit, Pursued by Taxman or Shakespeare's *Winter's Tale* Brought up to Date'
    © 2005 Fay Weldon; this version © 2006 Fay Weldon

'Little Joker Sings' © 2006 Peter Wells

'Available Light' © 2006 Jane Westaway

'Lolly' © 2005 Susan Wylie; this version © 2006 Susan Wylie

'Always Marry Up' © 2006 Spiro Zavos

Contents

Acknowledgements		11
Introduction	Fiona Kidman	13
Stories Bodies Tell	Maxine Alterio	21
Three Stories	Geoff Cochrane	31
Conan	Siân Daly	46
The Weakness of Women	Sue Emms	54
Surface Tension	Tracy Farr	66
Figures in Ice	James George	78
Thin Earth	Charlotte Grimshaw	92
The Thing that Distresses Me the Most	Lloyd Jones	102
Disconnections	Sue McCauley	108
Patrick and the Killer	Owen Marshall	116
Rocking Horse Road	Carl Nixon	125
Mrs Bennett and the Bears	Vincent O'Sullivan	149
The Sheep, the Shepherd	Jo Randerson	155

Julia	TINA SHAW	162
Something Will Change	ALICE TAWHAI	169
Exit, Pursued by Taxman or Shakespeare's *Winter's Tale* Brought up to Date	FAY WELDON	175
Little Joker Sings	PETER WELLS	183
Available Light	JANE WESTAWAY	194
Lolly	SUSAN WYLIE	205
Always Marry Up	SPIRO ZAVOS	216
Notes on Contributors		227

ACKNOWLEDGEMENTS

The stories listed below were first published or broadcast as follows:

'3 Stories' by GEOFF COCHRANE — *Sport 33*, Summer 2005.

'Rocking Horse Road' by CARL NIXON — *The Christchurch Press*, January 2006.

'Exit, Pursued by Taxman' (an earlier version) by FAY WELDON — BBC Radio 3, December 2005.

'Lolly' (an earlier version) by SUSAN WYLIE — www.bankofnewzealand.co.nz, 2005; *Hawkes Bay Today*, 2005.

Fiona Kidman

Introduction

SOMETHING WILL CHANGE. SOMETHING WILL *change*. That is the title of a story in this collection, by a writer called Alice Tawhai, who arrived in what we half-mockingly refer to as 'NZ lit' with the least fanfare of any writer since Janet Frame. I don't know anything about Tawhai and it doesn't matter. What I do know is that when her first book, *Festival of Miracles*, was published a year or so ago, some signals were already up. Something was changing in the way short stories are written in this country; first time around, Tawhai skilfully captured these elements, at the same time making a stand for the craft itself, rather than for grand-standing.

Her way of juxtaposing images reminds us that things are rarely as they seem, that there are seismic shifts between our expectations and what might loosely be called reality happening all the time. She begins her story by introducing a man of dark complexion called Snow, who has acquired his name by virtue of trying out, and being rejected, for the part of the Milky Bar Kid in a television advertisement when he was a child. So very New Zealand, yet it could happen in any multi-ethnic country: that's to say, pretty well anywhere in the world. I like the way dark (very dark) and light, a current of wry humour and a sense of displacement move alongside each other. What and who might be about to change is anyone's guess.

This quality of the unexpected, grounded in everyday life, runs through much of the third volume of *The Best New Zealand Fiction*. It's not so much a difference of form itself, or the shape of a story — although there are one or two exceptions here, such as Geoff Cochrane's 'Three Stories' — but a more charged awareness than in the past: an awareness of how the world operates and how people (characters) respond. The stories are neither blindingly obvious, nor so desperate to avoid the label of 'realist' that they obscure meaning; rather they have the subtle ring of truth about them, a kind of modern street wariness. I see these qualities particularly in Tracy Farr's luminous portrayal of two lovers' reunion, 'Surface Tension'; Lloyd Jones' unsettling domestic 'incident', 'The Thing that Distresses Me the Most' (perhaps the best story he has ever written); Charlotte Grimshaw's spine-tingling 'Thin Earth'; and Tina Shaw's moody, murderous story, 'Julia', with its intelligent referencing to Greek myth.

I began this series with Random House three years ago out of a personal and idiosyncratic need of my own. I read a great deal of short fiction and, during the past decade or so, have observed a world trend to the return of narrative storytelling as high art, rather than works that depended on visual and linguistic pyrotechnics to attract attention.

What I often found myself missing in New Zealand anthologies were stories as illuminating and generous about people's lives as novels, yet contained in the space of a single read. Many of the stories, with a few notable exceptions, such as in the work of writers like Owen Marshall, Barbara Anderson, Lloyd Jones or Vincent O'Sullivan, seemed locked into a format that demanded a single emotion, a single incident, and a shock or a crisis as its resolution. Much the way I began teaching short stories in creative writing classes thirty years ago; almost always the way they are written for local competitions (although it's welcome news indeed that the major Bank of New Zealand Katherine Mansfield Awards for short stories have altered their boundaries this year to admit longer and more adventurous stories).

I am interested in the notion of actuality disconnected from reality, of recasting life as a story, which is not the same thing as 'realism', so called. It's worth looking towards contemporary cinema, which shares many of the dilemmas of modern fiction. The ever-present desire to create something new sits uneasily alongside the necessity to maintain an audience. There is a particular resonance in the fact that, even now, cinema often depends on stories and novels to adapt for production. Where, for instance, would the makers of the New Zealand film *Whale Rider* have been without Witi Ihimaera's novel to draw upon? Or Maurice Gee's novel *In My Father's Den,* which was the founding text for the spectacularly successful film of the same name? Not to mention, further afield, Ang Lee's rendition of Annie Proulx's 'Brokeback Mountain' — although it is fascinating to observe Peter Wells' counterpoint story, and effective repudiation of 'Brokeback Mountain', in 'Little Joker Sings', a story collected in this anthology. In a new study of modern movie-making, writer David Bordwell maintains that narrative film is not dead, however many special effects, video-digital manipulations and short shot angles are employed.[1] Our 'realities' are altered, even in the retelling of the same story, as you will see if you watch modern remakes of old movies, but the semblance of narrative cohesion remains.

Amongst fiction writers, the Canadian Alice Munro springs to mind as an example of how familiar techniques have been skilfully manipulated to create a new take on the short story form. There can be few serious writers of short narrative fiction in the English language who have not been influenced over the past twenty or so years by the subtle complexities of her work. She has been taken up with admiration by Michael Chabon, Jonathan Franzen and a host of other young and international writers, not to mention local writers such as Marshall (or myself, for that matter), who concede a debt to her. Munro, whose own acknowledged literary debt is to Chekhov, has developed a form of layered storytelling that does not have boundaries in length. Her stories frequently 'turn out to be about something quite different from what [they] set out to discuss', as A. S. Byatt commented in a recent summary of Munro's oeuvre in the *Guardian*.[2] Or, as Harriet Allan, my publisher at Vintage, remarked to me recently, it's as if the pendulum has swung away from us believing all the things the media presents as 'true', towards an understanding that, even in sound bites, we need to know what lies behind the story. So too with fiction.

I am not suggesting for one moment that every New Zealand writer should write like Munro, or even aspire to; I am merely saying that it should be possible not only to write outside the formal conventions of what we once considered the well-made short story, but to be published in them.

When Allan agreed to publish the first volume of *The Best New Zealand Fiction* we had little idea of its chances. But she took a risk with my suggestions of a roughly equal mix of known and relatively unknown writers and the book was an instant success, quickly running into reprint.

The next year *Volume 2* ran out even faster. Some names reappeared, because the writers were simply putting out their best work on an annual basis (O'Sullivan will have appeared in all three); others are making a reappearance now in *Volume 3*. But there are also several names the general reader won't have heard of, such as Siân Daly, author of the grave and beautiful 'Conan'. I heard Daly read at a lunchtime programme organised by the International Institute of Modern Letters (IIML) in the winter of 2005, when she was still a student, and knew that I would want her work for this collection. I am grateful that she agreed. I have a feeling she will continue to be published but I'm not a clairvoyant. The thing is, we are now producing, each year, a relatively inexpensive book with a cheerful format that is for the here and now, and good writers have the opportunity to appear as often as they can produce the goods. So there is a kind of disposable quality about the notion of 'best'; some writers survive it, others may not. But it's perhaps worth mentioning here that Katie Henderson, who had had little prior publication when she appeared in *Volume 1*, has just won one of the world's most prestigious short story prizes, Ireland's Fish International Short Story Prize for 2006.

This brings me to a bone of contention that has been gnawed in one or two critical forums — what about the terrific writers who don't appear? Is it possible, for instance, to claim that these collections offer 'the best' without, say, Barbara Anderson? Well, I would love to have published her, and several other writers, but much depends on availability in any given year.

In case you are new to these collections of *The Best New Zealand Fiction*, here are our 'rules' again: we publish recent work, either complete fictions or extracts from work in progress, that has not appeared previously in book form, although it may have appeared in newspapers and periodicals, and we ask for stories that have a minimum length of 3000 words. We are absolutely committed to the first 'rule'. Although we toyed with the idea of dropping it once or twice, we decided that it must stand, or the floodgates would be open for a different kind of collection. We are a bit more relaxed about the word count, if we receive something wonderful, something clearly 'the best' — but not often. So, for one reason or another, we don't always get what we want, but with luck there will be more years ahead to capture the ones that have eluded us so far.

In the past two years we have published the work of visiting French writers to the Randell Cottage in Wellington, in order to see how living in New Zealand influenced the work of people from the 'outside'. This year I decided, instead, to actively seek out the work of some writers who were New Zealanders by birth or upbringing but who no longer live here. In my present existence I am particularly interested in the idea of writing from afar. This Introduction is being written in Menton, in the south of France, Katherine Mansfield territory, where I am the current Meridian Energy Katherine Mansfield Fellow. It is an odd sensation, writing of home from a great distance. For the moment, although I call this place home, when I write about New Zealand I am transported as surely as if I were clearing old man's beard from the boundaries of my section in Wellington: I am at once displaced from, and grounded in, the place I *believe* in as home.

I cast the net widely in my search for overseas writers, while aware that it was still merely a handful of those now working abroad, and in the knowledge that more poets live abroad than fiction writers. But two delivered — Fay Weldon, who came here to live as a child and spent some years in Christchurch (where she and her sister were famously painted by Rita Angus, as the Birkenshaw sisters); and one of New Zealand's most admired sports writers, Spiro Zavos, who lives in

Australia. Zavos wrote short stories earlier in his career, and is returning to the form. His first collection, *Faith of Our Fathers*, about growing up Greek in Wellington, won major prizes overseas; in 'Always Marry Up', an extract from a work in progress, he returns to this territory.

Weldon, an international literary icon, has long lived in England. Her story 'Exit, Pursued by Taxman' has the interest of being the Shakespearian play *A Winter's Tale* reworked, so here it is, that retelling of a familiar story on another plane again. The BBC recently commissioned a group of writers to do updates of Shakespeare's plays for radio. Weldon says: 'Free of the dead hand of script editors, able to cite Shakespeare as their excuse, writers were able to write what was not politically correct or motivationally sound.' But if the outcome of 'Exit, Pursued by Taxman' seems unlikely in some respects, we buy into it not just because it is Shakespeare, but because Weldon, as always, skewers the unexpected in human relationships with deadly accuracy.

Several other writers are removed in their stories from New Zealand, or their characters are coming here (or should I say there?), or returning in some way or another. Jo Randerson, young, sharp and exploratory in her work, sets her story, 'The Sheep, the Shepherd', in an international airport (Charles de Gaulle, surely one of the most confusing on the planet), and this terrifying examination of lost identity in a huge world disturbed me as much as any story in the collection. It is also, and unusually, deeply questioning about the philosophical and moral value of life. Vincent O'Sullivan's 'Mrs Bennett and the Bears' explores with an icy beauty the fleeting possibilities of love in an encounter in Japan; Susan Wylie's story 'Lolly', which won the Bank of New Zealand Katherine Mansfield Premier Award in 2005, follows an emigrant woman from her Polish home in war-torn Europe to life in New Zealand, Wylie's style drawing on beautifully wrought musical cadences; Peter Wells, in quite different vein in 'Little Joker Sings', follows the voyage, on a troop ship returning to New Zealand, of two men who have fallen in love during World War 2, and must now face the world as they left it. In a poignant aftermath he shifts to verse to explore the future. Another, and different, journey is followed by James George in 'Figures in Ice', which draws on a very contemporary theme of children spirited across borders, a story that also draws on musical references to enhance his text.

And, to return to Geoff Cochrane, his 'Three Stories' can be read as tiny stand-alone texts, which could be set anywhere, in the dark twilight zones of alcoholism and delusion, but read to me like one continuous narrative of displacement. There is a kind of schizophrenic quality about the characters in the stories, so that the reader is never certain whether they are reading about one or several people. Interviewed by Damien Wilkins for the literary journal *Sport* (in a piece worthy of the best *Paris Review* interviews), Cochrane says he finds himself 'constitutionally incapable of taking New Zealand literature seriously'.[3] Perhaps that is why his presence seems at home in this collection: he allows himself to do his best work without seeking out a 'position'. In introducing the interview, Wilkins remarks that Cochrane's 'continuing obscurity' is 'something like a cruel and stupid joke'. But I can't help wondering whether 'obscurity', real or not, hasn't been quietly relished in relation to the work. When approached for permission, Cochrane declared himself 'sanguine' about inclusion in this collection of 'the best'.

Death and old age rear their heads often in this collection. They are preoccupying themes, not just for those who are ageing, but for those who have responsibilities towards the aged and incapacitated. Sue McCauley's account of an old woman facing the insistence of her family that she enter residential care is tenderly and minutely drawn in 'Disconnections'. The act of doing up buttons becomes a metaphor that creates almost woundingly intense reminders of how our bodies break down at the moments when we most want them to co-operate.

Old age is just one of the considerations of a middle-aged woman going about her daily life in Sue Emms' 'The Weakness of Women'; if only men could see what we see, the story suggests. How ordinary and dull we seem from the outside — but just look in the places hidden from view, and be prepared for surprise. Maxine Alterio's 'Stories Bodies Tell' contemplates the aftermath of sudden death, but it's also a love story and, yet again, a story of such meticulously drawn forensic evidence it could take its place alongside that of top crime writers. Carl Nixon's 'Rocking Horse Road' is at once a richly intricate crime story, in the best sense of the genre, and a coming-of-age story. It is by far the longest story in the collection, and this is thanks to the editors of *The Christchurch Press*, who appear interested in promoting the same expansive opportunities as this volume offers, in their annual serial stories run over the Christmas season (last year we reprinted Annamarie Jagose's 'At Waimama Bay' from the same source). Although Nixon's work has been credited with some of the qualities and influences of storytelling master Owen Marshall, it's by way of coincidence that Marshall and he have both dealt with sudden violent death in the stories included here, and they are not at all alike. Marshall's story, 'Patrick and the Killer', looks at the lasting impact on a person who is witness to violence, a fierce examination of how extraordinary events can be taken and reshaped by the media, and the effect on individuals caught up in the issues.

It is alphabetical coincidence that lands Jane Westaway's name so close to that of Weldon, yet the two share some preoccupations. Westaway's novel extract, 'Available Light', is another comic take on desperate love. Being rejected in love is never funny when it happens, but in hindsight it can offer plenty of opportunities for wry mockery at the messes we can land ourselves in. Nor is it without resonance alongside the work of Emms and Farr, or, for that matter, Grimshaw, in her more domestic and always dazzlingly conceived moments.

Three volumes of *The Best New Zealand Fiction*: sixty stories, thirty-one by women, twenty-nine by men, over fifty contributors in all, one editor. Next year a new editor will decide what's best. I am not at all modest about these collections: they are brilliant. The writers ensure that they are, but the editor gets all the fun — and the grief, too — of selecting from such rich sources. Something has changed.

Fiona Kidman
Menton, 2006

[1] David Bordwell, *The Way Hollywood Tells It: Story and Style in Modern Movies*, University of California Press, 2006
[2] A. S. Byatt, 'Everything is Illuminated', *Guardian*, 4 April 2006
[3] *Sport 31*, November 2003

Maxine Alterio

Stories Bodies Tell

THERE IS A PLACE IN Central Otago where a fit day-walker with sturdy boots can skirt a water pipe, scramble over schist ledges, climb through a beech forest that years ago put down its roots halfway up a mountain, and tramp through tufts of golden tussock grass until the highest point is reached, which, instead of a peak, is a plateau. Such a walker can then turn 360 degrees, see he is alone, and realise that no matter what befalls him on this day, no one will witness it. Yet neither fear nor loneliness overwhelms one particular walker. Something about the vast, empty landscape enables David to garner those nebulous thoughts, which generally ride in on the wings of dreams and leave before they can be transformed into something meaningful.

High above the gorge in which flows a splendid river that once deposited gold into the pans of miners and where Gina, his girlfriend of ten weeks, sunbathes on a bank, David remembers being ten and waiting at the family crib for his parents to return from a climb in the same area. Even his grandparents, cajoling him with draughts and backgammon, could not make him budge from the window seat. Nor could they persuade him to put his binoculars down and come to the dinner table. He'd felt nauseous, as though his stomach was a miniature version of the agitator that swirled clothes and water around in his grandmother's washing machine. What if his parents were lost? Made a wrong turn? David played out increasingly desperate scenarios while his grandfather paced up and down on the porch and his grandmother shuffled pots around the stove. Directly above the simmering vegetables, the wall clock ticked as loud and wild as a defective heart, and insects buzzed against the window screens, attracted by the light inside, their unruly shadows adding a menacing presence to the warm night air.

An hour later, while his grandparents spoke in hushed tones about whether or not to contact the authorities, David had spat into the palm of his right hand and silently promised that if his mum and dad came home he'd never again let them go away without him. He had squeezed his eyes shut and pictured their descent through snow tussock and pockets of loose scree. Then he imagined them following the river until it flowed below the crib, where they'd emerge near the ginger-tinted willows and run up the track towards him.

He'd felt like a hero when they appeared minutes later. His father swung him in the air and joked that he'd grown five millimetres since breakfast. Everyone laughed, breaking the tense atmosphere, giving the impression that the fear that had accumulated within them could now evaporate, freeing not just them, but the land on which the crib — their waiting place — stood. Drinks were hastily poured and dinner served. Sitting at the table between his parents, David felt a heady mix of relief and power, as if he alone had been responsible for their safe return, a state he longs to replicate.

The closest he gets to them these days is on this plateau where the horizon and land blur and memories string themselves like flags across the mountain peaks. He stares into the big empty space until his eyes hurt, then turns away and lies face down on the ground. The earth smells warm and fresh, like Gina. He digs his elbows in and rests both hands on his jaw. How will he tell her? Where will he start? He compares the contours of the land around him to those of her body. Two smooth hillocks become her breasts and her stomach is a stretch of flat, golden land, while two hip bones jut from a rocky outcrop that is also home to a clump of soft mountain grass. He wants to run his hands up her legs and feel invincible.

Had his father felt this way about his wife, David's mother, when they first met? David will never know. All he has are facts. His father was still a junior doctor, and his mother a newly qualified physiotherapist, when they joined the same tramping club. Later, they travelled together through Asia and South America, working in small isolated villages, only returning to New Zealand for David's birth. Both thought their only child would benefit from day care, so that was his fate, five days a week, until he started school. He has a photograph of himself dressed in a junior school uniform, holding his mother's hand, a worried look on his face as though he already knew she'd leave him.

In a box at the back of a wardrobe in his bedroom at home are several drawings from those early years. He wonders if his parents ever noticed that he always drew them in black crayon and standing together in a doorway. Did they not realise those drawings reflected his sense of abandonment? Another thing: had their voices really lifted when they talked about their work or travels and dropped when he was the topic of conversation, or was that something he imagined?

Regardless of whether it is an authentic memory or not, David still equates tonal quality with levels of personal importance, which adds to his difficulties with women. Every time a woman lowers her voice, he assumes she's uninterested, so he slinks off. David has initiated more departures than a star baseball pitcher. And even on those miraculous occasions when he was upfront about being an embalmer and got past first base, as soon as he stroked bare skin, the recipient would whisper, 'That hand's been on dead people, hasn't it?' or something similar, and remember an urgent appointment.

  David wants Gina to stay around, so as the midday sun beats down on his long, lanky frame, he practises how to explain what he does. 'I am to a dead body what a makeover artist is to a news reader.' No, too pretentious. 'I prepare the dead for their biggest adventure.' That makes me sound like a reality show presenter. 'I take care of the dead. The longer I work with them, the more they reveal.' Yes, this is what David will say to Gina. Perhaps he'll start by comparing landscapes and bodies, each with their own ravines and passes, peaks and plateaus, contours and concealments. If things go well, he might add, 'Gina, you won't believe the stories bodies tell.' If she stops what she's doing, goes still and looks him in the eye, he will describe his work. He considers what to include and what to leave out. It's not easy. He doesn't know how she'll react. Some people are squeamish. They don't like to think about death. But he has to tell her.

  He could go for a condensed version. Just describe aspects of the initial preparation, such as washing the cadaver (although he'll not use this clinical word), placing an absorbent cottonwool pad between their legs and suturing the mouth and eyes. Then he could move to the stage where he decides whether the tissue requires hydrating or dehydrating, or if a yellow tint — evidence of liver or kidney failure — needs removing with specialised ingredients. That bit might be okay since she's interested in skincare. He hopes she'll also understand why he pays careful attention to the photographs family members bring in. It's important to get the skin colour right and pick up on minor details such as hairstyle.

  But what will Gina think about him talking to the bodies, describing what he does and why, sometimes asking, 'Who loved the pilgrim soul in you?' — a line adapted from a poem by Yeats. And how will he explain his need to know about their lives? He runs sentences around his mind as though they are trains on a track and comes up with a possibility. 'Their stories wait just below the surface, Gina. All I do is pay attention.' Yes, that has a captivating ring. Perhaps he should describe what he noticed and imagined about the last person he worked on. She was a forty-nine-year-old who'd had an appendectomy as a child and in adulthood developed thinning hair, stretchmarks on her buttocks and thighs. She'd had a lumpectomy in the left breast, a mastectomy for the right, and unusually smooth palms. These were the facts, what any trained professional would note on a worksheet. But David was equally interested in her history. So, during the one and a half hours it took to complete the embalming process, he constructed a plausible version.

The practicalities of the actual procedure were straightforward. He made a small incision in the muscle of the neck, just above the collarbone, and injected around eight litres of chemicals into an artery. With the help of a machine that acted like a heartbeat, these preserving agents were pumped through the arterial system, replacing the blood. Substances in the cadaver's main organs were then sucked up by a 40cm-long rod with a hollow centre.

David's imagined history of the woman was not so clear cut. He couldn't decide if the forty-nine-year-old had acquired her tan during a trip to a Northern Queensland resort with her property developer husband or by sunbathing in her back yard, believing, to the end, that she could somehow burn the cancer out. The depth and variation of her stretchmarks suggested two children, while the timespan placed them at university. Maybe neither had been overly concerned when their mother had the lumpectomy. Perhaps she'd downplayed the significance, especially if it was close to exam time. Her weight loss could have gone unnoticed, too, or been attributed to a new fitness fad. Did they berate her later for not telling the whole story?

Now, high on the plateau, David pictures the woman rubbing her hands together in anguish during her teenagers' emotional outbursts, then, after their anger is expressed and they have returned to their own egotistical lives, squirting a generous dollop of expensive lotion into her palms and stoically preparing to face the surgeon's scalpel for a second time. Why else would they have been so smooth? Gina might be interested to hear how he selected and applied the makeup, ensuring a close resemblance to a photograph. The cadaver's slim torso and pleasant face gave the impression that despite dying in middle age from cancer, she had managed, until the end, to retain some of the physical traits associated with youth. Perhaps love was partly responsible — that and good genes.

Until recently David could only imagine a love life for himself. While he never daydreamed about the cadavers, the lively young nursing students who visited his workplace as part of their training often played a role. Something about their respect for the dead and the way they solemnly asked questions appealed to him. Secretly he hoped one might see beyond his professional self and wish to become acquainted with his personal side. So, at the end of each working day he stepped hopefully through the side door into the carpark. The absence of a well-endowed nurse — for this was the type he fancied — waiting among the azaleas that lined the path did not deflate him. He was confident she'd appear at some stage.

Gina, who was a vet nurse — close enough — came into his life under quite different circumstances. He was leaving a fast-food drive-in in his gleaming white Chrysler when a late-model Honda shot in the wrong entrance and got hooked to his chrome bumper. After various attempts failed to dislodge it, during which time David noticed the owner's voluptuous curves and stunning violet eyes, he'd shunted Gina and her car around the corner to her flat, where they shared his chickenburger, chips and Diet Coke. Since David couldn't drive home without taking Gina's Honda, he offered to sleep on her settee, but Gina invited him into her bed, hoping to ward off the onset of post-traumatic stress syndrome. 'That car is the only decent thing I own,' she said as he curved his unpractised frame around hers. 'Take my mind off the accident,' she whispered.

David succeeded in this respect, not once, but twice. Each time he marvelled at the warm, silky texture of Gina's skin and the perfect curvature of her spine. Afterwards, he counted her vertebrae as if they were rocky ledges he'd been the first to climb, although it was clear from their encounters that she was rather familiar with the male anatomy. Back then he was happy to be subservient, as he was in every aspect of his life, except work. But now, lying under this wide, blue sky, a warm breeze licking at his brown hair, he wants to change. And he wants to begin soon.

'Tell me about yourself,' Gina had said that first morning as a shaft of bright sunlight glinted in her eyes. Just for an instance they'd reminded David of the clear plastic shields he places over those of the deceased to give them a fuller appearance.

'I work in the health sector,' he'd said, which wasn't an outright lie, but nor was it the entire truth. Before he could think of a clever explanation, Gina had nestled her gorgeous buttocks against his groin, which necessitated physical, rather than linguistic, action.

Gina had been happy to wait back at the campsite while he climbed. 'Don't use up all your energy, though,' she'd said as he bent to kiss her, tasting more than the peach she'd just eaten. Something like a future had slid from him to her and back again. But before he can relax and enjoy their relationship, he needs to tell her what he does and he has to do it soon.

Directly above, a harrier hawk soars on a thermal current. David envies its ability to cover great expanses of sky without feeling the weight of human complications. Whenever he climbed with his parents, something he'd done ever since making that desperate promise at his grandparents' crib, he was always acutely aware of his own insignificance, yet today he does not feel diminished, although he knows he must soon be truthful with Gina. He has no idea how she'll react. But if he waits any longer she'll think he's been evasive, perhaps dishonest. He decides to tell her this evening, after they've eaten and before they make love. It'll be dark. She'll be reluctant to leave the campsite. Anyway, there's nowhere to go. He'll have until morning to talk her around.

    On his way down the mountain he recalls being eighteen and, in a rare rebellious moment, deciding not to go climbing with his parents, citing too much homework. Even now, twelve years later, he is unable to erase his memory of gyrating to Queen on the stereo in the lounge, a beer in his hand and a cigarette hanging from his mouth, while somewhere in this mountainous area his parents disappeared. He still doesn't know how or where exactly. They just never came home. Hundreds searched for them. Some thought they'd tumbled off a bluff into the river; others reckoned they'd fallen into an abandoned mineshaft. Searchers were lowered into every known site, but nothing was found to substantiate either theory. His parents had vanished without trace.

    Their bodies were never found, which might explain his need to work with the dead, and why he always imagines middle-aged cadavers being the parents of inconsiderate teenagers. Why can't he forgive himself for not being with them and stop searching for answers in those he works on?

    A thin wisp of cloud curls like a corkscrew through the sky, its tail disappearing into the stark blue horizon. David leans against a schist outcrop and takes a drink from his water bottle. He hadn't given much thought to his reasons for becoming an embalmer until today. He'd seen an ad in the paper and he answered it. He needed to earn a living to keep the family home, in case his parents were found.

    Perhaps he should share his sorrows with Gina. Just let them pour out as though wild, underground streams. It might help her understand why he's hooked on his work. Right at this minute he wishes he was a builder or an electrician — then he could run the last stretch down to camp, take Gina in his arms and enjoy whatever came his way. Instead, a heightened sense of unease develops. He cannot bear the thought of losing her. His skin tightens as though it, too, is no longer willing to contain his secret. So much rides on finding the right words.

    He waves to Gina as he comes into the valley. She gives him such a welcoming smile that his heart skips as though it were a stone skimming across the surface of a lake.

'David, you look done. I put a bottle of beer in the water to cool. Let me get it.'

She pulls on a pair of light green shorts and walks across the dust-brown earth towards the river. His mother set off on her last day dressed in striped thermals and hot pink leggings. No one has ever arrived at the morgue wearing pink leggings. Thermals are common but none have been the exact pattern as his mother's. His father's blue and green paisley shorts have not appeared either.

The beer tastes good. He drinks it quickly. 'You should have seen the views, Gina, and the colours. The sun transformed all that dull grey schist into silver and gold and pink shafts of light. Everything shimmered, as though part of a sky-weaver's loom. The whole mountain blazed.' He's being overly poetic, trying too hard. Sweat runs down his back. He takes a deep breath, reminds himself that he's got all night.

'Sounds like magic. Perhaps I could come next time,' says Gina. 'I'd like to understand why people climb. Are you starving? I am.'

So there might be a future if he gets it right. 'I'll fetch wood for a fire. Dad always set his in a circle of stones. Less risk of a spark going astray, he reckoned.'

'My parents never camp. Luxury lodges are more their style. "Give us a spa and a gin," they say.'

'I went through a long period when I didn't like being outdoors at all. Now it's the place I most want to be.'

'Not the only place, I hope,' Gina says, nudging his groin with her foot and closing her eyes.

David leans over and eases off her shorts and loose muslin top. She lies completely motionless while he runs his hands over her body. He's struck by her ability to stay so still. Something enables her to enjoy being in the moment, whereas the minute she touches him, he worries that his body will betray him in some way. During his first year as an embalmer, he constantly examined himself for signs of disease or decay. Apparently medical students do the same, interpreting the slightest twinge as a deadly invader. He wonders if his father did as well. David wishes he could ask him. He has enough questions to fill a valley. Perhaps he could share them with Gina. Right now she's licking his throat. He tries to slow himself down but it's impossible. All his uncertainties spill into her.

Later they eat sausages wrapped in slices of bread doused with tomato sauce. Embers continue to glow in the stone circle. David rests his back against the gnarled trunk of an old apple tree, no doubt planted by a goldminer years ago, someone who left all he knew to come to this beautiful, remote land. Now all that remains of his wilderness sojourn is a crumbling stone chimney and a single fruit tree. David wonders what he will leave behind. More than a box of gloomy drawings, he hopes. His heart beats faster. 'Gina, you know how I work in health?'

'Yes. Me, too, remember? Only my patients are animals.'

'I don't work with living things.'

'What do you mean? Are you in a lab or something?'

'Sort of . . .'

'Do you put samples under microscopes and stuff?'

'Bodies are amazing, Gina. Don't you think it's incredible that most central nervous systems send out perfectly choreographed signals until the moment of death?'

'I haven't given it much thought but, yes, I guess it is quite a feat. You're a strange one sometimes.'

David decides to come at it from a different angle. 'You know how you said your parents prefer gin and other luxuries?'

'I'd hardly call gin a luxury, but yes.'

'Mine liked a drink with dinner but never while they climbed.'

'Do you actually like climbing or is something else behind it?'

'I did today — well, sort of. It's complicated.'

'Is it the challenge or the quietness?' Gina waves a hand in the direction of the mountain he'd been on earlier.

'Both. I can think up there. Yes. I feel close to things.'

'What things?'

'Things I've lost.'

'I sometimes think you're a bit lost yourself.'

A defensive streak rises. Before he can suppress it he says, 'I'd hardly connect my wanting to climb with being lost.' But it is related, he thinks. She's right.

'You know what I mean, David. Please don't get tetchy. I grew up with enough of that to last me a lifetime. I can't remember a single day when my parents weren't at each other's throats. They even argued over which of them I smiled or talked to the most.'

David thinks of his parents' close and loving relationship and is sorry that Gina will never meet them. 'Is that why you became a vet nurse? So you could work with less complicated creatures?'

'What do you mean? Oh, I see! You think dogs and cats and other animals don't get cranky or stressed. You should come by the clinic one afternoon. It can be a crazy place. Dogs are the worst. Some refuse to come through the door. They hunker down outside and won't budge. Not even when I wave a doggie treat in their direction. You wouldn't believe what goes on some days. I hardly do myself. How come you're so interested in my work? Most guys just want to . . . you know.'

'I want more than that. Like everything there is to know about you. What you think about when you're not with me. Stuff like that.'

'Which part do you want to concentrate on right now?' Gina wriggles closer to David and pokes his foot with her freshly painted coral toenails. Despite being tired and tense, David runs his hands over her legs. He wants to take her again under the stars. Daylight will come soon enough. He'll tell her then. It's not like she doesn't want to make out with him. She's already nipping his ears, something he'd prefer her not to do since it makes him think of his old fox terrier, Arthur, who chewed on his mother's bare toes every time she slipped off her shoes. If he keeps thinking along these lines he'll lose it. He runs one hand across Gina's breasts and the other through her hair until everything, even the air, seems electric.

Later they lie back and watch the stars in the night sky, each an entity in its own right, yet somewhat brighter in appearance when clustered with others.

David feels strangely emotional and senses that if he tries to speak, he might weep, something he hasn't done since Arthur died when David was twelve. His mother had helped bury the dog under a rhododendron. The T-shirt he wore that day is in a box under his bed, still bloodied and covered with dog hair. He wishes he could introduce Gina to Arthur and make his parents appear with another promise.

'I need to pee,' David says. This is not turning out the way I imagined, he thinks. I'm too stuffed to tell her tonight. It can wait until morning. A steady stream of urine pools on the ground as he compares the most basic functions of sperm and embalming fluid. The first makes you feel better, the second look better. On another level, each is a preserving agent, only one works at growing cells and the other at holding back decay. He, too, is holding back that which might flourish if given a chance. And it's driving him crazy. Perhaps he does deserve a future, despite that broken promise. Wouldn't his parents want him to have what they shared?

He fills an empty bottle with river water and douses the embers. After placing a tender kiss on Gina's sweet lips, he climbs into his sleeping bag. The big, still landscape settles around him. He drifts back to a camp he went on with his parents, not far from here, where land-locked salmon still return to breed. Whatever's in them is in me too, David thinks. I need this landscape as much as the bodies I embalm. It's part of me and always will be. Like Mum and Dad. He wonders if he could pay homage to his parents by forgiving himself. Is it unresolved guilt rather than his work that is interfering with what he wants with Gina? The possibility makes him feel overwhelmed and elated at the same time. Maybe he could start by telling Gina what he was doing when his parents disappeared. He's never revealed this to anyone, not even his grandparents. He'll sleep on it.

Just before dawn he wakes to her unzipping his sleeping bag, her gorgeous blonde hair spread across his chest. He feels free, as though a knot has unravelled during the night. The sun is already overhead. The sky buzzes with clear blue light. Close by, the river utters a wondrous roar, its great and terrible force washing over stones that have been here forever. He hears himself laugh, real down-to-your-boots laughter, not a choked up high-in-the-chest trill. His body ripples with power. He tells Gina what he'd like her to do. She lifts her head and smiles. Soon everything is on fire. He's flying. Nothing can stop him. She calls his name over and over. It sounds like a choir of singing angels.

Afterwards Gina perches on one elbow and looks at him. 'You're such fun when you let go.'

David sees compassion and maybe a hint of love in her generous, violet eyes. He caresses the tip of her nose with a finger, then does the same to her chin. Finally, he gives her a big full kiss that goes on and on and on, opening something deep within him, as though he's a brittle mountain plant that's been caught unwittingly in a dazzling sun. He starts to shake and cannot stop.

'Tell me, David,' Gina whispers. 'Tell me everything.'

Fear lodges at the back of his throat. Burning tears prick his eyes. He's afraid of what might happen once he starts to speak but there's no going back. The words are already rolling down his tongue. 'They left me, you see, my parents, in a million different ways. Yet all I do is search for them, here in the mountains where they went missing. Even at work. I'm an embalmer, Gina. That's what I do. You probably want to leave me now.'

Gina leans forward and takes his hands in hers.

David feels a rush of love mixed with hope. 'I don't know why they had me.'

'I do,' says Gina. 'They had you for me.'

David looks at this confident young woman sitting in front of him, and thinks, yes, that's enough for now. I'll simply enjoy their remarkable gift.

Geoff Cochrane

Three Stories

Down Through the Pines

Chapter 1

A postcard from a friend visiting Cedar Rapids, Ohio. It shows Einstein at the beach, a beach somewhere. And Einstein looks exactly like Einstein, Albert, physicist and Nobel laureate, but is wearing shorts and sandals. The Einstein face is graced by an expression of mildly amused braininess or pleasant imbecility, take your pick. The Einstein shorts are unremarkable, not particularly dated to look at, and the legs are okay legs, not too bad at all if somewhat hairless, but oh my God the sandals. They seem to have something of a heel; the peekaboo toes consist of dome-shaped apertures, vents like Turkish domes in silhouette. Onion domes or twirly confectioner's kisses.

    Yes: the Einstein sandals of 1945 . . . *are almost certainly a woman's.*

Chapter 2

My friend the postman has travelled to the four corners of the world. Travels every year on his meagre postman's pay to some fresh destination, there to revel in fresh discomforts and inconveniences.

    I leave the travelling to others. I stay at home and read and watch a bit of telly. When one's own habitation provides a sufficiency of annoyances, why go abroad? Letterbox and telephone furnish all the alarms I can cope with.

    My name is Bruno Swan. Some sixteen years ago I was coming to an end. The lights were going out all over Bruno. Today, I live a posthumous sort of life, one nonetheless replete with quiet satisfactions.

Chapter 3

My friend the postman is beginning to limp like a knackered dromedary. 'Seen anything decent recently?' I ask him.

'I haven't been to a film in months,' says Martin.

'No? My late father used to boast that he'd seen every movie made before the end of World War 2.'

'Quite. Some people simply swear off the cinema. Give it up, like smoking.'

'They do. But retreat perhaps to the reeking wasteland of television.'

As well as being a traveller, Martin's an omnivorous reader. His long brown face is handsomely lined, and has about it something of sage Arabian dignity, the wisdom of the oasis. 'Television? I'll tell you who likes television,' the weathered Bedouin says.

'Who?'

'Poor old Johnny Bray. Poor old Johnny Bray has taken to knocking on my door from time to time.'

'Ah.'

'It's late in the afternoon and there he is. Can he come in and play the piano? Can he come in and watch *Spongebob Squarepants*?'

'He's apologetic, but.'

'He laughs so much it's almost a delight. He laughs so hard at *Spongebob* fucking *Squarepants*, it's almost a pleasure to have him in the house.'

Chapter 4

Neil Young has a heartbreaking voice. Neil Young has a heartbreaking voice.

Somewhere back in the eighties, I stood in a bottlestore and watched a video clip of Young performing 'Like a Hurricane'. There he was on the screen above my head, singing and strumming while being blustered silly, stormily mauled by a wind machine, *I wanna dig you but I'm being blown away* . . .

The guitar work on 'Hurricane' is astral, titanic. Time and time again, I sit in the dark and let it do its thing, sit in the dark and let it take me apart.

Chapter 5

I'm stopped in the street by a bronzed, a blond young man. Levi's, T-shirt, designer stubble. 'What's that over there?' he asks.

His accent is English. 'It used to be a museum,' I tell him, 'and to the left you've got your carillon and war memorial.'

'Cool,' he says. 'Thank you.'

I walk along Arthur to the top of Cuba. On the corner is the house in which I spent the first few months of my sobriety, living above an empty shop.

It remains a sooty, dim, Dickensian address. Soon to be stomped by the new, obliterating motorway. In a bedroom at the rear I finished writing *Tartan Revolver*, the first of my three published books. I'd bought for the purpose a flat little manual in two tones of grey; when you pushed the plump red lozenge of a certain mysterious key, its carriage would track from right to left with an oily sort of thrum: *yoddle-oddle-oddle-oddle-oddle*.

Behind that window up there I completed a vivid, skinny novel, yes. And it might be fun to get a picture, to take a photo of those doomed, disappointed-seeming panes. A Fujicolor disposable would do the trick, but I'd have lots of film left over.

Chapter 6

My present address is temporary. No sleek, savvy cat dozes on the fire escape, nor are my neighbours prostitutes and members of Black Power, but I like and use the peace and quiet here. If I duck down through the pines to Wallace Street, I can be in the city in twenty minutes.

I keep the joint uncluttered, low on visual noise. The spines of a hundred books and a Chinese wall-hanging — I confess to finding colour enough in these.

Chapter 7

With regard to my worthless Chinese banderole: in search perhaps of balance, centredness, I sometimes contemplate its ghostly torrents, its floaty crags.

The Chinese seem to manage not to rear psychopathic monsters. The Chinese are sane and fill their jeans nicely (I've noticed that the young men tend to have good legs).

The truth of the matter is, I like the Chinese. I like their restaurants and cafés; I like their tanks of goldfish, their glossy black enamel, their lanterns with scarlet tassels. I like the sweet and sour of their temperate, amusable demeanours.

As the coal-burning city steams its way toward nightfall, I picture myself living in some muggy Chinatown, renting a room above a busy kitchen, playing noughts and crosses on a grimy little board of teak and porcelain. Smoking my opium.

'You wouldn't like it,' says Martin. (A dollop of clarification: my friend the postman is not of course *my* postman. We meet in town, if we meet at all, only when he's completed his route and is making his way home.)

'You're right,' I say. 'Forget the opium.'

'I'm not depriving you of your narcotic. It's just that you'd find the Chinese world too populous and hectic.'

'Probably. What with all that gambling, all those tong vendettas.'

'Quite. So what are you reading, at the moment?'

'Don DeLillo's *Underworld*. For the fourth time. *Underworld* is the book for me.'

'The one you take to the desert island?'

'Absolutely. There are more stories in *Underworld* . . . than are actually in *Underworld*. The Don DeLillo of *Underworld* extends to infinity in all directions.'

'High praise indeed.'

'Indeed. And don't get me started on the prose itself.'

Chapter 8

I seem to be forever buying milk. Buying milk or thinking that the blood vessels in my right leg are collapsing. And yet I've had my picture in the paper, been on the radio.

Chapter 9

My dream goes something like this:

Good Friday in a detox ward somewhere. The sweet, metallic smell of Wattie's canned spaghetti.

A pathetically sweaty Greek gangster has the bed next to mine. 'I'm shaking like a jelly over here.'

'Just hang tough,' I tell him.

'When's our next medication due?'

'God knows.'

'I can feel some kind of seizure coming on. I've wrought some fucking havoc in me time, but I don't deserve this.'

'What goes up must come down. Or something.'

'Them Nazis out the nursing station — the filph is *toffs* compared!'

My dead but ageless father appears. Suit and tie, hair parted wetly, familiar gold ring. 'I've always liked this town. Denny Mahon and I were stationed here during the early part of the war. I thought I'd take the bus out to the old aerodrome, have a look around.'

'Do that, Dad.'

'Will I see you at all, you know, when you grow up? Will there be a number I can ring?'

Dr Mephisto is next. Earring, three days' growth, soap-scented hands. (What do they want with me, these attractive young men?) 'Your pancreas is inflamed. Likewise your already fatty liver.'

'No kidding.'

'Ever had a shot of benzoethylcryptotriplicate?'

'No.'

'Hurts like hell, believe me. What are your thoughts on Dreiser?'

'I've never read him. The last ten minutes of *Carrie* were terrific.'

'You're referring to the William Wyler film?'

'With Laurence Olivier, yes. With Laurence Olivier being utterly tragic.'

'I put it to you that Don DeLillo is not the totally groovy, funky and together, hip wizard seer you think he is.'

'He's merely very good. Is what I think.'

'Don DeLillo sucks. Ditto Bruno Swan and *Tartan Revolver*. I'm tempted to reach for the hurty stuff.'

Sacraments

1

The city has Finnish-looking trams. Ferries, helicopters and Finnish-looking trams.

A tennis court stands next to a cathedral. A sandwich bar embarrasses a theosophical temple.

Some of the smaller banks have tinted windows, science-fiction panes the colour of petrol. And the Yohst and Kubrick Centre in Bilton Square wears copper epaulettes; at night, it's painted by floodlights of lime and guava pink.

As 3 am approaches, the station settles down, achieves a degree of equilibrium. It loosens its belt (as it were) and breathes a little easier. And the mad and the bad and the sad in the cells downstairs? They admit defeat and shut up — finally.

Detective Mark Traven rises from his desk. Time to empty the bladder and stretch the legs. In white shirt and loud floral tie, Mark looks like a shoulder-holstered Mormon, trim and youthful and smoothly truculent.

He drifts toward Stella Greybill's desk. She's up to her armpits in folders papers files, her messy hair a storm of golden wisps. 'Cut your crap, Traven.'

'I haven't said a word.'

'This place stinks of fries and hamburgers.'

'Yours and mine,' says Mark, 'but mostly mine.'

'Ain't that the truth.'

'We should be the subject of a study. The scientists should study us long and hard. Nutritionists with clipboards, probing the mysteries of our bright eyes and bushy tails.'

'Grow fucking up.' Is what Stella says.

'I'm closing fast on my next cigarette. I'm cruising stealthily.'

'Not me. Not this detective. What I want is beef tea, if you're passing the machine.'

'Beef tea? Since when? These are questions the machine itself will ask.'

'The secret is not to bully it. The secret is to let it do its thing.'

2

The convent is that of the Sisters of Abiding Comfort, a dwindling community of tough, cheerful souls. The nuns have their business in the city, with the desperate, but their home stands on the side of a bushy vale in a quiet eastern suburb.

Convent and playfully Gothic chapel: few people know of their existence. A circumstance that Robert Sharland does his best to perpetuate.

He's here again this morning, in the first pew but one. He likes the altar of white marble, the lilies and the candlesticks of blond brass. Enjoys the windows and the watery stains they impart, palest tincturings of lemon and rose. His bodyguard is armed and wired for sound and sits one row behind his principal, apparently unfazed by the dour Latin Mass.

Bread and wine are at hand. Chalice and ciborium. The sacrament achieves its overcast plateau, and the priest says the occult words of consecration. How does Matthew have it? '"This is my body. But behold the hand of him who betrays me is with me on the table."' Something like that, Sharland thinks. And Matthew's is a Rembrandt-esque effect, with candlelight and gloom interpenetrating.

The nuns like Sharland to breakfast at the convent. Swap pleasantries with the visiting celebrant.

Two places have been set at one end of a long table. The room itself (a small refectory?) has plastered walls, a floor of reddish tiles. Sharland's bodyguard seats his employer, places a cellphone beside Robert's plate and retires to a chair just inside the door.

Stripped of his vestments now, dog-collared Father Conway makes his appearance. 'It's toast and jam and boiled eggs, I see. The sisters seem to want to feed us up.'

'Good morning, Father.'

The smiley little priest's as plump as a sparrow. And layman and cleric are by no means strangers. 'You turned in a brisk performance this morning.'

'Did I now,' says Conway. 'Perhaps I'd counted the house.'

'You'll have noticed that I never take Communion.'

'I've noticed that your minder sometimes does.'

'I'm a product of my education, Vince. I believe in the Mass without believing.'

'Surely not.'

'I believe in the Mass. Without believing.'

'Well I wonder now how that can be. I do.'

A nun arrives with more triangles of toast. Orange juice in a stainless-steel jug. 'Shall I do you another egg, Father?'

'I think not, Sister Joan, on this occasion.'

Sharland waits until the nun has gone. Resumes his 'confession' in a somewhat cooler tone. 'I'm a powerful man, Vincent. I make things happen. My puissance flows out into the world to sink and saturate, penetrating systems from top to bottom.'

'Oh?'

'I trickle down. Through structures, institutions. I might be likened to the Holy Ghost.'

'Hubris. Blasphemy. To say nothing of the lesser sin of rank hyperbole.'

'I export and import and rake in dividends. Power begets wealth and wealth begets power. But among my hobbies is dealing in pictures. It's well within my competence to annoint struggling artists, and this it amuses me to do. I make their reputations and begin to sell their paintings for surprising new sums. I feather their nests while also upholstering my own. Does this make me virtuous, or am I merely acting out of self-interest?'

'Both. You're having a bob each way, like most of the rest of us.'

Robert's cellphone trills. He picks it up and jabs its Answer button. 'You've reached Sharland. Speak.'

The bodyguard approaches and addresses Conway. 'The Rolls will soon be brought to the side door, Father. Can we offer you a lift anywhere?'

'That's thoughtful of you, Taube.'

'Sell sell sell,' says Sharland. Talking of course to his dinky Nokia.

3

It's Tuesday morning, and this is Eric Jones. He's sporting the maroon thumbnail, the big black shapely fuck-you Druid's hood. Yes, hooded is exactly how he likes to feel.

For a period of time. For a period of time, he stands in the doorway of a camera shop and watches the mall. He has money in his pocket and blood in his ralph. He has crisp new notes in his wallet and blood in his tackle.

A blue mid-morning whim flares like a match in him. Prompting him to stir and straighten up, muster and marshal forces.

Bamboo Grove Apartments are tricky to get into. You have to wait for a citizen to exit, then duck inside with no apologies. On the third shallow floor lives Henry Hawke, the oldest surviving junkie in the realm, notorious and grey.

Notorious and grey and pigeon-chested. Like some derelict knight of yore, bony and big-knuckled. 'Look what washes up. Just as I'm about to have my lunch.'

'Lunch? You?'

'I pick. I pick.'

'I'm Eric if you've forgotten.'

'Yes. No. I remember you from that Narcotics Anonymous meeting. So how's the battle, Eric?'

'I slipped. I crashed and burned.'

'So what the fuck is new? But never mind. Would you like a cup of coffee?'

The man himself, at home. A steely cook and chemist of the old school, ground and sanded to a narrow-shouldered skeleton, a bristly skull with Auschwitz-ashen temples, skin as grey as dishwater. 'The name of Henry Hawke has entered the textbooks. I've outlived any number of quacks, addiction specialists and hepatologists. To say nothing of cops and probies.'

'Hepatologists.'

'I buried my own lovely brother. Also several arseholes of whom I was fond. But Craig lies in a quiet place, and I know I could have taken better care of him.'

'Yeah?'

'Yeah. And how are you having this coffee of yours?'

A Buddha here, a crucifix there. Many antique LPs are angle-parked along the skirting-board. The silent Panasonic is tuned to the horse-racing channel, its screen a brilliantly colourful display.

Henry lives on Nicorette gum, with hogget and tepid gravy delivered by Meals on Wheels. And Eric Jones observes him, and not without respect. 'I graduated from smack to methadone. I got my shit together,' Henry continues, 'and even began to drink. Imagine it. I took to the grog and thought I'd joined the human race. Methadone and Mogadon and wine. With taxis to the pharmacy, the bottlestore. Plus also I smoked to the level of national representative.'

'Carbon monoxide. Tars.'

'Where are you stopping now?'

'Here and there. I'm seeing a chick.'

'And you're keeping your hand in, I suppose.'

'Xylox. I'm moving a little Xylox.'

'What can I tell you? You've got to get back on the horse, begin again. You should at least continue with the meetings.'

'I could maybe handle a treatment centre. When I'm good and ready, like.'

'Shrinks and cardiologists and kidney guys — they all despaired of me. Said I was in for death or insanity.'

'They love that line.'

'Years passed. Decades. And then one day I couldn't do it any more. I was sick of the hideous weight, the unabating demands of my addictions. I was sick and tired of the huge responsibility of being me.'

As a maker of instant coffee, Henry is not deficient in technique: the milky brew he hands to his guest at last is free from undissolved clots of powder. 'I need a lucky break,' Eric ventures.

'You need a lucky break, which is what I got. It was as if a clock had wound itself down and finally stopped ticking. Some sort of inner, organic clock, the thing that had craved and hungered through thousands of days and nights. Silent now, defunct.'

'This gives me hope. No shit.'

'I can't see why. My very own brother lies in a quiet place.' Henry indicates a framed photograph. 'The pair of us at the races. Seventy-six, that was. I guess you can tell by the Starsky and Hutch costumes.'

'Disco lives.'

'And what about yourself? Do you have any brothers anywhere?'

Eric shrugs. Sips at his coffee and makes a face. 'Christ. Point me at that sugar bowl, Henry.'

4

The city grows ever more concrete. The city grows ever more abstract and abstruse.

He smokes a little weed, shifts a little Xylox. And Eric has his hood deployed again; the modelled, glans-like cowl seals and finishes him.

Wednesday afternoon. A whitish glare replaces shadows, contrasts. This is the whiteness of X-rays and photographic negatives.

He's in a mood to maybe go again, trouble the flame a second time, for Henry Hawke has something Eric needs. Not that Eric can put his finger on it. Not that he can know quite what he's in for.

Henry's front door has been snibbed and left ajar.

Eric knocks on the jamb — with no result. Calls out Henry's name — to no effect. But Eric was born to push and probe, to test the elasticity of boundaries and borders, to ease himself forward with pre-emptive stealth.

The beautiful telly thrives, a colour-oven. Old Spice talcum powder scents the air, and a towel lies on the carpet near Henry's ivory foot. Henry himself is wearing a khaki bathrobe. He has obviously showered and clipped his toenails, and now he's resting up. Is sitting on a chair at one end of his Formica table, his back to the wall and his softened eyes in neutral.

And he could indeed be watching *Charlie's* fucking *Angels* — except that he's plainly far too dead to be watching anything.

This is Eric's first dead body. Seated as if relaxedly, its left arm supported by the table, it seems a thing of touching poise and lightness. And Eric is not afraid to bend, incline his ear to the slightly parted lips, glance into the clement, disconnected peepers.

No breath, no sounds of breathing. No pulse in carotid, jugular. And Henry Hawke's grey cheek feels less than living, even less than fleshy. No point really in attempting mouth-to-mouth; no point either, much, in ringing for an ambulance. Also, and of maximum importance: the person reporting coming across the corpse is always of interest to the cops. Becomes in fact a popular interviewee, where foul play is suspected. But Eric can detect zero signs of violence.

Best to do the bizzo and clear off. Best to take what's up for grabs and fuck off out of it.

He swishes the $375 he finds in Henry's wallet, but what else is of value? Henry's vintage LPs are useless to Eric. Even if he knew what he was dealing with (Iron Butterfly, Jefferson Airplane and Tangerine Dream, for instance), he has no means of playing them. And then he discovers the. And then he discovers oh Jesus yes the gun. He opens a kitchen drawer and there it is, in the roomy part behind the wells for knives and forks: a bluish, satin-finished .38 that fits and fills his hand, making him feel both smart and ballsy as.

5

CONFIDENTIAL TRANSCRIPT

Laszlo Sinclair is twenty-three and works as a theatrical electrician. He was the subject of surveillance from June to September of this year. A number of charges have been laid (see attachment).

DETECTIVE STELLA GREYBILL: I'm sitting here. I'm waiting.

LASZLO SINCLAIR: (Inaudible.)

GREYBILL: Fill me in, Laszlo. Illuminate this mess.

SINCLAIR: (Inaudible.)

GREYBILL: You don't think you can? So make like a thing with a spine and give it a shot.

SINCLAIR: Xylox is very kind to one at first, but it soon becomes this total preoccupation.

GREYBILL: Now there's a surprise.

SINCLAIR: I went to Larsen's Crossing in the early hours of Sunday morning. I'd swallowed a tab at final curtain, and I went to Larsen's Crossing with a member of the cast. And in this actor's shitty little flat, with a neon sign for beer just outside the window, I saw the gods.

GREYBILL: You saw the what?

SINCLAIR: Ken plays Mungo in *Walking Tall*. We'd gone to a neighbourhood bar, slurped some suds and walked back to his place. Thunder and a deluge just as we got in.

GREYBILL: And?

SINCLAIR: Kenneth crashes out, goodbye and thanks a lot. Just me and the cat and the beer sign after that.

GREYBILL: Just you and the cat. Go on.

SINCLAIR: I look at my watch and it's four o'clock. When I look again, it's ten minutes earlier, the second hand's adopted an anticlockwise sweep and it's welcome to psychosis Lasz' you sorry fuck.

GREYBILL: Xylox. The *good* shit, right? A Day-Glo-orange tablet with a wee X on it.

SINCLAIR: The beer sign stops flashing and the cat stops breathing. And I myself am dead, stopped and null like a disused abattoir. And then I see the gods in their hundreds, the brown gods in their thousands. Tier upon tier of them, back and back to infinity, a sort of tessellation of sage brown faces.

GREYBILL: (Inaudible.)

SINCLAIR: Sage brown faces, back and back and back.

Tattoo

Marcus was released from the clinic on a grey, humid, drizzly day in April.

By five o'clock that evening he'd found a suitable flat. The block itself was situated in a sodden little gully of a street.

Behold a tiny kitchen like the galley on a trawler, its stinky black stove petite and personable! Marcus was also beguiled by the rest of the mouldy dump — he'd long aspired to living in just such a windowless bunker: a womb without a view.

'It could do with an airing,' said the woman.

'Who the hell are you?'

'I'm Mrs Sykes. From the floor above.'

'Goodbye, Mrs Sykes.'

Marcus wore his wheat-coloured coat in the continental manner, leaving the sleeves empty. When the Salvation Army van arrived, he directed operations like a caped gendarme, disposing the junk he'd bought earlier in the day. Mattress, blankets, small cuboidal fridge: these and an armchair were all his possessions now. Well, almost.

He opened his only suitcase. Sandwiched between two of his best shirts, the tastefully gilt-framed oil was small and square; Marcus took the painting from the case and stood it on the seat of the armchair.

'Shall I fetch you down a cuppa?' the Sykes woman asked.

'No. Enough already.'

'You can tell me to mind my own business, but you shouldn't wear jeans with a nice coat like that.'

'Should I not?'

'It's a great mistake, in my opinion. What's your line of work, if you don't mind my asking?'

'Demolition. Boom.'

'I don't know how to take you, I'm sure.'

Marcus lifted a bottle from his suitcase. The poison of his choice was Tattoo, a vodka-and-cranberry cocktail with a red and green dragon on the label. Bold, romantic, maritime Marcus! He swigged a mighty swig of dragons and tattoos, mentally toasting distant Shanghai.

'I don't think much of that painting,' the Sykes person announced.

'You really must stop barging in like this.'

'A country road with bits of snow and mud. There's not much to it, is there?'

'Not much at all. Deliciously.'

'Would I know the artist?'

'I shouldn't think so. His name was Maurice Vlaminck.'

'?'

'A motor mechanic by trade, he played the violin in the gypsy orchestras of Montmartre.'

'!'

'Derain gives him a pipe. A painter and a poet, was Vlaminck. Billiards he liked, and tennis—and wrestling and cycling and driving racing cars.'

'You seem to know an awful lot about him.'

'In 1945 he published a book called *Radios Clandestins*.'

'So what are you really? A writer?'

'No no no no no, Mrs Sykes. My name is Marcus Darke and I'm an actor.'

'Like Peter O'Toole and Al Pacino?'

'Like Peter O'Toole and Al Pacino, yes.'

'But have I ever seen you on the telly?'

'I prefer to work on the stage.'

'Mind what you're doing with that bottle! You're slopping your dripper, Mr Darke.'

'So I am. How careless of me. Would you like a snort yourself?'

'I think not, under the circumstances.'

Marcus considered the cold lights in his bottle. 'I prefer to work on the stage, but I don't get the parts any more. I'm resting, Mrs Sykes, and I have been for some time. I've been resting yes for years and now I'm slopping my dripper, and soon I'm going to throw you out and take my medication.'

'Medication, Mr Darke?'

"'I could be bounded in a nut-shell, and count myself a king of infinite space, were it not that I have bad dreams.'"
'Nightmares, Mr Darke?'
'But not just at night, Mrs Sykes.'

Siân Daly

Conan

His name is Conan, like the barbarian. But he's smaller. He is standing in front of me and breathing in and out as if he's having a fit or an asthma attack. He's imitating me. It's because of yesterday.

Yesterday I found him out in the back yard dismantling my bike for parts. He's been modifying his own to make it lighter for trick-riding and jumps. He has taken parts off my bike three times before. Four times was too many times.

'What am I going to do with no brakes?' I said.

'Ride slow,' he said.

'Put them back,' I said.

'Make me,' he said.

Then I pinned him to the ground because I'm still bigger than him, so I can. I was so angry all my breaths were shallow and fast. It's called hyperventilating.

Now he's pretending to do it too, just to make me angry again.

'Spastic!' I say, aiming an acorn at his thigh.

'You are!' He ignores the acorn strike and waves his hands about in front of his face. I suppose he is pretending to be a spastic who is also hyperventilating.

'Conan,' I say, 'You're not all there!' That's what Mum said when he kicked a hole in the bedroom wall while he was having a tantrum. It shuts him up.

It is Christmas Day. You may wonder why we are not being nice to each other. We are not being nice because we had our Christmas last night. It's over. We already have our presents and have thanked each other for things. We had Christmas dinner on Christmas Eve, the way they do in Scandinavian countries. We are trying something different. Mum wanted to. Today, there is just a drive and a picnic, so that we don't waste the 'lovely summer's day'. Luckily it is actually a lovely summer's day. There are only a few clouds and they burn away before your eyes, if you can watch for long enough. I was doing this before Conan started giving me a hard time. I saw one whole cloud disappear into blue and I only blinked five times.

We are waiting to go to church because although we are trying something different, we are also doing some things the same. We always go to church on Christmas morning. Personally, I don't believe in it. I've told Mum. She said that it is my own business what I believe or do not believe in, but I am still going to church with the rest of them and will have to do this until she says it is time to stop. She is considering letting me stop going to doctrine class on Wednesday evenings though, especially after Sister Mary's phone call.

Sister Mary is this year's teacher. All I did was ask her who was actually in hell. She said, 'Sinners are in hell.'

I said, 'I thought God forgives all our sins.'

She said, 'Yes, but first you have to pray to God and ask him to forgive your sins.'

I said, 'What if you'd meant to pray but you'd just forgotten that one time and then, suddenly, you died. Would you still go to hell?'

She said, 'You have to remember.'

I said, 'So hell is full of the forgetful.' She didn't say anything. She just rang Mum. Mum talked to me and told me that hell is not full of people who forgot to pray. They are in purgatory. So it still pays to remember.

Sometimes, on a Sunday, there are people still gathered outside the red-brick front of the church when we arrive. They stand around, crunching their shoes on the tiny gravel pieces. It is always the same people who stand on the semi-circular steps going up to the double doors. I think they arrive early to get in first. Today, there is nobody outside. We are late. This means we will probably have to sit in the soundproof room where people who are late and mothers with babies go. There is a soundproof window so we can see the Mass and some speakers so we can hear the Mass, as if it is happening underwater. It's hot in there and there are always flies buzzing on the glass. Besides, I didn't take my first communion so I could stay in the 'fly box'. I'm allowed to be in the church and go up to receive the body of Christ.

I do like to sing the little chants. 'Oh, lamb of God, who takes away the sins of the world, la la la la.' I also quite like to bend one knee and cross myself before sitting down. Genuflection makes me feel important. It makes me feel like I might know something, some secret thing in my heart that is mine and only mine. I kneel down and close my eyes when I pray. I try to look for the secret in my heart but I quite often lose my train of thought.

The one major thing I don't like about being in the church for Mass is if I am sitting on the edge and have to turn to someone else, not in the family, and shake their hand. And say, 'Peace be with you,' or, 'Also with you,' if they say it first, which they normally have to because I don't like to be touched by strangers and I don't really like to look them in the face and stuff. Besides, I know they'd rather shake hands and wish peace to another adult. My wish of peace doesn't count as much.

I also hate it when we are late because there is no holy water left in the little fonts to cross yourself with. Even if you push your finger down into the sponge, there isn't enough to feel it on your forehead. I made a good joke once when the sponge was dry and I said to Mum and Dad, 'How unanointing!' I'm pretty sure they got it, but you can't laugh out loud in the house of God.

Maybe because it is Christmas, we don't go into the 'fly box' but into the main part of the church. We walk in, not even creeping, and sit at the back. Unfortunately, Mum and Dad sit on the outside with me and Conan together in the middle. While Father Morgan is saying Mass, Conan reaches his hand around the back of my head and taps my other shoulder. I shake him off. Then Mum slaps his knee. I give him the weasel face, pushing my teeth out over my bottom lip and screwing up my nose. He does a few silent hyperventilating breaths. I ignore him and look straight ahead. He hates it when I ignore him, so after a while he tries the same trick as before, reaching his hand around my back. Dad makes Conan get up and sit on the other side of him. After that, Mass seems to go on for a very long time.

When Mass is over the altar boys hand out chocolate fish to all the children at the sacristy door. Then we put the Christmas flowers on the grave of a stranger, and we are finally ready to go on the picnic. It must be nearly lunchtime already. I'm starving. We drive away from our house and along the straight road until we get out past town and are heading towards the hills. Then the road turns and winds. Every time we go around a bend to the right, I slide towards Conan and try to squash him against the door. He does the same to me when we go around ones to the left, until I tell him to cut it out because he's not even using gravitational pull or anything. He's just throwing himself at me, which is against the rules of 'corners' and he is disqualified. He says, 'There's always more gravitational pull on a fat person.' I give him a dead arm and say, 'No returns, ever!'

We are not deciding exactly where we will go but we're heading in a general direction. Mum says we will let the car take us somewhere.

I look over at Conan and screw up my face. He rolls his eyes. She says stuff like that . . . like we're in *Chitty Chitty Bang Bang* or something. Dad still seems to be driving the car so I say, 'Dad, is the car giving you an idea?' Dad says, as if he is in a trance, 'I see black swans, black . . . swans.' Black swans are on Lake Ellesmere. So I suppose we'll be going past Little River.

Conan and I stayed in the car for hours one day when Dad was in the Little River pub with some people after we went with him up the Kaituna Valley and into the bush on a job. We had two bottles of lemonade each, with a straw in them, and two bags of potato chips. We were supposed to stay in the car but we went across the road for a bit. There was a stream and we looked for tadpoles. Also the water had flooded some flat grass so we played 'paddyfields' for a while, which is a game where you pretend you are harvesting the rice by hand in China and you are Chinese. Conan was only six and not very knowledgeable about Asia, so he didn't enjoy that game like I did. Then he got his shoe stuck in the mud. It got sucked off his foot and filled up with water. So that was the end of that and we went back to the car.

Conan started crying because he was cold and his feet were wet and it was getting dark. I was sick of it all too, so I sent him into the pub. I knew little kids in pubs are generally frowned upon, so a crying one with muddy clothes and one shoe on would be especially disliked. I walked Conan up to the door and said, 'Go on. Say we want to go home.' He said, 'Come too,' and tried to hold my hand. He had snot coming out of his nose. I said, 'No, you go,' and pushed him in the door. I ran back to the car and got in the front and then Dad came out with Conan and we went home.

Conan says he will have all the red cars that pass us. I wish I'd said red first but I didn't think of bagsing cars, so I say I'll have green. I only get one VW Beetle car and Conan gets a sports car without a roof and a Vauxhall Viva, which Dad says is burgundy and that is a type of red so that is allowed. He also gets a red stationwagon with a white roof, which is also allowed because it always goes on the main colour of the car. I stop playing then. I say I just want to look out the window. I wish I'd bagsed the red cars.

We pass Lake Ellesmere, which is always like a mirage because the water seems to spread across the land in shining lines, just like a mirage does. Except Lake Ellesmere is real and it creeps across the grass, never having a proper lake edge. It is only separated by a beach from the sea. It is big and seems very shallow and flat. It creeps like the start of a flood, getting bigger. Some parts of it are salt water and some fresh water. I love the swans. Only black swans swim on Lake Ellesmere.

They sit on top of the shining lines like they are painted.

Then we drive on to Birdlings Flat, which is where we are having lunch. I think it's a bad choice. There are so many stones to walk over to get to the sea and it's a bit smelly. But we're hungry anyway, so it doesn't matter. Mum pulls out the folding chairs and the folding table. Dad gets out the chilly bin. Mum hands us the plastic plates and the matching plastic cups. Mine is a green plate and cup. Conan's is orange, which is a bit yuck, but that's what happens when you don't get to choose your colour first.

I pour a lemonade for Conan and a lemonade for me. Mum gives us cold potatoes and chicken and lamb and salad and some mint sauce. I don't want chicken and lamb on the plate at the same time. I don't really like them to mix. I ask Mum if I can just put the chicken off until I've eaten the lamb. 'Put it into that little compartment away from the lamb,' she tells me. She's pointing at the round place which is the holder for the matching green cup. I sigh. 'What will I do with my drink, then?' She just reaches over and takes my drink out of my hand and puts it on the table. That's not very convenient for me, because I'll have to put my plate down to get it again. So, whenever I want a drink I just say, 'Would you pass my drink please, Mum?' I'm very polite. And then, 'Would you put my drink back on the table please, Mum?' Now she is my drink holder.

After we have finished our lunch Conan and I go exploring. We are not allowed to go all the way down to the sea. We walk quite a long way from Mum and Dad but are still in sight, as we were told. When I stand up on the hilly rise of stones I can still see them and I wave out to show them we are here. Then we go a bit further, looking for the perfect flat stones. It's a competition. That's the thing about Birdlings Flat. Almost every stone there is round and flat and grey. And there are miles and miles of stones.

We have to find a flat stone within the count of thirty and then compare them to see which is better. Four times out of five, mine are better. I say to Conan, 'Every one you pick up seems better than the one you already have.'

'Yeah,' says Conan, and he shows me one he has. 'Look at this one. Why are they all here? Maybe God was experimenting and these are all His try-outs.'

'So where is the absolute perfect one He finally made, then?'

'Out there, somewhere.' He sweeps his hand out in front of us.

'Let's try and find it,' I say. We both look at all the stones.

'What if we've already found it and then we threw it back?' he says. I bite my lip. I look at the stones around my feet. I don't suppose it would matter. What would it matter if you had the perfect one or a nearly perfect one? But I wish I could hold in my hand the rolling soft edges of the absolute perfect stone. Just to know what it would feel like.

'Would you want one perfect one or a whole heap of other pretty good ones?' Conan asks me.

'The perfect one.'

'I want lots and lots of stones!' Conan yells, and he kneels on the stones and gathers them up to his knees with his arms, sweeping them in towards him until his legs are covered.

I bet Conan that he can't make a better flat-stone tower than me. He rushes into things. He may make it faster but it won't have better stones. He says, 'Okay, but there's a time limit, so you'll be finished before we have to go home.' I agree to a time limit of half an hour. We pretend to synchronise watches. Conan isn't wearing one. So I count down to the start. 'Ready, set . . . go!' And we go.

You have to make a base first. Otherwise the whole tower will fall over. Then you need bigger flat rocks for the lower parts and getting smaller and smaller to the tiny ones on the top. I ask Conan if he really believes God made all these stones. He says he does.

'But is it the God at church?'

'I don't know. Maybe.'

'Because, why would He?'

'What?'

'Make lots and lots of flat stones, all slightly different?'

'So we can make towers.'

We keep on building. Conan's tower is getting higher than mine. He's always been good at constructing things.

'Do you pray?' I ask him.

'Not really.'

'Why not?'

'I only pray when I have to. I haven't got anything much to pray for. Everything's okay already.'

'What about asking Him to forgive you?'

'I don't have to. I just tell Him you did it!'

'Ha ha. He knows you're lying.' I put my hands on my hips.

'I win,' says Conan. He stands back to observe his tower. I look at my watch.

'There's still ten minutes to go,' I say and keep working on mine. Then I step back and knock his over. It's an accident. But he still belts me in the arm and marches off to tell Mum. I run after him. Mum's frowning and giving him a hug when I get there. I pour myself another lemonade and say to Mum, 'It was an accident.' Then I pour some lemonade for Conan and say he won.

It is late afternoon when we pack up to head back home. First we have Christmas cake and say 'Happy Christmas' again. Mum says she thinks it has been a very successful Christmas and we should do it again like this next year. I'm hoping she forgets about it during the year because I've missed having the presents on Christmas Day, really. We are driving along when Mum sees some cherries on trees where an old house used to be. They are under a steep rocky slope and a cliff with a high ledge. Another cherry tree is clinging to the ledge with branches laden with cherries, hanging out over the edge and throwing a shadow on the ground below. Dad stops the car and Mum gets some bags for us to collect the cherries in.

Conan and I run through the long grass and he climbs one of the trees with his bag. I climb up another tree with my bag. Mum and Dad pick the ones from the lower branches. Soon we have lots of cherries. Mum goes to the car to put the bags in and see if there are any extra bags or anything to put a few more cherries in, because there are just so many. Conan and I start to climb up the rocky slope. Conan keeps climbing higher up. He wants to get to the tree up there because there are millions of cherries on it. I stop on the ridge at the top of the rocky slope, under the cliff, and look up at Conan as he scrambles up to the tree.

'You haven't even got a bag,' I tell him. He says he'll shake the tree and I can pick them up when they fall down.

I'm busting for the toilet now. Conan is up in the tree. He shakes a branch and lots of red cherries fall onto the ridge. Some tumble away over the rocks and roll down the slope. I pick up some of the cherries that are around my feet. 'You're just bruising them,' I say. 'Wait till we have a bag.' Then I yell out to Mum that I need to go. She yells back that I should go in the grass.

'Everyone can see me.'

'Nobody will look.'

'Conan can see everything from up there.'

Mum looks up from the back of the car and yells, 'Conan, get down from there!' Then she calls out to Dad and he looks up at Conan.

'Get down, son.'

'It's okay,' yells Conan. 'There are heaps of good cherries in this tree. Mum, we need some bags.'

'I need to go to the toilet!' I yell. 'I'm really busting!'

'I need some bags up here,' Conan says to me. 'Go and get some.'

'Shut up, Conan. Just get down.'

Conan shakes the tree again so that cherries fall onto the rocks all around me.

'Are you going to wee in your pants?' He laughs.

I turn to throw the cherries I am holding and as I am turning my head there is another shake of the tree. Then there is the sound of wind whistling. It is right near my ear. Conan falls at my feet. He is looking up at the sky. He breathes out, 'Uhh.' And he is still staring up at the sky.

I call, "Mum!" She is already halfway through the barbed-wire fence. A barb tears a strip of her purple T-shirt away from her back. And she just keeps going. She is carrying plastic bags in one hand. She calls out in a strange voice with no real words.

And I am standing at the edge of the narrow ridge, with my hands held out, still cupping the cherries. Dad is running up through the dry long grass to the bottom of the rolling rock slope and then there is no sound.

Sue Emms

The Weakness of Women

THE HOWL OF CATS FIGHTING under the house doesn't wake Louise: she's already awake. She has been for seven minutes and is trying to decide whether she should get up. It's only 3.59 but the sheet is twisted and the blankets — which Ian insists on because he can't bear duvets — are heaped on her feet.

Her shoulders are cold, her legs hot and she thinks she would give anything for the light weight of Dacron, for the smooth sweep of a duvet. She is gritty-eyed with the need for sleep, and wide awake.

Ian sleeps on beside her, in spite of the thump-bump-shriek under the house. It sounds like a fight to the death. There's a particularly loud thud, then silence. Thank God.

Ian sits bolt upright. 'Thassthecat?' He stumbles out of bed as he speaks and gropes around for a pair of shorts. He still sleeps in the nude — that hasn't changed in all the years they've been together.

But getting up in the middle of the night to rescue their old fat cat, this is new. Louise watches his shape as he bumbles around in the dark. There was a time when he had barely tolerated a pet in the house. But now he anxiously calls the cat, frets if it doesn't eat enough, combs it every week to remove its dead hair and buys it fake rats to play with. He calls it Fatso and Fluffybum in a soft doting voice.

And he gets up in the middle of the night to rescue it from the feral toms that prowl, starving and angry, through the neighbourhood.

Louise wonders if it's a kind of displacement anxiety. Ian refuses to accept that Brent, their son, is anything but perfectly placed in life.

A despairing wow-wow-wow sirens up from under the house. Louise hears Ian make his soothing noises and, a few minutes later, just as she has sorted the blankets and snuggled down again, he arrives back with the cat. They both get into bed, Ian stroking and patting and saying there-there while the cat talks back in purrs and chirruping meows.

Louise wonders if maybe it's not displacement anxiety after all.

The cat adores Ian, has done so from the day it arrived in the house, and maybe Ian's just succumbed. He is its god, its hero, and it must be nice to be loved so absolutely.

Whatever.

Whatever it was, she doesn't want to share her sleeping space with a cat. Sighing, she slides out of bed. 'I give up,' she says.

'Okay, love,' says Ian.

Louise envies him his ability to drop straight into sleep.

She pads through the house to the kitchen, not bothering with lights because they have lived in this house for so long that its crooks and corners are as familiar to her as her own skin. Past the bedrooms with the wobbly doors and high brass handles; past the guest room where her father stayed after her mother died.

She pads, barefoot, over the thinning carpet down the big wide hallway, her fingers trailing over the polished hall table. She touches the gilt-framed picture of Great-Aunt Julia, steps around the brass elephant Jessie brought back from Thailand on her big OE, and pauses in the place where Brent rode his trike into the wall. He was four then, and that was when he broke his arm for the first time and Louise lost the baby.

Ian had decided to plaster the wall himself. 'Save some money,' he'd said at the time, but it wasn't just the money, Louise knew. Sometimes you just had to keep busy.

Louise loves the imperfection Ian's handiwork has left, in a way she suspects is slightly mad. But when the sun shines down the hallway, the painted bump glistens like a small pregnant belly.

At first, Ian had offered to have it fixed.

'One day,' Louise had answered, but she moved the table to cover the bump until Ian forgot all about it. Now, it is a part of the house, forever. Or as long as it is possible for forever to last.

She is aware, as she moves into the grey-lit kitchen, that forever is a word that belongs to the fierce sticky hugs and solemn promises of childhood. I will love you forever, Mummy, I will.

She wonders again how such an all-encompassing love can switch to active dislike. But these thoughts are fish-hooks, and she's been caught before, for too long already, and she turns away from thoughts of her son.

You can only grieve for so long.

She begins the routines of her day — a couple of hours earlier than usual, maybe — and a wry smile tweaks her mouth as she fills the kettle and scoops ground coffee into a plunger. More time to fill.

Once, she had planned on going back to uni and finishing her degree, but couldn't muster the enthusiasm. Did the world really need another sociologist, she wondered, and the answer was always no. She could get a job, she thinks, but has no qualifications and even less experience. She's spent her years supporting Ian in his work, in bringing up Brent and in nursing her mother, in comforting her father when his wife of fifty years finally died.

Louise wouldn't mind a job. She suspects, though, that she would end up as one of those over-made-up women fussing around in a specialist kitchen store, selling a spoon for every task, a knife for every chop. It's not an appealing image. But it's a job that would reflect much of her experience.

'Bugger it,' says Louise. She stares outside. It's light enough now to make out colours and the eastern sky is a shimmering liquid edge. A pheasant awk-awks up on the bank, a thrush clears its throat, and a quail calls for its morning smoke: tobacco, tobacco. Soon the stir of birdcall will be a full-on shout to the day.

The best hour of all, thinks Louise, and decides to make some meals for her dad. He might be in a rest-home but he still prefers her cooking to anyone else's: so she assuages her guilt at not caring for him as she did her mother by taking him pottles of soup, small dishes of mild curry and chicken fricassee; slices of lemon meringue pie, chocolate cake and shortbread biscuits. When it's the right time of year she picks the strawberries from her garden and makes him tiny pots of chunky jam: she preserves the feijoas from the tree he gave her twenty years ago as a house-warming gift and she grows tomatoes so she can make him relish, just the way her mother used to.

Her father is grateful, she knows. But since his stroke, he eats less and less. She's seen her made-with-love meals and preserves in the hands of nurses, visitors and other residents. She doesn't mind. If her dad can't eat them himself, it will be giving him pleasure to pass them on.

By the time she's washed, chopped, sliced and diced the vegetables and sautéed the chicken mince, by the time a batch of muffins is cooling on a rack and a potato-top pie is bubbling in the oven, it is gone eight o'clock. She makes fresh coffee, and carries a cup up the hallway.

'Ian,' she says. Her husband is still asleep, flat on his back, his mouth open and the cat curled on his chest. The cat opens one eye; Ian snores on. Amused, Louise places the coffee on the bedside table and gives him a shake. 'Not going to work today?'

'Wha?' Ian is not a good waker. 'Saturday,' he mumbles and rolls over. Fatso slides off but, forgiving as ever, simply kneads her paws on his back and begins a rumbling purr.

'Bad news, hunny-bun. It's Friday. And it's past eight, so if you don't hustle, you'll be late.' Louise is pleased with her unintentional rhyme. 'C'mon, sleepybones.' She pokes Ian again, and he scrambles up to sit on the side of the bed, a stocky man with long, thinning hair and a well-rounded potbelly. He blinks up at her and looks exactly what he is — a middle-aged, small-time accountant.

Louise has always loved him, and she leans down and kisses his mouth. He grins at her. 'If I'm late,' he asks, 'does it matter if I'm later?'

'Not to me,' she says, and lets him pull her back into bed. She tries to feel guilty that it is Rob's hands she imagines caressing her breasts and stomach. But guilt eludes her: she is just filled with a greater longing than ever. She wants.

'Wow,' says Ian. He's breathing hard and has a slightly stunned expression on his face. 'I should wake up late more often.'

When he has rushed off to his cubicle at the bank and Louise has showered, she sets about portioning the meals she has prepared for her father. She keeps a supply of plastic containers for the job. They're just the right size for his small appetite, and because they have hinged lids he doesn't have to fumble with plastic wrap.

She thinks of his hands and the way they have become weak and pale, the way they lie in his lap, trembling, and grief and love tie knots in her chest. Get a grip, she tells herself: he's okay. She pulls open the cupboard where she keeps the containers. It's empty.

Resigned, Louise stares at the spot on the shelf. She's not the most organised of people and is used to running out of things. Still. She's visiting her father later: she'll buy some containers on the way home and put the meals together then. It'll make no difference if he gets them today or in a few days' time.

She tries not to think that it wouldn't make a speck of difference if he never got them at all.

Her life, she thinks, is made up of tenuous threads and if even one were to snap, the whole fabric would unravel.

Her father doesn't notice her when she first arrives and she pauses in the doorway of his room, mustering the strength to smile and say, You're looking good today, Dad. Only he doesn't look good. The stroke has left him split in two. Viewed from the right he is a proud, elderly man, stooped and a bit scrawny, but who still carries something of the bearing that years in the British Army gave him. His mind is sharp, and on a good day his eye gleams with intelligence and humour.

Viewed from the left, it's easy to see the damage the stroke has inflicted. His face droops. His left eye weeps constant tears and his arm and leg are withered. He is reduced to using a walking frame and needs a nurse to help him shower and shave.

His heart is broken along with his body, and Louise knows this. But he's made an effort and is dressed today, and sitting, propped with pillows, in a La-Z-Boy armchair. 'Hi, Dad,' she says.

'Louby-lou.' His face lights up. 'How's my sweetheart?'

'Great,' says Louise. She feels guilty as she always does. It seems an insult, somehow, to come charging in full of vitality and health among these grey and dying people. It is even worse that one of them is her own father. She pulls up a chair and sits close to him, takes his hands in hers.

'That young man of yours?'

'Went to work whistling.'

Her father's good eyebrow quirks upward and she grins and kisses his cheek. She chooses the withered side, refusing to let his disfigurement affect her love for him.

'Jessie?' he asks. This is their routine — the queries about family and friends. Jessie was Brent's girlfriend a few years ago; she had his baby about the time Brent lit out for distant shores. She has done the decent thing and kept in touch.

'Jessie is good and so is Ryan. They're coming to see you Sunday. It's Ryan's birthday and she thinks you'd like to see him.'

Her father grunts. Children exhaust him, but he loves his great-grandson in small doses. He has reservations about Jessie, doesn't understand why a woman wouldn't follow her husband around the world. Not that she and Brent were actually married, but he doesn't really understand that either. 'Brent?' he asks.

The final, painful question. 'Dunno,' says Louise. 'Haven't heard for a while. Somewhere in Canada, I think.'

'Silly boy,' says her dad.

'Dad,' Louise begins.

'Got something to tell you.'

They both pause, but Louise waits patiently. She has learned that when her father breaks with routine, his processes take longer. She can do nothing for him except give him her time: the only thing which she has in plenty. Her father has so little of it, she thinks, but she knows that the little he has is exhausting to him.

'Louby. I'm tired of this lark,' he says.

'I know.' She does know, and grieves for him. Old age is a tyrant. 'But what can we do except make the best of it?' They've had this conversation before.

'We can end it,' says her father.

'End it?' echoes Louise. They've not had this conversation before. She stares at her father, at his weeping eye and twisted mouth.

His good, strong eye holds her gaze steadily.

'After Sunday,' he says. 'I'd have liked to seen that grandson of mine, too, but we can't always have what we want, can we?'

'Sunday.' Louise is dazed. 'Are you serious?' She knows he is, but has to say something.

He nods. 'Will need your help, but.'

'Help,' she looks at him helplessly. She doesn't ask why, doesn't need to. 'How?' she asks. 'How?'

'Usual way.' His expression is tender and understanding. 'Pills. I've been saving them a while now. It's time.'

'Oh, Dad.'

'Don't you get upset now,' he says. 'Can't stand emotional women.'

It's a joke, an old joke. Louise's mother was a crier. She cried for joy, for beauty, for love, for pain, for sorrow. Old joke or not, Louise doesn't feel like laughing. She doesn't know what she feels. Not surprise, she knows that much. She wishes she did. 'I'll miss you,' she blurts.

Her dad nods. 'Goes both ways.' He's silent for a while and then says, 'But I'm looking forward to seeing Cora again.'

Louise is glad her father believes in something. She doesn't know if she does, not any more. She can't imagine heaven with its streets of gold or a flame-filled hell. She can't imagine ghosts and spirits hanging around this earthly plane. She can't imagine her parents, restored to youth and running through flower-filled fields. And if it is all real, what about the baby boy she lost before he was fully formed, before his fingernails had grown and his eyes had opened?

Who would he be in that unimaginable afterlife, Louise wonders, which leads her to the age-old question: If Ellis had lived, would he have been happier than his brother? Would Ellis have loved her more than Brent does?

'You'll come Monday?' asks her father.

'I'll come,' says Louise. She kisses him again. His good cheek this time, and then has to leave, quickly, before the numbness cracks apart. She doesn't want to feel anything, not yet.

'Good girl,' she hears her father say. 'You're a good girl.'

She is home before she remembers she meant to buy plastic containers. She stares at the muffins, the potato-top pie and the casserole she made only a few hours before and for a moment she wants to smash everything, to scream and to curse, but the numbness holds and she decides, instead: one last time.

One last time she will take her gifts of love to her father.

She heads outside to the garage. Ian is bound to have some plastic containers lying around. He saves the trays the meat comes in, the empty yoghurt pottles and ice-cream boxes and other sundry plastics. 'What for?' Louise has asked him.

'Might come in useful,' he says.

'What for?'

'Screws and stuff,' he says, which always amuses Louise. Ian's handyman skills never did improve and mostly, now that they can afford it, she calls a repairman when something breaks.

She pauses at the garage door. The garage is Ian's domain and she rarely enters it — she parks her car in the carport attached to the kitchen where it's convenient to unload groceries, where she can go from the house to the car without getting wet when it rains.

Her eyes widen as she looks around. It's a regular garage with room for two cars and shelving along the walls, a workbench tucked in a corner. But — good God — everywhere she looks she sees plastic containers. Dozens of them — maybe hundreds. They are stacked along the workbench and piled in corners. Towers of plastic all, as far as she can see, carefully matched for colour and shape. Round with round, square with square, rectangle with rectangle: white, coloured or transparent, with remnants of writing such as Apricot Yoghurt and peeled-back labels declaring a cost of $2.31.

'Good God,' says Louise. Ian has got a bit carried away, she thinks, and then her gaze falls to a stack of banana boxes on the floor next to a white melamine cupboard. The top box is full of red plastic bowls, the kind that Christmas puddings come in, and there are dozens more of them than she and Ian have ever eaten. Where has he been getting them from?

Dazed, she moves the box and sees that the second box is full too, and so is the third. 'Good God,' she says again, and coldness seeps through her. She opens the cupboard. It is jammed full of plastic containers in all shapes and sizes. They are stacked neatly according to size; all fitted in together like a giant, bizarre pile of children's stack-a-cups.

There must be thousands of plastic containers stacked in the garage.

'Oh, Ian,' says Louise. Oh, Ian. When she trudges back to the house she is clutching an armful of plastic and feels as if the ground is swallowing her whole.

The message light on the phone in the lounge is flashing. Two calls while she was outside. She pauses to listen.

'Hi, Louise, Jessie here. I'm getting my chakras balanced this evening — can you look after Ryan for an hour or two for me? I'll call around later.'

The second message is from Rob. 'Louise . . .' There's a pause. 'Are you going tonight?' Another pause, as if giving her time to answer. 'I'll call around on my way and give you a lift, eh?' Rob is awkward with words, but Louise doesn't care.

She plays the message again, just to hear his voice. The 'tonight' Rob is talking about is folk night at the local pub, a monthly event when a disparate bunch of musicians and singers get together for open-mike sessions. Louise sings a little and goes along when she can to add her voice to the chorus. It's fun and something different, but when she's being honest with herself, she admits she only goes so she can see Rob.

Ian is a bounce-in-the-room and be-the-centre-of-attention kind of person. He always has a joke and a smile, is the first to crack open a bottle of wine. Rob is quiet and contained and often has a distant, closed expression on his face. Sometimes, she feels there is a wide and empty desolation in him and she wants to fit herself against him and hold him close. She wants to fill those spaces. She feels connected to him, and doesn't understand why. But sometimes, when he glances at her, Louise thinks he feels the same kinds of connection she does.

Other times, when she catches a glimpse of herself in a mirror — her greying hair and ageing face — she thinks that if he does know how she feels, then he would feel nothing in return but pity for a flabby, middle-aged woman with a crush.

No matter what he thinks, she goes to Folk Club; she sings and drinks beer and is happy because she's in the same room as him. This is the way he makes her feel.

'You poor sad cow,' she says, very loudly. Perhaps she'll stay home this evening after all, especially if Ryan is coming round. She sees too little of her only grandchild.

As she cooks dinner she tries not to think of her father, hoarding his pills for God knows how long in the bottom drawer of his dressing table. She tries not to think of Brent, backpacking somewhere in North America, searching for Utopia in needles and pills and drifts of smoke; and she tries not to think of the contempt he feels for his staid, boring mother.

She tries not to think of Ian saving his plastic containers and forgetting which day it is and turning into a sentimental old man.

She tries not to think of Rob and his desolate centre and is glad when the door bangs open and Ian yells, 'Honey, I'm home.'

'Hi.' She squints a smile at him and carries on making gravy while he crashes around pouring a whisky and dry. 'You're a bit late,' she says. It's unusual for him.

'Yeah. Would you believe I took a wrong turning?'

'You what?'

'Went the wrong way. Must've been on my way to visit Al.'

Louise doesn't know an Al. 'Who?'

'Zeimers,' Ian says, grinning. 'Al Zeimers, geddit?'

'Oh.' She knows she should laugh, but suddenly she is weeping, bent over the stove with a wooden spoon clutched in her hand.

'Lou? You all right?'

She straightens up quickly. 'Fine.' She smiles, wide as the sky. 'Dad was a bit poorly . . .' She wants to tell Ian about what her father has asked of her, and draws a deep breath.

'Better,' Ian says, 'if the poor old prick were to just cark it. You know?'

Louise is left stunned beyond pain or sound. But any stray thoughts she'd had of staying home and talking to Ian disintegrate. She doesn't want to be in the same house as him, not for one moment longer.

He can be chief babysitter.

Ryan is a sweet and rowdy little boy who looks nothing, to Louise's relief, like his father. Jessie drops him off, but almost before she has finished saying hi, Ryan is off demanding horsey-rides on Poppa's back. Poppa doesn't take much convincing to get down on his knees. 'God,' says Jessie. She is smiling. 'Isn't he gorgeous?'

Louise looks at her husband of almost thirty years galloping across the carpet on his hands and knees and throwing back his head and neighing. She thinks, He'll pay for that tomorrow. With sore knees, aching back and a stiff neck at least. While Ryan, clinging and wobbling and giggling helplessly, will wake with an exuberant yell and demanding food.

'Nana-nana look at me!'

Louise is looking. 'Gorgeous,' she agrees softly, but she wonders how it is that these gorgeous, beautiful, perfect little boys turn into such broken men.

Rob arrives for her at seven in his ute. His guitar is in the back, along with a scattering of magazines and books, and as Louise swings into the seat beside him she has a feeling of coming home.

'How are you, Rob?'

'I'm okay. You?'

'Okay,' Louise says, and she is: okay and softly happy. Rob, she thinks, is quieter than usual and withdrawn. She wants to flow around him and say, Let me heal you, Rob, and suspects this is another of her small insanities.

'I'll have to let you out,' he says. 'The door's jammed.'

At the pub Rob buys her a beer, then wanders off to tune his guitar and talk with the other musos. Louise takes a seat in a horseshoe-shaped booth, and soon she is squashed in by a group of regulars: Sam, Ellen, Quin, Gerry and Shona, all talking and laughing and being themselves. Lucky them.

Louise pretends she is someone else: not a mother, not a wife, and definitely not a daughter, and she starts to relax.

Shona stands and taps her glass with someone's coffee spoon, as if she were an MC. She is a big woman, loud, with a sharp wit and sharper eye, a voice that raises goosebumps and a liking for filthy limericks. Her eyes gleam as she looks around for a victim. She settles thoughtfully on Sam.

'Aw, Gawd, not me.' Sam is new to the group, in his twenties, and from out of town.

'There was,' begins Shona, 'a young man from Thames, who played his guitar with his friends. He played hard and long,' Shona's tone is suggestive, 'till the strings caught his dong and now he's no longer a mens.'

Sam laughs as hard as anyone, even though his cheeks are scarlet. 'C'mon, buddy.' Shona slaps him on the shoulder. 'I'll buy you a beer.'

This is the thing about Shona, Louise thinks. She is just who she is, with no pretences. She is both kind and cruel, loud and soft, she wears garish flowing skirts and beaded waistcoats; she teaches guitar and lives alone in a house she has painted scarlet and blue. It is quite possibly the ugliest house Louise has ever been in, but she loves how Shona has made it an extension of herself. How she is boldly, unashamedly, gloriously herself.

Ian wanted their house to be understated. 'Timeless,' he called it, and Louise gave away dreams of buttery yellow and soft greens. They'd ended up with a home in shades of grey and white and gold. Classy, Louise supposed, but often she just thinks it dull. Cold. Shouldn't, she wonders, your own home reflect who you are, somewhere, somehow, sometime?

Even with compromises for your husband, shouldn't one room echo your own heart? She thinks of deep rose pink, of purples and blue in misty swirls. A flash of turquoise, maybe.

Ian would have a heart attack.

'Ooh, that Rob's dishy.' Shona is back with a bottle of wine and a jug of beer, which she slops on the table. Everyone squeezes around to make room for her again, and Louise finds she is perched on the edge of the seat. She has a perfect view of Rob, who leans against a pillar and watches the guitar player in the corner. He is dishy, in a worn, remote kind of way. It pleases Louise that other women agree. She slides off her seat and crosses to him.

'You okay?'

He smiles, but his eyes don't light up. 'Long day.'

'You should've stayed home.' She has to step closer to him as someone squeezes past behind her; he has to lean down to hear her speak as new music bursts from the corner.

'Yeah,' he says, 'but I wanted . . .' He stops abruptly, but it is all Louise needs. She feels that their chakras line up, throat to throat, heart to heart, belly to belly. She wants to press against him, place her wrists against his, touch her heart to his chest, her mouth to his. 'Rob.'

He turns from her. 'Take you home, eh?'

He has to get out of the ute and come around to open her door again and for a moment they stand in the darkness. 'See you next month?' says Louise.

'Na. I'm heading off.' Rob doesn't look at her. 'Seems for the best.'

'Oh.' Dismay and hurt rise in her chest like small acid tides. Am I going to lose everyone? she wonders. 'I'll miss you,' she says, and thinks of her father.

'I already do,' says Rob, and now he looks at her. 'Miss you.'

She moves into his arms then, and understands it isn't enough, will never be enough. He needs all of her. She wants to give him all. Their hug is platonic.

Ian is in bed when she goes in, though he's not asleep.

He's left the hot tap running in the bathroom. Louise turns it off slowly, watches the last of the water running down the dark hole of the sink. Am I going to lose everyone? she wonders again, and thinks of her sons. She goes through the routine of checking the house — making sure the doors are locked, the windows closed, taps shut off — before she climbs into bed.

Fatso is curled up in her spot, and she gives the cat a shove. Across the valley, an owl calls morepork twice and falls silent, waiting for a reply.

'Have a good night?' asks Ian.

'It was okay. How was Ryan?'

'Good, great. My knees are a bit sore, though.'

Good job.

'Listen, Lou. I'm sorry about what I said before. About your dad. It came out wrong, you know?'

Louise doesn't want to give him easy forgiveness.

'Honey? I really am sorry.'

'I know.'

Louise lies in the darkness, longing for sleep, the blankets heavy on her legs. Ian snores beside her; Fatso-Fluffybum purrs on his chest.

She is thinking of her son, lost on another continent. She is thinking of murdering her father on Monday morning, of the train that's thundering down Ian's track. She thinks of Rob and how he is leaving.

Grief claws at her chest.

The morepork calls again from across the valley and she waits; waits longingly, achingly, vainly, for a reply.

Tracy Farr

Surface Tension

Nick smells like a jumper you smoked hash in a month ago, then threw to the back of the cupboard: sweet, must, fug and dust. He has always smelt like this, with or without drugs. The smell is the sweat in his hair, curling down towards the tip of her nose as she tiptoes to kiss him on the cheek. The memory of the smell is dredged up from the base of her brain: she remembers the smell with her whole body, head to heart to cunt to toenails, the smell of her youth.

'Helen.' He kisses against the top of her head, holding her in a tight hug as they stand, just out of the rain, framed by the front door of his house. Music is coming from inside the house, just audible under the high, animal wail of a tiny baby. 'Come in and meet the family,' he says.

Helen follows Nick down a long wide hallway, past doors opening onto his life: steel grey office, sun-yellow lounge room, deep red bedroom, sour-milk baby's room. The hall ends in a big, open space. There's an impression of light, even with the darkness outside, the rain clouds and early morning.

Though she's never been there before the room is familiar to her, from the photograph of it in the newspaper clipping that her mother sent her last year. The paper had run a series of features over several weeks, 'A New Architecture for Australia', and of course they'd featured Nick — so lucky to have him back, internationally acclaimed, signature work in London and Hong Kong, settled back home with beautiful young wife. And so on. There was a photo, a fish-eye view of this room, Nick in the foreground distorted by the lens, with the thin, backlit figure of Young Wife in the background, sitting on the wide window ledge, her legs drawn up under her chin like a sulky teenager.

In the room now, Young Wife sits with a dark-headed baby at her breast. She looks up from the book she is reading, eyes beaming smiles from under curling dark hair.

'Eva, this is Helen. Helen, Eva. And our little Nina.'

The baby lifts her hand from her mother's breast, as if to wave hello to Helen. Nick stands watching them all, grinning.

'Hello, Helen, I've heard so much about you. Good to finally meet you.' Eva smiles at Helen, that beatific smile.

'You too,' Helen says. 'I can't believe we haven't managed it before now.'

'Well, cuppa?' Nick asks.

'Thanks, I'd like that,' Helen says quickly, welcoming the thought of something to do with her hands, something to hide behind.

'Water for me, darl,' Eva tells him, 'and can you bring me the macadamias? Sit down,' she says to Helen, 'make yourself at home. Every time I sit down to feed her a message goes straight to my brain. Ping! Macadamia nuts. It's costing us a fortune.'

'I was the same with Liam. Roasted almonds. Here, I brought something for Nina,' Helen says, foraging in her bag. She brings out a lumpy gift, leans across and places it on the table in front of Eva.

'Helen,' she says warmly, 'thank you.'

Nick brings a glass of water and the bowl of neat round nuts, places them on the table by Eva. He picks up the gift, starts to unwrap it.

'Thanks, Hel.' He drops the paper and holds up the stocky wooden bee, spins the rounded red wings with his finger. 'It's great.'

'It's a Buzzy Bee,' Helen tells them. 'It's a New Zealand thing, one of those classics that everyone had when they were a bub. They're mostly made in, I don't know, China or something now, but this is a true blue Kiwi-made one.'

'It's lovely, Helen, thank you, she'll love it.' Eva smiles that smile again, beaming it in Helen's direction.

Nick squats in front of Eva — squats easily, Helen notices, watching him in profile. None of the old-man groans Tom's started making when he kneels or bends or folds himself into a small space. Nick waves the bee close to Nina's head. 'Look, Bubba, Kiwi bee from Helen and Tom.' He turns and shrugs, smiling, at Helen, 'Thanks, Hel. It's great,' puts the bee down on the sofa next to them, and places his hand gently on the suckling baby's head.

'Isn't she beautiful,' he says quietly. It isn't a question, and he means Eva as well, Helen thinks, not just the baby. She remembers, vaguely, years ago when her boys were new, Tom looking at them — at her — like that. Nick turns his head to look at Helen, a sideways look, and she's struck again by how little he's aged, how much he's still the young man she remembers from all those years ago, when he was hers.

Nick gets up — Helen listens especially hard for the creak, the crack, the under-his-breath oof, but doesn't hear them — to tend the whistling kettle, then brings mugs to the low table the sofas cluster around.

'It's chai. Decaf. With honey.' He takes the piss as he tells her. 'It's all we've got at the moment. Eva's made me empty the house of anything with caffeine.'

'Fine, fine.' Helen holds the mug to her face, inhales. It smells like wet dog, but sweet. She watches Eva and the baby over the steaming tea. Nina has dozed off, her mouth slipping away from the long nipple leaving a trail of saliva and milk joining mother and child.

'I'll take her,' Nick whispers, and settles back into the sofa as Eva lifts the baby and places her in his arms.

'You forget how tiny they are,' Helen says. 'I know it's a cliché, but you do, you know. When they grow up.'

'How old are your boys now?' Eva asks, reclining now against the arm of the sofa, her feet (her tiny, soft feet, Helen notices) against Nick's leg, rubbing gently.

'Liam's twelve, James'll be ten in August.'

'God, are they really?' Nick whistles. 'I remember when you called me, when Liam was born. I was in—'

'Hong Kong. And we were in Seattle.'

'Was it that long ago?' the two of them say simultaneously, then 'Snap!' They all smile at that, smile over their drinks at each other. They're quiet for a while, the rain clatting on the roof, the tea keeping them occupied.

'They're lovely when they're like this, aren't they?' Helen says, nodding at Nina. 'Is she sleeping at nights? Are you sleeping?' I'll bet you are, she thinks. You can't look like you both look and not be sleeping, not with all the new-baby-bliss hormones in the world.

'She's amazing,' Eva confirms, 'we're so lucky. She's slept through every night, a good nine or ten hours.'

Fuck, Helen thinks, remembering the endless, sleepless months when her own boys were little. 'Mmmm,' she tells them, 'lucky you. Makes a difference. I remember being so knackered, just constantly knackered.' But you have youth on your side — bitch, she thinks, then mentally takes it back.

'Hey, we still going out for breakfast?' Helen asks. She feels the need to get out into the world, be on neutral ground, away from the perfect warmth of their house.

'Yeah, let's—'

'Darl, would you mind if I didn't? Helen, I hope you won't mind. I'd love to come, but I really should have a lie down while Nina's sleeping. You two must have plenty to catch up on.'

'Oh, sure, I know how it is. You sleep,' Helen says, relieved and ashamed at feeling relief.

'I'll take Nina with me, babe. I can take her in the frontpack, she'll be fine. Give you a real break.'

Eva reaches up to Nick's ear with her toe (with her toe!) and strokes it. 'Thanks, darling,' she coos. She unfolds her legs from the sofa, stands up, yawns and stretches, and reaches out to take Helen's hand. Eva's hand is cool and warm at the same time. Soft. Small. 'So lovely to meet you. We'll talk again before you go home, yes? You should come around for dinner. She's in a fresh nappy, darl. Have a lovely breakfast,' and she turns and leaves the room, padding down the hallway. Helen hears her humming, hears doors opening and closing, a tap running. Then quiet. Nina snuffles, still asleep.

Nick looks across his daughter at Helen. 'Shall we go, then?'

'Yeah.'

'I'll just grab a few things for Nina, won't be a tick. Would you hold her?'

'Sure.'

Nick stands, hands the sleeping bundle to her, then busies himself filling a bag with nappies, spare clothes, a distracting toy: the simple paraphernalia of the tiny. Helen's body remembers how to hold a tiny baby — how long has it been? — but she is still surprised by the lightness of her, and the heaviness, the density, at the same time. 'Hello, Nina,' she whispers at her. 'I used to be in love with your dad. I'm Helen.'

They drive towards the coast in Helen's rental car. Nina is strapped into her capsule in the back, behind Helen, where Nick can turn around and see her easily, touch her, touch the plastic keeping her safe. There is a quilted fabric star hanging above Nina on the handle of the capsule. She is asleep, oblivious.

The roads have changed, the houses of Helen's childhood gone, and she is always shocked when she visits to come this way, to see the great walls of roadway where the little dark houses used to be. She turns the car into North Street, pointing straight at the sea. They pass Lyons Street a few minutes later.

'Your old street,' Nick says, grinning at her.

'They sold it ten years ago,' she tells him, smiling, thinking, He remembers, he remembers about me.

'They happy where they are? Mandurah, right?'

'Yeah, yeah, they seem to be. Dad's got his boat, Mum's got half the street organised into book clubs and coffee mornings and god knows what else. The house is all new and shiny — well, ten years new, but you know. Yeah, I think they're happy. They don't miss town.'

'God's waiting room down there, isn't it?'

'It's not so bad; it's nice for them. It's their fiftieth wedding anniversary next week, that's mainly why I came over. We're having a big party — all the old cronies, people I haven't seen for decades.'

'God, fifty years. I can't even begin to imagine what that must be like.'

'Tom and I will've been married twenty years next August.'

'Shit, I guess so. Shit. It seems — recent. And forever ago.'

'You'd already gone. You were in Sydney,' she tells him, surprised at how well she remembers, at her lack of hesitation in remembering.

'So I was. Well.'

'Well.'

'Well, wish them all the best from me, eh. Your mum and dad. They probably don't remember me.'

'Oh, they do. Mum adored you. She always asks me what you're doing, as if I have some kind of wireless connection to your diary.'

She turns the car into Marine Parade and the ocean is there, dark blue for winter, the noise of it, the glory. The rain has stopped as they've driven, and the sun's out, as if the rain was never there. Helen pulls the car over, swerves across the road and stops, skewed, looking at the water, out to sea.

'God, it's gorgeous,' Helen says under her breath.

'I know. It's why I came back, you know? I fucking love this coast.'

Helen winds the window down, closes her eyes and listens to the surf, smells it.

'It's so warm. For winter. Wellington's freezing at the moment. Well, always.'

'Serves you right, living there. I never could understand why you went. Christ, New Zealand! Traitor.'

'Bugger off. Dag.'

They smile, sit a bit longer. Nick turns back towards his still-sleeping daughter, pulling the rug up towards her chin. He leaves his hand on the rug as he turns back to Helen.

'I check her about a thousand times a day, you know? Is the blanket too far up, can she breathe, is she warm enough, is she too hot, too many clothes on, not enough. I've never felt like this before. I'm taken over. She's so beautiful. I don't want anything to happen to her ever — nothing bad, nothing imperfect. Such perfect feet; they've never trodden ground.'

'It's true. I remember, when they're this little you can't imagine them being bigger than they are, being — violated isn't the word, I don't mean anything as strong as that. Changed. Affected by the world.'

'Yeah.'

'Then all of a sudden they've got big tough smelly feet, just like us. Scabs and cuts and dirty toenails, sticky hair and sour breath. At least, boys do.'

'I'll put my Nina in silk slippers with sheepskin lining. Keep her perfect and soft and untouched,' Nick grins at Helen, not meaning it, meaning it. 'Put her in a convent. Only let her listen to k.d. lang.' They both laugh. 'Come on,' he tells her, 'I'm dying for a coffee. I'm sick of fucking chai.'

The café is already crowded when Helen and Nick walk in. Nick cups Nina's sleeping head in his hand, her body strapped against his chest in the frontpack.

A couple is leaving a table by the window directly over the beach, and Helen and Nick replace them, polite smiles as they manoeuvre around each other in the too-small gaps between the tables. Seated, Helen leans against the window, looking out at the beach. There are swimmers, young and old, despite the temperature, despite the early hour. There are always swimmers at this beach, every day of the year, never mind the weather, Helen remembers that from when she lived here. She remembers thinking they were mad, the ones who swam in midwinter like these ones — she was only ever a summer swimmer, would wait until the water was as warm as it would get. Now, living in Wellington, she hasn't swum in the sea for years. Not since the boys were little enough to need her to go in with them, and even then she could usually count on Tom to do it.

A girl drops menus on their table. 'Coffee? OJ?' she asks, her smile as abbreviated as her language.

'Latte, please,' Helen tells her, 'and a croissant. With jam.'

'Flat white, thanks, and a smoked salmon bagel.'

'Right.' The girl leaves them to it, scribbling on her pad as she focuses on the next table.

'I was swimming for a while,' Nick offers, tilting his head to the side, towards the ocean and the tiny figures shivering behind the glass. 'Every morning, rain or shine. It was good. Good start to the day.'

'Why'd you stop?'

'Don't know. I was away last winter and I got out of the habit. Kept meaning to take it up again, but I never got around to it. Then Eva got pregnant — I don't know, it was just one of those things that fall away, out of your life. I'll take it up again sometime. It was good, good for me.'

'Something's been good for you, anyway,' Helen says before she can stop herself. 'You look great. Pact with the devil? Painting in the attic? What's your secret?' She looks at him then, really looks, and finally, this close, she can see the lines around his eyes, at the side, the depth of the lines running from his nose to the edges of his mouth. Laughter lines, etched deep. He's doing it now, utters a loud laugh.

'Clean living.'

'Bollocks. Tried that, and look at me.'

'No, you look great,' he says quickly, too hearty so she knows she doesn't.

'Thanks, Mr Magnanimous. Good for my age, you're supposed to say.'

'You're only my age,' Nick says.

'Don't remind me. I feel like your mother.' Because she does. Helen knows that Nick will be noticing how like her mother, how like her father, too, she's grown in the years since they last saw each other. That she's put on her mother's heft and wobble; that her face has set, like her father's, into its plain, Anglo-Saxon, meat and potatoes heritage. She has faded to the pallor of wall putty after years in the cool, unbeckoning sun of Wellington. Next to Nick's slim, dark face and body — melanzane and vino rosso, his dad was the same, she thinks, skinny as a rake, young until he died — she feels a generation older. Come on, she tells herself, shake yourself out of it.

'Eva's lovely,' Helen says. And young, and beautiful. Especially young.

Nick just smiles back at her, an almost embarrassed smile — acknowledging, thinks Helen, that he knows exactly how lovely Eva is, how lovely to wake up next to, and how slim and beautiful is her body to hold.

'How's old Tom? Say hello to him for me,' Nick offers, to match her Eva-talk.

'Fine, he's fine, same as always. Busy, of course,' because her dear Tom is always busy, and always fine, and always the same. Always has been. Her Tom is the same as he was when she met him: her pillar and post, her support, her brace. As he was all those years ago, when he picked her up and buoyed her up and cheered her up: when he put together the desperate pieces that Nick had left her in after he'd torn out her heart.

But her heart doesn't hurt any more, not from Nick. It's been too long; the hurting stopped years ago. When she sees Nick now, it's as if he's a long-lost, well-loved relative, someone she's delighted to remember is related to her. Except that he's not, not really related, except by shared memories of long-ago passion, flared bright with youth. She looks across the table at him now, cradling his daughter, and loves him like a brother — but not a flesh and blood brother. Fluids, that's what they shared. He's a fluid brother: long-ago shared spit and come and her own distant wetness bonding them surprisingly tightly still, like wet clothes sticking to hot skin. Or as a coaster holds tight to the bottom of a glass, lifting with the glass to the lips of the drinker. Surface tension binds them, with the molecular memory of the long-ago action of fluids.

The girl brings their coffee and food, and they smile their thanks, drink, eat a little, comfortably silent.

Then, 'I was going through boxes when we moved back,' Nick tells her, 'and I found that old poster for *The Merchant of Venice*.'

'Oh god, you had it on your wall for so long! You used to stare down at us from that poster — remember? You had it over the bed. Your eyes used to follow me around the room, I swear.' His hooded eyes, Helen remembers. 'I've got the programme at home somewhere. Among all the other junk.' She smiles as she thinks of them, so young. 'We felt so old, remember? We were the oldest ones in the Drama Society — they were mostly first years; we felt like their grandparents.'

'Yeah, we were twenty-two.'

'You were the only one for Shylock. Remember, everyone said you looked Jewish enough—'

'Yeah, Italian, Jewish, what's the diff?'

'—and of course you were so old—'

'And you were so pissed off that you didn't get a part.'

'As always. They made me the dramaturg. I was always the fucking dramaturg, and no one outside the English Department had any idea what one even was. I don't know why I kept going back.' Helen laughs at herself, at growing close to anger even from such a distance. 'It got under my skin, you know? I wanted to be on stage, and all I got to do was bloody dramaturgy. God, I still don't even know how to say it properly.'

'You were good at it,' Nick tells her. 'You used to boss us around. I'd never noticed you before that.'

'I'd noticed you. You were the reason I kept going back. I wanted desperately to do the trial scene opposite you — I had this grand plan to subvert the text and sexualise it.' She takes the piss as she speaks, but it was true, it had been her plan. 'You know, all that talk of flesh. "This bond doth give you here no jot of blood: the words expressly are a pound of flesh." I had it all worked out. You were powerless.'

He is looking at her, fraternal, all notion of sex gone, a mild smile across his face, as if amused to remember that he and Helen, that the two of them, that he and the middle-aged woman, that they ever were. The sexual tension is gone — as it should be, she reminds herself. Nothing like the smell and electric loin-stirring of the *Merchant* nights, the rehearsals flowing into notes, flowing down to the pub and eventually into his bed — but not until after the last night. A full house, the crowd loud and loving it, the great surge of whatever it was that lifted and bound them all backstage, in the dressing room after the last performance was over. Bubbly, then too much beer, then someone had a bottle of rum, and then just the two of them and a calming joint, sitting on the grass across from the pub, by the river. The talking had stopped, stilled by the smoke, and she'd placed her hand on his back and found that it belonged there, and he'd turned to her and smiled that bewildered smile and that was it, their mouths had fallen together and the kiss had lasted an hour, longer, and he was glorious and she smelt him and her hands travelled the country of his body as they lay on the cool grass, under the dark night sky, and she rolled him over and he was hers, his flesh was in her, slick, and the night-time smell of the river was all around them, wet — like them — and as glorious.

Helen looks at Nick across the table again, chewing her lip. Her heart doesn't hurt any more. It doesn't. There is Tom, there are the boys: the heart-stopping beauty of their boys. And things are good; her life flows along with equanimity. There is little rush any more — not from sex much, not from anything, really. She assumes this is the business of age, that this is the shape of a human life. And it is gentle and calm, and she cherishes this. Yes, she must cherish this, that's the way: celebrate the calm.

'It's all so long ago, that's what I find hard to—'

Nick breaks off from speaking, looking up as a deep voice shouts — maybe a word, maybe 'God' or perhaps something less formed, a gutteral grunt — at the counter of the café.

'Christ,' the woman at the table behind them says under her breath, then 'Oh, sweet fuck!' from across the café, then there's shouting from the beach, wafting to them through the windows. Helen and Nick look up from their coffees, look at each other, then down onto the beach like the others in the café, but it takes them some time — only seconds, but everything is starting to happen more slowly, time becomes strange at this point — to focus on what is happening. There is splashing in the water — but it's a beach, there is always splashing. There is shouting from the beach — but there is often shouting. It's the tenor of the shouting that helps them make a sense of it. The shouting is shrieking, and the shrieks are of terror.

There is a bigger splash then, a flash of dark, a bullet, an intensity, that most feared thing. There is a shark, breaching the surface. And, as quickly, the shark is gone. Or has become unseen. And Helen realises that there is a swimmer in the water who is not moving, that there is something strange about the swimmer's shape and lack of movement. And that there are two other swimmers in the water, heading to the still swimmer. Two strong swimmers, two men, stroke matching stroke as they pound towards the still one. Everyone else is getting out of the water; they are standing, shivering, lined up staring at the sea, watching the strong swimmers as they reach the still swimmer. One of them grabs the still swimmer in rescue hold, around the neck; they swim as quickly the long fifty metres back to shore, to the shallows, and collapse on the sand in only intermittent reach of the fingers of foaming water.

There is no blood, not even a drop to pinken the water. No jot of blood. She had expected blood. But there's the flesh: there is the torso in the shallows where the other swimmers have dragged it: legless, one arm missing, like a shop-front dummy waiting to be dressed. The strong swimmers lie, exhausted, either side of the torso. Three other men lift the body from the froth of the surf, lift it from the shallows and stagger up the beach, place it gently on the sand, above the reach of the water, then one of them kneels at the head, places his hands at what's left of the neck. Other watchers reach for the two men, the rescuers, help them up, drape them with towels, with jackets, warm them. As she stares, unable to move her eyes, someone covers it — the body, him, she tells herself — with a cartooned beach towel. The shape of his body fills the shape of the cartoon cat, raises it lifelike above the sand. A second person covers the cartoon towel with a plainer one, appropriate, coloured blue-green like the ocean.

Helen hasn't heard a sound for the last several minutes. It is as if the noise of the people in the café has stopped, the cars have stopped, even the waves have been making no sound. But she realises, as the noise slowly starts to filter back into her mind, that her brain must have blocked out the noise, that her poor senses had more than enough to take in without the crash of the waves, the frightened shouting from the beach, the sharply inhaled relief — it wasn't me — of the people in the café. As her hearing returns, Helen hears the thumping whirr of helicopters, that sound of war zones and traffic reports, vulturing in for a stickybeak.

She tears her eyes away, looks shyly at Nick across the table. Nick, still staring through the window, covers Nina's sleeping eyes with his hand, as if to shield her from the horror.

'Oh fuck, oh fuck, oh fuck oh fuckofuckofuckofuck,' he whispers, on and on and on into the salt, sweet, chill air carrying death in through the barely open window.

They drive to Nick's in a silence broken only by the quiet whimperings and snufflings of the restless baby in the back seat. Helen stops the car on the verge outside his house. Nick lets himself out, then comes around to Helen's side to unbuckle Nina. He reaches his hand in through the open driver's window and lays it over Helen's, clenched around the steering wheel. His hand on hers is cold and sweaty. Shock, Helen thinks.

'Hel,' he says quietly.

'Yeah,' she says to the steering wheel, 'look, tell Eva I had to go, I can't—'

'Yeah,' he says. 'It's okay.'

She looks past him and down at the staring, black-eyed, perfect baby.

'Hey, Nina,' Helen says to her quietly, and the baby stares back at her in an understanding way, 'look after yourself.'

When she gets back to her sister's house there is no one home, but Ruth has left her soup for lunch, and a note telling her to help herself, that she and Tony have gone to meet friends for lunch, they weren't sure when she'd be back, XXX, see you, R.

Helen can't take her eyes from the sheet of paper in front of her. The lightness, the lack of shark and flesh and horror in her sister's note hurts her, makes her heart ache for the sister, the wife, the daughter, the mother, the lover of the dead man on the beach. For his flesh, ripped and cut and torn: forfeit. To bait fish withal.

She reaches across the bench for the phone, presses the numbers that will take her home. Five rings and the machine clicks on, and it's James's voice, her baby: 'You've reached the Flannery household. We've all been abducted by aliens, so we can't take your call right now. Please leave a message after the beep and we'll get b—aaaaaaaaaaagh, the aliiiiiiiieeeeeeeens—' The message dissolves into a gurgle of alien noises, she can hear Liam's voice as well as James's, then laughter, muffled. She hears the beep and breathes in deeply.

'Tell those aliens you're entitled to one phone call. I'm at Auntie Ruth's all day. Call me. Love you all.'

She turns to the stove, lights the gas under the soup. She takes an open wine bottle from the fridge and pours herself a large glass. She raises her wineglass to the window of her sister's warm house, out through the window to the trees. It has started to rain again, and the garden is dark and glistening. Water coats the outside surface of the pane; drops join to form rivulets then part again, becoming singular, individual.

James George

Figures in Ice

Nathan

CC sits still, holding the banjo against her. She stares over my shoulder. I turn to the window but there's nothing there.

'What was it, honey?' I say, but she doesn't answer.

I let a chord chime on my mandolin, play a quick run to jolt her back into the here and now. She gives me a smile.

'Sure you can keep up with me?' she says. 'Should I play some senior stuff?'

'In your dreams,' I say.

I play a few licks, the fastest runs I know, trying to challenge her. Until about a year ago it did. Now she aces me.

People marvel at how she can play so well when she's only fifteen. But they haven't seen the hours every day she practises.

CC

Dad leans forward, looking down at his mandolin. Grey hairs sprout from under his hat brim. He's taken to wearing that hat all the time now, since he started going grey fast. Last week I knocked on his door with his morning cuppa and he reached and put the hat on even before he swung his legs over onto the floor.

But I still saw the grey, fading like dead branches.

When they announced the music prize, giving me six months being tutored in the US, Dad had a smile as wide as the harbour bridge. Then all of a sudden his face went as grey as his hair. We hugged, and he whispered something I didn't get.

'What was that?' I said.

He didn't answer, just held me real close.

When he let go, his smile had come back.

NATHAN

When she was a baby she had red hair like her mom. A few wisps at first, then a few more strands appeared, week by week. By the time we left the States and came to New Zealand she had near to a full head of the stuff. Shame I had to dye it black.

In time the black grew out, just like she'd grown out of her name. Her birth certificate said Melissa Jane but she came into this country as Catherine Carlene, and she's always answered to CC.

One of the first banjo players to record was a guy named Dock Boggs. Came from up in the mountains of Virginia. He was a coalminer and sometime moonshine runner. In those hill towns there were musicians way beyond being virtuosos, but most of them never recorded. Just played with their buddies or families, now and then putting on something at a church fair. But old Dock saw a sign taped against the glass of a furniture store one day, about a guy coming from a recording company in the city, trawling the back roads and mountainside cabins for musicians. So Dock goes back on the allotted date, sets himself down with his banjo and starts a-playing. Playing the songs he was near enough born singing. In a voice that wasn't singing as such, more the rasp of boots with the soles coming off on miles of country roads. Pickaxes and bandsaws and mine whistles and TB coughs and graveside crying.

When CC was eight years old she got a bronchial infection that turned into a chronic condition. It meant she had to stay in bed day after day. It was as if something had curled up on her chest, like some fat, angry cat. When she spoke it spoke, when she coughed I could hear its claws around her throat. Even on the medication she never seemed any better and the paediatrician would say something about how it needed to take time.

Time. Sounded to me more like it needed to take my little girl.

We saw a specialist who took me aside after the consult, while CC lay wheezing on a bed in his white-walled surgery.

'The patient's chances of recovery are reasonable,' he said. 'When a subject is so afflicted, anything can happen. Monitoring will tell.'

I leaned close.

'You're talking about my daughter here,' I said, 'not some goddamned subject.'

She wasn't supposed to get up out of bed but I didn't have the heart to stop her. She'd lean puffing against the window frame of our caravan, watching the other kids going past the trailer park gates.

Barefoot kids walking along the road with wet swimming trunks and towels. Skateboards and bikes and skipping ropes. Then one day I heard her humming a piece I'd been working away at on my mandolin. She asked me to play it for her, so I did, sitting on the edge of her bed. She reached out and touched the fretboard, made a crazy note ring. We laughed. We hadn't laughed since that fat cat curled up on her chest. I handed the mandolin to her, showed her how to fret it. She fingered a minor chord, staring at the window. I had an old banjo I'd picked up in a yard sale before we left home, so I went and got it, plucked at it while she sat there strumming the mandolin. She stopped, reached for the banjo. She could only just hold the damn thing as it dwarfed her hands, but she tried to fret it anyway, leaning back in the bed, her head raised on three pillows.

I bought her some thumb and finger picks, showed her stuff she could plunk-plunk-plunk out on the banjo while I played the mandolin. Little melodies over my chords. Basic bluegrass stuff. She lay there coughing now and then, her breath harsh against our music, trying to pick away on this glorified tin drum, strung with what sounded like chicken wire. I turned my head away, looked at the wall. She didn't need to see my cheeks all wet.

Then I remembered old Dock and his songs of crop failures and whisky stills and cops on the take and coalmine owners busting up union meetings with wrenches or fowling guns. If she was gonna fade away, I'd rather she at least had music to keep her company.

I sat up playing my mandolin one night, unable to sleep. On the edge of my bed with my eyes closed. Old-time stuff I had to reach back through my granddaddy's ears to find. I felt the light go off of my face and looked up to see CC standing in front of the lamp, holding the banjo. She began to play along, watching me for the chord changes, feeling her way. Some bum notes but a whole bunch of them good 'uns too.

The weaker her body got the stronger her playing became. Like it was her sword against the thing. Then one day her body began to come on back to us.

By the time her cough started to dry up at last the bum notes were rare.

By the time that fat ol' cat had gotten up off of her chest and slunk off to strangle some other poor kid, she was playing smooth as applebutter.

CC

She was pretty, I guess. As pretty as your mum can be. We have a total of two photos of her. Two. I know the story off by heart. I made Dad repeat it enough times. He met her in the States, when he was playing mandolin in a country band. She was with a party of 'beautiful people', that's what Dad called them, slumming it at the dives on the edge of town. She stood watching him play, then came up to him at the bar.

'That's an exquisite mandolin,' she said. 'May I?'

He looked down at her hands. She had long, graceful fingers.

'Are you a musician?' he said.

'No. I'm an artist.'

'Paint and such?'

'No. I only use things I find. Old wood, stone. Ice.'

'Ice?'

'Yes.'

He lifted his hand off the mandolin and she picked it up, ran her thumb over the wood. She didn't try to make any notes ring, just turned it over and over, felt the wood's texture. Dad glanced down and she followed his gaze to the reflection of both of their faces in the mandolin's woodgrain.

They left the States and arrived in New Zealand when I was only about a year old, lived on a commune down by National Park.

That first winter Mum caught pneumonia and died in a shed made from fibrolite and corrugated iron. With snow on the ground and ice in the eves. He laid a garland of candles in a half moon around her silent face.

She's buried in a little cemetery behind the town.

I've never seen her grave.

'Do you know where Mum's parents live?' I said to Dad as we were jamming on some country blues last week. 'Maybe I could look them up when I'm in the States.'

'Too far away,' he said.

'We could at least tell them I'm going. See if they can make it to some place I'm passing through or whatever.'

He shook his head.

'Everyone else I know's got four grandparents,' I said, 'and I've never met any of mine.'

'They'd bore you, just some old people. You've got more interesting things to do over there.'

'It wasn't a big deal. Just a thought.'

I hit the strings hard, felt the thumb pick digging into my skin.

NATHAN

Can't blame her wanting to look up her mom's parents. I'd like to look up my own folks, but I can't.

My old man.

Shit.

I can still hear him, back when I first told him I was quitting the classroom, going touring with the band instead.

'Hellfire, boy,' he said, 'what's wrong with teachin' school? You all too fancy for that now?'

'Pop, look—'

I looked to where he sat with his chairback leaning against the kitchen wall. The shadow of his rainslicker hanging on its hook by the door. His falling-to-bits boots on the step.

'We didn't bust our butts to pay for your college fees for you to be some damn fool musician,' he said.

'I know.'

'Hell you do.'

'Pop.'

He closed his eyes, leaned further back against the wall. There were cracks in the paint, like a desert floor.

I never saw him again.

I lost touch even with his name, when Joseph John Kendrick became Nathan Watts to get on an aeroplane. A guy in a backstreet shop in Houston, Texas, saw to that, holding the forged passport up next to the real one and asking me if I could see any difference. I shook my head, handed him the money.

Dock Boggs had the godawful luck to be recording and travelling as a musician right as the Depression hits, 1929, and his career goes on the same skids as a coupla million jobs. People want to buy his records, but who can afford them? So Dock walks back on up that road he came down from the hills on. Sits back in his kitchen, playing his banjo till his wife starts hollering for him that they need to get back to earning some actual money to eat on. He leans his banjo against the rear wall of a cupboard and goes back down the coalmine and doesn't reach into that cupboard again for thirty years.

It was the folkies that resurrected him. In the early 1960s authentic American rural music was hip again. Dock was an old man by then, stooped and short-sighted and ornery fit to burst.

'Hey,' they say, 'didn't you use to be Dock Boggs? Man, you were there at the beginning.'

He picks up his banjo again, starts singing the same old songs in a voice tireder now, meaner with the ways of things that bore down on him. But under that scarecrow face and rockslide voice maybe there was a last surviving sprig of sweet summer grass.

CC's mom used to sculpt figures in ice. She'd walk out into the winter woods behind her folks' vacation cabin we stayed in for a couple of years, up in the Catskills in New York state. Walk out dragging a little sled on a rope behind her. I'd watch her vanish into the white, her red hair like a lantern amid the snow. She'd come back with a block of ice on the sled, haul it in through the doorway of her workshop.

She'd work away for hours on her ice, her tools laid out in precise order on the table. Sometimes she'd ponder a single cut for a half-hour, sitting on the edge of a sawhorse, tapping a chisel against her jeans. There were guys around used to take to car-sized blocks with chainsaws, carve out huge dragons and such, but Sara worked in intimate sizes, no bigger than her head, sometimes no larger than her hand. In the February chill her sculptures might last a couple of weeks or more. She'd display them in the towns and resorts around. An ice owl, a bunch of frozen flowers, a woman's face. When she was pregnant she sculpted a baby lying in a pair of arms. Then the spring thaw hit. Day by day the baby began to melt, its ripe cheeks thinning as if they were ageing with the passing days. But ageing backwards, shrinking down to a foetus, then back to an egg floating in water.

Then just water.

By the time CC and I left the States for New Zealand the only ice her mom was still sculpting were the lines of cocaine she cut with the edge of her credit card, to suck up into the paper tube and snort until her eyes glazed and she lay back staring at the ceiling.

CC

At the final contest night for the prize, I played a version of 'Foggy Mountain Breakdown', though only parts of it at the supersonic speed of the original. I interspersed it with some slow bluesy stuff Dad had taught me. Light and shade. Where he came from in Texas they didn't do bluegrass music as such. Browngrass, he used to call it, or Deadgrass.

'No-grass?' I said.

He smiled.

'Bout the size of it,' he said.

He taught me Tex-Mex, some Mississippi Delta blues. Some N'awlins shuffles and English folk music. Bit of everything he'd heard and assembled. So I don't sound like some Foggy Mountain Boy, but a little piece of everything. Little piece of everywhere.

Bits 'n' pieces.

'Dad,' I say as we sit ready to tune up, 'why don't we ever visit Mum's grave?'

He looks up.

NATHAN

Sometimes I see Dock Boggs' coalmine in my mind. Not the pithead and the tracks and wagons, but the tunnel. The darkness.

CC

I fly out for Los Angeles late tomorrow night.

But.

But there's a place I need to go first.

The train leaves Britomart station at eight in the morning. I've packed two changes of clothes, a few sandwiches and a water bottle into my backpack. I carry my banjo in its case. The train guy checks my ticket, hands me a boarding pass and nods towards the second carriage. The luggage dude reaches for my banjo case.

'Nah,' I say, 'I'm cool with this.'

I left a note on the dining-room table, propped up against the old Jack Daniel's bottle Dad uses as a vase. I was out of home this morning and on the bus well before he was awake.

> *Dad,*
> *Something I have to do. Be back tomorrow, in time to head*
> *for the airport.*
> *CC*

Auckland seems to go on forever. Houses after houses after houses. Then space clears at the edge of the tracks, there are fields instead of concrete. Cows instead of cars.

My cellphone rings and I glance at the caller ID.

'Hey, Dad.'

'CC, where are you?'

'On a train, heading south.'

'South? Where south?'

'National Park.'

'Honey, you shouldn't have.'

'I need to, Dad.'

Silence. I wonder for a sec whether the cellphone reception's gone. Then he speaks again.

'CC, there's stuff I should've told you. Should tell you.'

'I'll be back tomorrow.'

'No, I mean, I mean important things you have a right to know.'

Silence again. Even over the train's rumble I imagine I can hear him breathing. Like when he'd sit alone in his corner of our caravan when I was sick. Sit looking into the shadows, showing those shadows the tears he always thought he hid from me when he smiled.

'Dad—'

'CC, I need for you to forgive me,' he says, 'or at least to understand.'

'What are you talking about?'

More silence, then, 'I'm not making sense,' he says. 'I can't do it like this.'

'Dad?'

No answer. He must've been cut off. I wait for him to phone again but he doesn't.

Sara

I do the same thing every year. Get another candle and put it with the others and light them all. There's fifteen candle-holders now, all lined up across the doorway to what would've been her bedroom. I light them every March 4th. Her birthday. I only step over them to go in and dust the windowsills, sweep the floorboards or put on a different bedspread. A bedspread on a bed no one has ever slept in.

Sometimes I talk to her, almost beneath my breath, when I see something that I imagine maybe she'd like, as if we're both looking at it together.

'It's my birthday next week,' she'd say.

'Yes,' I'd say, 'I know.'

'Just checking,' she'd say, and we'd laugh.

I keep an eye out for things all year. So her room has fifteen presents also: teddy bears, colouring books with crayons, dolls, a dollshouse, a framed montage of horses, a glass sculpture of a dolphin . . .

CC

There's morning mist in the gullies between the hills; every now and then a pond appears, or a half-hidden tree. The train stops in the middle of nowhere — 'waiting for a work crew to vacate the track', says the voice over the intercom. I lean back in my seat, my face almost against the window glass. There's a rider on a horse, sort of zigzagging up a steep hill rising next to the track, ushering a lazy group of cattle forward. The horse is careful, wary, the rider not seeming to be forcing it, just pointing the horse's head where they need to go. I open the little sliding window, taste the cold air. I stand and pick up my banjo case and walk out to the little viewing platform between this carriage and the next, stand watching the horse and rider.

I take out my banjo, begin a slow country blues over the low hum of the train's motor. Our little band: an idling train, a horse's hooves on wet grass, a banjo. I slip into some old Delta stuff, the strings ringing out in the morning cold. The rider turns, looks through the mist at me, raises the brim of their hat to me, and I see then it's a woman. She looks forward again and steers the horse on up the hill and I go back inside.

The mist clears as we go through Otorohanga and Te Kuiti, then head into a kind of canyon country all the way to and past Taumarunui. We slow again and the voice on the intercom says we're into the Raurimu Spiral. The tracks climb as we go around, the engine pitch rises and dips. Even the air seems to change, purify. I take a deep breath, turn to watch the white mountaintops rise beyond the copper-coloured grasslands.

I keep on playing, playing to the railroad tracks, to the grass and flax bushes and blue sky. People come and go, look down at me. One guy reaches down with a two dollar coin, tries to hand it to me. I smile, shake my head.

The town of National Park stands stark against the volcanoes and flat plains. We stop for lunch, but this is the end of my line so I step off and nod goodbye to the train dudes and walk into town. First shop I come to I go in. There are furry hats and scarves and booties on the counter.

'Hi,' I say. 'Where's the cemetery?'

'Eh?'

'The cemetery.'

The woman looks me up and down, shrugs, gives me directions.

There's a glade of wind-scarred trees, scrubby grass beyond. Should be right about here. I scale a rock wall, do a 360, yeah, there.

Some of the headstones are in rows, some of them are in a jumble. The oldest ones are the least ordered. Since there's, like, no map, all I can do is walk every row. So I do.

But.

But there's no Sara Watts.

Sara

The hardest time is when the candles burn down to nothing one by one. Each year I buy an extra one, larger than the others, so each time they burn down they last that bit longer. When the tallest of them gets low, down to a stub of wax and the last plume of wick, I turn all the lights in the house on, so when it goes out nothing will change.

A week after her fifth birthday I took her to her first day at school. When she was nine I sat watching her in dance class, her tiny body reflected in the floor-to-ceiling mirror. Teetering on one leg, her other leg trembling as she tried to raise it out over the wooden boards. At ten she fell off her bicycle and I crouched in the faded fall leaves rubbing her knee while she frowned into the grey sky. Then one day I sat and talked to her about what it would mean to become a woman. The changes that were going to happen to her and how she shouldn't be scared of them.

All of these things floated in the smoke of those shrinking candles, the only place where they lived. There and in my imagination.

He and I weren't like that perfect, plastic couple you see on top of wedding cakes. There was never any question of that. His road was slippery with booze, mine with white powder. The first coke habit I had cost me time I can hardly now remember. The second, after he and I had married, did something far worse. It took away my little girl.

He used to look at me when I was high, that 'check out the poor little rich girl' look he'd get. When he was sitting there sculling bourbon so fast the liquid never settled from the time he first opened it until he dumped the empty in the trash. But he wised up before me, got clean before me, took her away — 'for her sake', he said. Then I got clean, away from my old haunts and bloodsucking contacts. Three months in rehab in California, another six in therapy.

'Paid for by your old man's money, I reckon,' he said.

'So what if it is?' I said. 'Where's my Melissa?'

'Oh, so now you care.'

'I haven't stopped caring. Where's my daughter?'

'I don't believe you.'

'You don't believe I love her?'

'I don't believe you're really through.'

The lawyers were brought in. He thought he had a strong case, but my turnaround was genuine. I had changed. I'd been off substances for a year by then. I had testimony from counsellors and yes, the best lawyers money could buy. But he never showed in court. The police looked, the FBI looked. Interpol. Private detectives my folks hired in Canada, Britain, Australia.

I haven't seen my baby since.

CC

I go back along the rows again, check out the jumbled stones, even wander out of the cemetery to see if there are other headstones around, but there aren't. I sit against a tree, looking at all the stones, pale against the brown grass. I pick up my banjo and sit playing. Sit there for a couple of hours, playing in the sun, watching the tree shadows move across the grass. Play until I hear the crackle of boots on the stones of the path, look up to see Dad standing there, our car small in the distance behind him.

'She isn't buried here,' he says.

'I don't understand. You always said she was.'

He takes off his hat, runs his fingers up through his grey hair and puts the hat back on. He walks over, sits on the grass next to me. He takes a gulp of air, glances across at my water bottle. When I pass it to him his hand is shaking. The shimmering water sparkles in the plastic.

'Where is she buried?' I say.

SARA

I'm glad I moved from California back up into the Catskills, back up to the old place. I'm glad to feel the seasons change again. Be able to see the leaves turn. I've cleared out the old barn I used as my workshop. My tools were covered in cobwebs and dust. One of the windows had broken and the wind blew in dust and leaves and snow. There's damp leaching up the walls. But my sawhorse is still here and I fitted a new leg in place of the broken one on my old work table.

I moved Melissa's bed up from California, too, set the candleholders in the doorway.

NATHAN

She sits there on the grass, looking at me.
    'Where, Dad?' she says.
    I lean and pick up her backpack.
    'Let's go home, honey,' I say.
    She puts her banjo back in her case.
    'Dad?' she says.
    We drive out of town. The hills are dry, a pale, barren fawn.
    'When we left the States it was just you and me,' I say. 'Your mom didn't come with us.'
    'Why did you always say she came too?'
    'It was easier.'
    'How was it easier?'
    'She isn't buried anywhere, Seece. Well, not that I know of.'
    'She's alive?'
    'Yeah, I guess.'
    'You guess?'
    'I haven't had any contact with her for years.'
    'How many years?'
    'Since you were a baby. Since we left.'
    She turns and stares out the car window.
    'But why'd you tell me she was dead?' she says. 'All these years I asked you things about her.'
    'So you wouldn't want to get in touch.'
    'Stop the car.'
    'I'm sorry, I'm not explaining this very well.'
    'Stop the fucking car!'
    There's a rest area up ahead. I pull in, stop at the edge of the asphalt where the long grass runs down to a river. CC gets out and half walks, half runs through the grass, carrying her banjo. I call after her, then follow. Near the riverbank her Nikes slip and she flops down hard onto the dirt. She doesn't get up, just sits, leaning over her banjo case, rocking.
    'I could've written to her,' she says. 'Talked on the phone. Done all sorts of stuff.'
    'CC.'
    She looks up. Her curls hang ragged over her eyes and cheeks. She doesn't brush them away.
    'Or did she just not want me?' she says. 'Is that it?'
    I sit.
    'I thought that once,' I say. 'But it wasn't the truth.'
    'Then what?'

I reach into my jacket, lift the envelope from the inside pocket, set it down on the grass. She glances at it, then back up at me.

So I tell her. Everything. When I've finished she sits staring across the river, into the reeds and tall grass on the other side. I lift the envelope from the grass, hand it to her. She takes it, without touching my hand.

'What is it?' she says.

'Open it.'

She tears the envelope's edge, lifts out the photo. An ice sculpture of a baby, before it began to dissolve.

'I don't understand,' she says.

'Turn it over.'

475 Cedar Way,
Catskills, New York
Tel: 1 845 655 4296

'Her folks will never have sold the place,' I say. 'They loved it too much. So someone there will be able to put you in touch.'

She sits staring at it.

'I wrote that stuff on the back for you years ago,' I say, 'way back before you even got sick. I've tried to give it to you a hundred times.'

'Why didn't you?'

I look down into the river, where the trees on the far bank and the clouds beyond the trees are reflected in the water. There are dark shapes of rocks beneath.

'Why, Dad?' says CC.

CC

The international terminal is full of people coming and going. Banks of TV screens with all the flight stuff on it. In, out. I sit holding the photo. At first I thought it was glass.

'No,' said Dad, 'it's ice.'

'Ice? It wouldn't last.'

'But look how beautiful it was.'

The voice on the intercom says I should go through the gate. I turn to Dad.

'You know what it'll mean if I phone this number?' I say.

'Yes,' he says, then again. 'Yes.'

People begin to queue beneath the arch over the entrance to

the escalators up to the departure lounge. I point towards the gate.

'I have to,' I say.

He nods. He moves to hug but I don't, so he leans and kisses my cheek. Then I'm gone, boarding pass in one hand, photo in the other. Banjo snug in its case over my back.

SARA

I set out my tools on the cleaned and polished work table. Chisels and knives stepping up in size from one to the next. Some steel wool and sandpaper. Last night brought a fall of fresh, late-winter snow. I get my sled and wind the rope around my hands and head off into the woods. Hard ice has formed on the rocky outcrops, where snow and rainwater fell.

There are pieces large enough to sculpt an owl or a teddy bear or a dollshouse.

Perhaps even a child.

Charlotte Grimshaw

Thin Earth

I LOOK BACK ON MY marriage, searching for patterns and clues. I think about the good times and the bad times, and I try to work out why things turned out the way they did. Sometimes I get an idea and decide to write it down, although I don't have much faith in my scrawled notes. There's no point talking to Max. He doesn't believe in analysing. 'Best to move on,' is what he says. 'No need for post mortems.'

Last night I had a dream about our trip to Wanganui, when we were still married and Charles was still at his private school. I remembered how I'd loved the town, and how it seemed to have a special flavour, particularly because of the bad thing that had happened there. The way I dwelt on it, as if it had been laid on as a special entertainment just for me! I see myself, hair-trigger alert, alone, running through those silent, dusty small-town streets. And then later, on the trip back, something happened that made me feel, not different, but, I don't know, more reflective. Perhaps I understood better what the bad thing had meant to the people whose lives had been crushed by it.

Anyway, the dream set me off thinking about that holiday. It was high summer in Wanganui. There I was, flustered, one eye on Max junior, the other on the local newspaper spread out on my knees. Max lounged beside me, his gaze fixed on Charles, who stood out on the cricket pitch, a slim, elegant figure in the hot light, poised to deliver his killer bowl . . .

Charles was playing in a four-day cricket tournament. It was just before the end of the school holidays, the hottest days of the year. We'd come down from Auckland with him for the fun of it, to see the town and stay in a motel. Charles and the rest of the team were billeted in the dormitories at Wanganui Collegiate. Karen and Trish's sons were playing; they'd come with their husbands, along with a lot of other parents. They were lined up along the edge of the field with their deckchairs and umbrellas and picnic baskets. It was early but already it was hot, cloudless, still. The grass was faded; the ground was hard and dry. Simon Lampton, strenuously jolly, his nose covered with white zinc, was handing around boxes of juice.

The parents, the milling kids. Karen and Trish waving. I, fiddling with my glasses, looking down at the paper, pretending not to see. I didn't want to sit with those two. I was reading about the murder.

There were streets cordoned off near the river when we'd driven in. It had been on the radio. A young woman, a barmaid, had finished work, stayed for a few drinks, left the bar and vanished. She'd been found in the Whanganui River, floating by the bank. She was twenty-one years old.

'Slow down,' I'd said to Max as we passed. There was a caravan set up, some policemen. Those tapes they use to cordon off crime scenes. I see myself as if from outside, the car slowing, my face pressed against the glass.

After we'd unpacked that first day I went for a walk. The motel was by a railway line. Heat rose off the stones, the grass was withered. I looked along the train track to where it disappeared around a bend, the trees forming a green tunnel over it. The streets were quiet, full of misty light. There was hardly anyone about. In the suburban streets around Wanganui Collegiate there was silence, hush, closed windows and gates, streets so thickly covered by trees that the sun shone down in thin beams of light. Empty gardens. Green shade. Walking, I kept looking behind me. Thinking of that girl.

But it wasn't here she'd been killed, in the prosperous suburbs around the Collegiate, but down near the river, where the houses are small, shabby, poor — tiny workmen's cottages, ragged bungalows. These were the streets we'd seen as we drove in. I wanted to go down there.

The police had no early leads. They were 'building a picture' of the girl's life. A 'lovely', 'bubbly' person, she was the daughter of regular churchgoers (Baptist). She was 'always willing to help someone in need'. She had ambitions beyond working in a bar. There was no regular boyfriend, but a wide circle of friends. A popular young woman. Her parents too devastated to comment . . .

That first day of the tournament, Max and I watched the game for an hour or so. I finished reading the paper. 'I might go for a run,' I said.

'It's a bit hot, isn't it?'
'Will you look after Maxie?'
'Yeah.'

Little Max settled down against his father. They looked very alike: handsome father, white-blond child. I felt a silly pride looking at them.

I said, 'You know the murder? I think I'll go and look for clues.'

Max laughed.

'*Go on*, Mummy,' Maxie said. Big Max patted my leg and lay back. I went away feeling happy.

I changed into my running clothes at the motel. The room was stifling. I locked it and set off, across the main street and down towards the river. The further you got from the Collegiate, the poorer and more ramshackle were the houses. The streets were just as empty down here. Occasionally a dog looked up from a porch, or a figure moved between washing lines, behind a slatted blind. I recognised the name of one street: the young woman had lived there with her parents. There was a tiny Baptist church on the corner, where they'd held her angry, desolate funeral. I reached the river and stopped. The river was wide, stretching away into a blue summer haze. I ran along the path looking down. Somewhere near the bank, in the shade under the trees, the body had been found, floating. I looked at the long grass along the path, thinking I would find something. I stopped a couple of times to look at bits and pieces lying on the ground, knowing it was foolish yet hoping to find something, a real clue.

A man wearing a hood passed me, his head down, his face hidden. His hands were heavily tattooed. He turned once and looked back, as if he'd sensed me staring. There was the black shadow under the hood, an absence of face. He turned away, with a flounce almost, a quick rotation of the hips, something smooth and furtive. I checked my watch. Murderers often return to the scene of the crime.

I didn't find the exact spot. It was too far along the river. I came to a railway bridge. There were rowing boats and spectators along the bank. I was getting to the end of my strength. Max would be wondering where I was. I rested, watching the boats. Then I turned back.

I went a different way. Three young men sat on a veranda, their feet resting on old beer crates, silently watching me. Two little girls played outside a rundown house, the door open, a shape moving behind the flyscreen. Towards the main road a van pulled out of a liquor wholesaler, nearly running into me. I called out, 'Hey!'

The driver's shaven head sat necklessly on his shoulders. He had a beard, a gold earring. The van's back windows were blacked out and it was daubed with symbols: suns, moons, stars, crosses. Painted along the side, in black Gothic lettering, were the words 'Sinister Urge'. The man glared, reversing out. I saw his face behind the windscreen, reflections of leaves sliding across it. He had missing teeth, a tattoo on his cheek. He drove off with a dramatic little squeal of tyres.

That night in a café on the main street I was describing him to Max. The van with its blacked-out windows, the painted words: 'Sinister Urge'. Imagine him parked outside a school! I said, 'But if he was genuinely sinister, if he wanted to abduct people, he wouldn't want to advertise it, would he? He'd drive an anonymous car. So why just threaten people? Why does he want to do that?'

'More wine?' Max said. He was trying to get Maxie to eat his dinner. The little boy was slumped, exhausted, in his chair, red circles of sunburn under his eyes. Max held a piece of garlic bread under his nose. Maxie gave it a weary swipe.

'Did you find any clues?' He signalled for the waitress.

'No. I probably saw the murderer though.'

'The freak in the van.'

'No, a guy in a hood.'

'Oh, right.'

I looked at Maxie. 'He's sunburnt,' I said.

'Well, while you were looking for *clues* I couldn't find his *hat*.'

'Oh. Sorry.'

Maxie slumped moaning into Max's lap.

We walked back up the main street under the hanging baskets of flowers, Maxie on Max's shoulders, asleep. I looked at his little brown leg, Max's big hand holding it.

'It's so nice to get away, out of Auckland.' I put my hand in Max's back pocket. The town had woken up. Boys cruised down the street in low-slung cars, stereos thumping. There were groups of teenagers. A band was setting up on at outdoor stage. A banner behind them read: 'Subhuman'.

'Jesus, look at them,' Max said. There were three boys, twanging their instruments, testing their microphones in that humourless way they do: 'Two two. One two.' Their faces were painted, their clothes ripped. Their heads were shaven at the sides. Dreadlocks sprouted from the tops of their heads.

Max eyed them. 'Imagine if your kid turned out like that.'

One of the boys had black lipstick and eye paint; another had his face blacked out.

'Fucking nightmare,' Max said. He hitched Maxie up higher.

'You never know,' I said, 'they might be Collegiate old boys.'

'Over my dead body,' Max said vaguely.

One of the boys donned an oxygen mask. Max applauded. 'Oh, tremendous, that. Nice touch.'

I laughed. 'He's got quite a nice little face, the one with the makeup.'

'Nice? God!'

We walked on companionably, through the warm dark.

In the night the motel room was hot, pitch black, silent. I woke from dreams that were loud, garish, raucous; they came at me and receded and I lay spinning in the dark before I sensed them coming again, points of light rushing across the blackness, a mad caravan: their flaming torches and whirling figures, their fires.

The next day we went out for breakfast, then to the Collegiate fields. Trish arrived, clambering down from her husband's SUV. She was wearing an extraordinary outfit, all stripes and pleats and ruffles. Maxie stared.

'I've got a red waine hangover!' she called. 'Saimon and Karen haven't even got up yet!' She sank down next to us and talked lazily to Max for a while.

Women liked Max; he had a kind of restless, rogue air. I listened and smiled. I wasn't at ease with Trish: she brayed and talked about money and never stopped fundraising and ordering people about. What was it about her and the Lamptons that made me uncomfortable? — their stifling 'respectability', I suppose. Deep down, some small, fierce part of me despised the way they behaved, although I was faintly shocked at myself. But already I was thinking of running away, down to the river, through the hush of the Collegiate neighbourhood, then the treeless glare of the poor streets with their rickety fences and scruffy gardens, and finally the river with its gorgeous misty distances, its blue beauty glittering under the pearly sky — its beauty and what it held within it, things hidden below the surface, terrible things.

Here came Simon Lampton trudging across the field, a pair of fold-up chairs slung over his shoulders. He stood waiting for Karen, who was carrying a tiny shopping bag. She told him where to put everything. Karen and Trish talked about their night out.

'You were a raiot. You nearly got Saimon into a faight!'

'It wasn't quite like that,' Simon said, embarrassed.

Trish let out a screech of laughter. It carried in the still air. Out on the pitch the boys and their coach looked up. Simon glanced at me, wrinkling his forehead. He was a big, awkward man. He held up his hands, as though to quell the cackling women. Max stretched out, sexy and languid on the grass. I caught Trish eyeing him and giving Karen a look. I imagined them over their red wines, the lewd things they'd say.

I said to Simon, 'Have you been reading about the murder? I went down to the river, where she was found, the dead woman. The town's different down there. It was spooky on the riverbank.'

I stopped. Consternation in his eyes. 'The murder?'

'Yes, I went looking for clues,' I said, trying to charm, ingratiate. Oh, funny little me.

He looked pained. 'How horrible.'

'Mmm, awful. A young woman, bludgeoned to death . . .'

I was getting this all very wrong. There was a look of revulsion on his face.

'It is terrible,' I said hastily. 'I'm being frivolous. Sorry.'

He gave a weak smile. Silenced, I watched the cricket. I listened to Max murmuring with the women, his louche, cynical chuckle. Why wasn't I horrified by the idea of the dead girl? I just wanted to go back there. I wanted to go down to the river and find the exact spot this time — where they fought, where he picked her up and threw her dead body down the bank, down into the speckled shallows.

I surprise myself. I can run faster and further than I ever could before. I'm running away from the playing fields, genially dismissed by Max, who doesn't mind looking after Maxie, whom he adores, released from squawking Trish and nervous Simon, running away, down to the river. What is it in me that wants to stand in the very spot? Is it just that I want to be right at the point of something, anything, so long as it is at the highest, hardest pitch of feeling? Or is it that I do not understand something that Simon Lampton does? I remember thinking as I ran: I don't know if Max loves me. I don't know. *How can I know?*

I didn't see the man with the hood again, nor the man with the sinister van, although I looked for them, running each day through the silent, heat-shimmering town. I loved the place; the more I ran through it the more it turned away from me, charming, secretive, elusive. I felt as though I were following some important thing that I couldn't quite catch, only saw it at the corner of my eye, fading into the leafy shadows. In the afternoons, drugged with exercise, I watched the clouds moving across the sky, the boys on the field, thin figures in bright light.

On the fourth day, at lunchtime, Charles ended the tournament by whacking the ball away for four. We clapped and cheered. There were little speeches, a prizegiving. Dependable Simon lugged out a chilly bin full of iceblocks. And then we were getting in our cars and heading out of town, the boys tired and silent, Max cheerful and smelling of the peppermints he'd sucked to mask the smell of the matey cigarette he'd shared with Trish behind the trees.

We drove past the crime scene, deserted now, the evidence tapes hanging limp, the police caravan with its torn posters. We were heading to Rotorua: the boys had requested a trip to the mudpools. We drove for a long time in contented silence, my hand resting on Max's thigh.

At a motel in Rotorua the boys played minigolf. We sat on the balcony in the hazy evening light. Max smoked, his feet up on the railing, his gaze fixed on the boys. He jumped up to get Maxie a sweatshirt, thumped down long-sufferingly to help free a trapped ball. I remember his smoke curling up into the air, the boys' voices, the tiny thwack and scuttle as the golfballs rattled through their courses. There was an orange street-light outside the window of our room; it blinked and buzzed in the night like an incensed eye, peering between the blinds while Max and I made love.

The next day at Whakarewarewa, told of the price for a family ticket, Max said, 'You're kidding!'

Something formed, shaped itself up in the face of the woman in the booth. Lips parted, downturned mouth, nostrils widening.

'Is there a problem?' she said.

Max shrugged, and thrust the money through the hole. The woman fell to hard laughter with one of her colleagues. A whiff of brimstone hung in the air.

'God, Max,' I said. 'Don't have a fight before we're even in.'

He laughed, wiping sweat from his face. Here it was even hotter than Wanganui — boiling water under the earth, white fire pouring out of the sky. It felt as though you could get sunburnt through your hat. Below the bridge children were diving for coins, their brown bodies sleek and shining. Charles and Maxie threw in some coins and the boys surged up onto the bank, shouting, spitting, calling for more. We moved on into the village. Neither Max nor I had been before. We were struck by the bucolic shabbiness of the place, its tumbledown fences and tiny dilapidated buildings. There was none of the touristy artificiality we'd expected.

'It's sort of raw,' Max said wonderingly. Between the buildings there were glimpses of battered cars, washing lines, back doors lined with gumboots and stacks of beer crates.

'Well, it's a real village,' I said.

We stood at the edge of a briny blue pool, the water steaming. Bags of corn were cooking at the edge. Heat came up in waves, along with the rich, oddly enjoyable sulphur stink. A woman wandered past with a walkie-talkie and a voice crackled out of it, asking whether the corn was cooked. Our boys ran about, marvelling at the plopping mudpools, the steaming vents. Across an expanse of rock and clay and scrub, over which clouds of steam wafted, a geyser suddenly shot water high into the air.

The boys shouted and pointed. 'We want to go to the geyser. Over there!'

We walked towards it but came to a locked gate. Trying to find our way, we headed up behind the village, past a hall in which a concert was being held for a tour group. A fierce child eyed me from a doorway. Behind a flyscreen, a woman jigged a baby in her arms.

A rough track led up a hill and we followed Max, who was determined to find the geyser for the boys. We walked through low scrub past mudpools, the white clay crusts all pitted, the water letting off waves of steam. I enjoyed the heat. We stood on a point looking down on an emerald-blue pool. Then we walked down into a shallow dip of the land, a crater. Amid the scrub there were white clay banks; bubbling pools; still, chemical-green puddles. A sign said: 'Danger. Thin earth. No responsibility taken.'

I caught up with Charles. 'Listen,' I said.

We could hear water trickling under the earth. I called out to Max.

He waited for me. He'd picked Maxie up.

I said, 'We shouldn't go off the path. There are signs saying Danger. Thin earth. And listen.'

There was the sound of water running under our feet.

'That water's hot,' I said. 'If you fell through . . . '

Max grinned. 'You'd be cooked.'

'Don't go off the path.'

He was already walking away. Charles ran to catch up. I followed. I heard water again, right under where I was standing. I didn't like it. When I caught up with Max he was putting Maxie up on his shoulders.

'We're going to cut across there,' he told me. 'To get to the geyser.' He pointed across an acre of scrub, steam drifting across it.

'There's no path there. What if you fall through?'

Charles was already walking ahead, around the edge of a mudpool.

'You can hear the water under the ground. Listen!'

Charles laughed. 'Don't freak out, Mum.'

I ignored him. I hated him siding with his father, laughing at me. 'Max! You can't take them across there.'

'We'll be fine. Come on.'

Little Maxie watched me patiently, not unsympathetically: poor Mummy, making a fuss again.

'I'm not walking on that,' I said. 'It says not to.'

Max shrugged, and followed Charles across the clay. It looked thin, dry, brittle. I felt frantic watching him.

I couldn't make myself walk where they'd gone. I turned away, my eyes stinging. I was furious, ashamed. I went back along the path. Had I abandoned my own children out of fear? But they were not abandoned. They were with their father. I thought about Max's power, his separateness. His love for the boys, their love for him. That he could carry them away and I would be left with nothing but the sound of my angry pleading, the ground trickling away under my feet.

Thin earth.

I waited at the bridge, watching the local boys diving for coins. The sun was an angry white eye. I waited for a long time. After an hour I walked back over the hill but there was no sign of them. I went to a hut near the gate. Two guards, a young man and young woman in floral shirts, were sitting behind a desk. I asked how I could get to the geyser.

They glanced at each other. 'You can't get to it from here. It belongs to the other guys.'

'Other guys?'

'The neighbours!' They exploded into giggling.

'How do I get there?'

'You have to go around the road, go to their gate and pay them.'

You keep that quiet, don't you, I thought. That the main attraction isn't in your bit of the park. I said, 'Can I borrow your phone?'

They were kind, getting out of the way and letting me ring Max's cellphone, allowing me go on trying when there was no reply. Then he answered, and suddenly I was calm and reasonable, laughing along as he told me they'd crossed the scrubland and been caught in the neighbouring park without the right ticket, that they'd been briskly ushered out, having viewed the geyser, and were walking all the way back around the road.

I met them coming back. The boys were eating iceblocks. I laughed over my stupid attack of nerves, admired Max's acumen in getting what the boys wanted. Max, adopting a faintly cynical and patronising air, allowed me to praise him.

'Silly old Mummy,' the boys said. We straggled back to the village and opened up the car to let out the heat.

I found myself thinking about the girl in Wanganui. The funeral. Her parents. How it must have been. There were boys playing cricket, the sun was shining, rowboats were racing on the sparkling river, and their daughter was dead. I thought of them burying their only child. I watched as Max carefully buckled little Maxie into his seat. I thought: I must take care of my boys, love them, guard them. I must take care.

The baking concrete, the furnace glare of the afternoon sun. Max straightens; we face each other over the bonnet of the car. There is something in his expression. A moment of hardness, clarity between us. A bird, turning and turning in the air above us, gives a high, sad, warning cry. I think of that expression Max likes to use: 'Over my dead body.'

He believes, with justification, that I am incompetent and hysterical. These are our roles — I dizzy, he rational. These are the parts we play. But a kind of communication passed between us then, as if, for a moment, we had abandoned our lines and were confronting each other, free of script, on an empty stage. He nodded and stared off at the hillside, absorbing the thing I was telling him.

If you leave me, you go alone. *Over my dead body* will you take them away.

LLOYD JONES

The Thing that Distresses Me the Most

LET ME START BY SAYING THIS. My husband is not a bad man. I don't know the others all that well — Don Seeward, another from Auckland, Phil someone, James More from down south; 'Macca' I think they call him. Two others as well. Jim? I don't know. It doesn't matter. I've met Don once. The others I must have spoken to when they've rung the house for Stuart. They all work for themselves. Stuart knew Macca at university. The rest of them he's picked up over the years in different jobs.

Once a year they get together to discuss 'engineering issues'. This year it was Stuart's turn to host the occasion. They flew in a few weeks before Christmas. It was a Saturday, a gorgeous day.

On the way to taking the kids to the beach I stopped by Stuart's office to drop off a quiche and a cake. I could see them in the window gathered around the table in serious discussion.

'Knock, knock,' I said as I came in. They all leapt up like a bunch of thieves. Soon as they saw the food they gushed with compliments. Don gave me a hug and a kiss. Stuart introduced those faces I'd spoken to on the phone. They were happy about the food, and I was happy to leave them to it. I had the kids waiting outside in the car.

I saw them again, about five that afternoon. I drove by with the kids to find out Stuart's plans for dinner. I slowed down, and from the street I could see them in the window. They were standing now, beer bottles in hand. Someone must have been telling a joke because I could see Stuart in a convulsive fit with a hand over his mouth and Don, more expansive, as he leant back, mouth open wide. I thought Stuart could ring home later and let me know his plans.

I was glad to get home. Clara and Bella were acting up in the car. Both of them had got too much sun. At home I ran a bath for them. I made that old-fashioned emulsion my grandmother used to drum up from vinegar and rubbed it into their sunburn while they squealed and shouted. They were hungry, and around six Bella started whining for pizza. I said let's wait and see what your father's plans are. It would be like Stuart to invite everyone back here; that would mean a quick run down to the supermarket. The pizza place is on the same block. I didn't want to make two trips. To take their minds off their stomachs I switched the telly on. I thought I would ring Stuart's office. But each time I picked up the receiver to dial I put it down again. If they were having fun I didn't want to be that grumpy bitch who brings things to a close. So I thought I would text Stuart. But the moment I had the idea I saw he'd left his mobile on the table. It was sitting with some papers I think he had meant to take to the office.

At seven o'clock I went to get pizzas. The girls came along for the ride in their pyjamas. There were half a dozen people in the shop so we had a bit of a wait. After giving the pizza order I thought I'd run by Stuart's office and gauge the mood. This time as I slowed down the blank window stared back. If anything the letters in the window were more bold — S. Richards. Engineer and Quantity Surveyor. Bella asked why we were back at Daddy's office. No reason, I said.

I thought they must have gone off for a drink somewhere. A phone call to that effect would have been nice. But then perhaps Stuart was planning to come home soon anyway.

At home I put the pizzas out on the table and left the girls to it. I walked over to the phone and picked up the receiver. Bella looked up, a wedge of pizza jammed into her mouth. I put the receiver down and poured myself a glass of wine.

The girls watched the Saturday night movie on Two. I tucked them into bed at ten and without complaint from either. This was as late as they had ever been up. They seemed to know that something about the night was different but they didn't want to know what it was. While they were watching TV neither one could shift their eyes from the screen.

There was some washing to bring in, and outside under the clothesline I looked up at the night. We live in one of the inner-city suburbs. There must have been some cloud about because the sky over the city was a sickly yellow. I heard a siren, and closer, maybe two streets over, the godawful noise of a boy racer tearing up the night, and more distantly the steady rumble of the city. The washing still contained the airy warmth of the sun from earlier in the day, and for some time I stood there under the washing line with Stuart's shirts bunched in my arms, just listening.

I thought I would wait until midnight before taking further action. I sat on the couch watching the minutes tick by. At the stroke of midnight I picked up the phone and rang the police. I was surprised to hear a woman's voice answer. It made me hesitate — just a bit. 'I don't know where my husband is,' I said. There was a pause at the other end, and in the intervening silence I heard the silliness of my complaint. Stuart wasn't missing. I was sure he knew where he was. I apologised and hung up.

There was nothing else to do but to go to bed. I pretended to read. I managed to stay awake until one-fifteen before I switched off the light. Some hours later I woke with a start. I sat up in bed bright as a whistle. I got out and walked to the phone in the hall. I picked up the receiver. There was no message. I thought about calling the police, but I was afraid of getting the same woman again and telling her the same thing. I suppose I was afraid of my embarrassment. So I returned to bed. This time I slept; I slept well. When I woke, sunshine was pouring in the windows. I could hear the TV blabbering away at the other end of the house.

I got up and looked into the spare room in case Stuart had come home in the night and got lost.

It was 11am before his Subaru wagon pulled up in the drive. I watched from the living-room window. Stuart had on his sunglasses. In the strong morning light he looked pale. I watched him walk towards the front porch. I came out to the hall. I heard him fumble with the key. I could have unlatched the door, but I thought, bugger him. Eventually he got the door open, and as he staggered in I could smell the alcohol on him. His shirt was torn. There was a nasty scratch on his cheek.

'I feel sick,' he said.

For a moment I thought he might mean something else, but no, he leant against the wall rubbing his head, his other hand on his stomach.

'It's eleven o'clock on Sunday morning,' I said.

He held up a hand — to stop me.

'I'm sorry,' he said. 'I'm really sorry. The night just got away on me.'

The night just got away on me. What a wonderful expression that is. Like it was the night's fault. The night was a bull he'd wrestled with and finally submitted to, but not without a fight. Is this what he meant?

Still, I was surprised by my own calm. I said, 'What do you need? Coffee?'

'No. No. Jesus, no,' he said. He waved a soggy arm at me and leant against the wall.

I ran him a bath and helped him out of his clothes. In the bath he lay back like a man dying. I got a cold cloth and held it against his forehead. I wondered about the scratch on his cheek. A red crescent tapering off to broken skin. A proper fight and there would have been bruising. A fight with a man, that is. It's funny, isn't it, where your thoughts lead you? Not in a million years would I have thought that one day I would be led down that dark path by a scratch on my husband's cheek. I handed him two Disprin and a glass of lemonade. I watched him gulp down the Disprin, and sip at the lemonade. I waited, but nothing more was said.

I went out to the front room. I switched off the TV and sent the girls outside. Then I went into the bedroom and closed the curtains. A moment later Stuart came out to the hall, a towel around him. He saw me staring at that scratch. He said, 'It's not what you think it is.' But that's all he said. He said he needed to sleep. He would explain all later.

Bella was due at a friend's birthday party in an hour. I ran down to the bookshop and picked up a gift, then I dropped her off on the other side of the city and left Clara at my sister's.

When I got home Stuart was up. He was in the kitchen waiting for the jug to boil. As I came in he barely looked up. I pulled up a chair and sat down. 'Okay,' he said, 'this is what happened.'

After the office, the younger ones had wanted to go to one of the bars. Stuart and Don had lamely followed. Stuart is forty-one years old and Don is perhaps a year or two older. I am thirty-seven. The other engineers who'd flown up from the South Island for their 'conference' are younger still. According to Stuart the younger ones led the charge. And one thing led to another. Or, more true to say, one bar led to another.

Around eleven o'clock it occurred to Stuart to ask the others where they were staying. Well, that was the funniest thing, according to Stuart. It seems none of them had stopped to think that far ahead, so Stuart led them to a backpackers, where the engineers checked in their bags before heading back out to the bright lights.

It seems . . . well, it doesn't seem so much as it happened . . . they headed off to a well-known strip club. This wasn't so much a surprise, I have to say, as Stuart admitting to it; as a result I feel able to trust the rest of what he had to say.

At the strip club, one or two or more, god knows, paid for lap dances. It doesn't matter who, though Stuart did mention names, but a few of them headed upstairs to pay for a woman. That's when I found myself looking back at the scratch on Stuart's cheek.

'So. That's it?' I asked.

'More or less,' he said.

'You spent the whole night in the strip club?'

'No. They did. I didn't.'

Stuart said he left them; he doesn't know what hour that was. He'd had enough, he said. He says he couldn't remember where he'd left the car, which is a good thing. And he'd forgotten about the room he'd paid for at the backpackers. He says he didn't have any idea where he was headed. It was late, but not that late, he claims. Anyway, he says there were still lines of people waiting to get inside the more popular night spots.

Within a block he'd left behind the noise and the lights and the crowds. He was on one of the streets running down to Te Papa on the waterfront. His legs carried him on. He says there was no decision in head or will left in his body except for in his legs, apparently. Somehow he got himself across those lanes of traffic on Wakefield. I shudder to think. Then, he says, he walked around to the seaward side of the national museum and that's when he saw the flax bushes. As soon as he saw them, he says he knew what to do. He crawled into the flax, where I suppose he passed the rest of the night, and which, I gather, accounts for his torn shirt and the cut on his cheek.

In the morning, as he woke in the flax bushes, he says he became aware of others — drunks, I suppose, hoboes, I guess, whatever you wish to call them, street people. That's the company he kept that night sleeping in the flax bushes outside the national museum.

Now, if someone else was telling this story, in other words if all this was being recounted by someone else and it involved someone else's husband and family, I wouldn't know what would have appalled me the most. The lack of a phone call — at any time that night. The binge drinking. The strip club. The lap dancers, or the business upstairs in the strip club. But no, the thing that distresses me the most is the thought of Stuart crawling into those flax bushes. It is the thought of the man I married in good faith waking in the flax bushes with all the other drunks of the city, and it is also this: he is really no better than them, and that fact would be known to everyone if he didn't have a home to go to.

Sunday night I ironed a fresh shirt and left it on the bed. Monday morning I dropped Stuart off at the office for an early meeting with a client. Later I went along to Te Papa as a parent helper with Clara's Year 8 class. It is that time of year when teachers cast around for activities outside the classroom. We took in the Maori waka, and after that the kids scattered and flew like moths to the voices of piped history in various parts of the museum. The trip ended up on the marae level overlooking the waterfront. From there I could look down to the flax bushes where my husband had spent Saturday night.

Already it felt like history. And here I suppose this story might have ended. I might try and forget it, and move on, as everyone says. But while standing there with the rude wind in my face, I felt a nagging that had nothing to do with it or the cries of squabbling children over my shoulder. I decided to take myself down to those flax bushes.

A woman office worker sat on the lawn, smoking and sunning her bare legs while she tackled the crossword. She didn't pay me any attention though. She didn't see an anxious middle-aged swamp hen creep into the shrub and the flax. It was easy to see where people had burrowed through. The ground was well trampled. I poked around. You could see where sleeping bodies had lain, and in one or two places there were plastic and glass bottles lying among the bark chips. One of the other women, the mother of one of Clara's friends, yelled out to me. What was I doing down there? What on earth was I grubbing about for? I could hear her laughing voice rallying above the gusting wind. But I pretended not to hear, and went on looking for a piece of Stuart's white shirt.

Sue McCauley

Disconnections

THE BUTTONS ARE SMALL. TOO small. They slither away from my fingers, from my clumsy finger and thumb, which today seem bigger than I expect them to be. Not swollen, but solid and wide as if they have refused to diminish in pace with the rest of me.

I can remember a word like diminish yet not the name of my first daughter. Nor the word for these buttons, which are tiny and thin and shine in the way of that thing that's found in the sea. I know the word, of course I do, everyone knows the word, but all that my brain can find right now is shell and that's almost it, but not quite.

I give up on the second button and try for the third. At least numbers have stayed with me; though what is there these days that I need to count? My poor limbs have lost patience with me. Or perhaps have simply rebelled after too many years of loyal service. Enough, old girl, give us a break. Ah, I'll reword that — give us a rest.

I know that is silly and fanciful. These crumpled hands, those scrawny legs, are mindless minions temporarily disorientated by erratic signals from headquarters. That temporarily seems a little optimistic but the doctor says it is so. The neurons are damaged, but not, as one would suppose, worn out. The damage can be repaired, but not by the doctor; it's all up to me and my faulty neurons. With sufficient effort and determination normal operations can be expected to resume some time in the future. The question is, will it be worth it? Will I still be around to enjoy my restored co-ordination?

And, if I am still around, will I still be here in my own little house? And, if not, will I want to be still around?

Two more buttons to go. The trick is not to hurry. I bought this blouse in Hong Kong when we went over for my brother Robert's wedding. His first wedding and heaven knows how many years ago that was. The great thing about silk is how warm it keeps you. It got on the tight side and I packed it away for many years. Now it hangs on me like a shepherd's smock and is no doubt utterly out of fashion. Even the word has lost favour; you mustn't say blouse any more, it's become some kind of joke. You're supposed to say top. And trousers and skirts may as well become bottoms, for only us old folk would roll our eyes.

Not that blouse was ever a word I was attached to, but at least it's one my defective brain still readily delivers up. Besides, it seems to me there are more than enough changes around and words are something we should be allowed to rely on.

Hard not to hurry and fluster my fingers, for while I am dressing they are assembling in my . . . in the room with the sofa and chairs. I shall have to walk in and have them watch me inching my wayward leg forward, an awkward stick-clutching crab. That, or the frame for ancient toddlers? Either way not one of my finer entrances.

The stick. It must be the stick.

Yesterday my friend came, the one who lived next door to us a long time ago. Jenny, I think her name is. Or possibly Margaret. We were neighbours for years. Her husband was never much chop, and then he ran off with the locksmith's wife and my friend went back down south to be closer to her family. She's much younger than me, nearer in age to my eldest daughter.

She came to see me in the hospital — my daughter, that is. She came in, I think, a number of times. My brain, at the start, was foggy, but I hope I remembered her name at least once or twice. Now it's gone out of my mind entirely, though it's not an uncommon name, I'm sure of that.

She's gone back to Australia. My first daughter, that is — not my friend who called in yesterday because she was passing through with her new man. Not new to her, of course, but to me he was. Or I thought he was, so it was a relief when he assured me we'd not met before.

He said he needed to stretch his legs and went off for a walk. When he'd gone she said he wasn't much into sitting around with women, but this time she'd been lucky for he was a good, kind man.

That was as far as her luck had stretched. She looked well to me, but it turned out she wasn't. She was in the early stages of the dreaded dementia. That wasn't the word she used. Now it's called something else, a name I know perfectly well, but it's gone. A terrible thing, and she's still young, but she knew she had it even before the doctors agreed.

So there we were — it was actually funny — the two of us comparing what we couldn't remember. And what we could. Not a great deal in my case, but she remembered the past. Each day a little more of it would come back to her in astonishing detail. She came up with things I'd long forgotten: the big yellow vase that stood in our hall, her little girl drowning the chickens by teaching them to swim, the man down the road who had a dozen or more old toilet bowls sitting out under a . . . big old . . . the one that grows everywhere and sheds those skinny, spiky leaves.

My friend can remember things like that, yet some days she has no idea what she did the day before, or where she's put the marmalade or how to open the oven door. This is hard on the good husband, who had to retire earlier than he planned in order to stay home and watch his wife grow dottier every day. This, she said, was the thing that upset her the most.

But I would rather be in his shoes than hers. It must be like drowning, inch by inch, day by day. No amount of willpower can save her, so I am the luckier one. Yet the thought of reliving a life by way of unearthed memories is appealing, and there were things I wanted to ask her but didn't in case they would seem nosy. Were her memories, I wanted to ask, mostly happy or at least inconsequential? Reliving all the bad ones could be a kind of purgatory. Almost there, why do they make buttons so small?

Also I wanted to know if her memories came in context, each moment leading into another like a film playing in her head. Or did they arrive out of the blue, randomly jogged from the past, as my own memories do? The woman with scars on her face who lodged in my parents' house and kept her bedroom locked even when she was in there. The unknown man in a brown leather jacket who bent forward and nibbled my bottom lip. I was on a train. Why? Where was I going?

I may, of course, have dreamt this. Or read it, or seen it — for real, or on screen. The margins became indistinct a long time ago. Do my friend's recollections, I wonder, come with some kind of authentication: a genuine memory from the life lived by . . . ?

And do they, perhaps, run in reverse — the recent past all the way back to entry point? So that, if only she had retained her faculties, she would be able to gauge the amount of time she had left.

My second daughter, whose name I have no trouble remembering — she is Janine — and my daughter-in-law, whose name will come back to me any minute, are in the kitchen opening biscuits and setting out cups on my behalf. Is this a moment they will recall in their distant futures? My hearing aid is behaving for once and along with the noise of cups I'm catching ripples of politely obliging laughter. No one has come to check on my progress, so I can't yet have taken too long. There may be some who have not yet arrived. I'm not sure who's coming, though Janine must have told me. Check the buttons. One doing its best to slip the noose, but otherwise all done up. Where is my stick? Could someone have moved it? Please don't let it have fallen; reaching down to the floor is a tricky manoeuvre.

That is my lawyer's voice, reminds me of sand sliding. Nice of him to come — those people are always so busy. He's quite a young man but he seems to know what he's doing, and these days one needs to be on the ball when it comes to money. He's made me into a family trust. This was for tax reasons, but the joy of it is I'm saved from having to make endless tiring decisions. 'Leave it to the professionals,' my son is fond of saying. 'That's what they're there for.' I'm sure it's good advice but it always sounds like he's blowing his own trumpet.

Whateverhisnameis, the lawyer, isn't just a professional, he's almost a family friend. We used to know his parents and they were decent people. He even came to visit me in . . . the place with the doctors. Didn't have to, but he came. And he tried to tell me I had the wrong idea about retirement homes. I remember that because it got on my goat. 'Just go and look at one or two places. They're nothing like they used to be. I think you'll be pleasantly surprised.'

As if I haven't spent half my days in those places over the last dozen years. Rest-homes, villages . . . whatever you like to call them, the bottom line is the same: you're shunted away from everyday life. No matter how cosy or self-contained the rooms may be, you're surrounded by collapse and decay; the only young people you see are those who are in charge of you.

How many friends and relations have I visited in those places? Too many to count. And then the funerals; my dead outnumbered the living a long time ago — proof that I've lived too long.

My sister-in-law who used to pop in quite often is now away across town in the place with the rhododendron garden. Her house is still on the market for an outrageous price. And Peter — some sort of cousin and almost blind — is paying through the nose to live in a fancy unit he can barely see. Perhaps I said this out loud. 'Won't cost you a penny,' the lawyer told me. 'The beauty of a trust is the state has to pay. No need to sell off the family silver.'

Found my stick; I must be blind. Heading the same way as cousin Peter. Which side am I meant to hold it? They've told me over and over, but the more they tell me the more confused I get. My good leg is now the bad leg and my bad leg is my better leg, so it should be the opposite side to what I was used to, but I think I was doing it wrong all these years and no one told me. Some things you do it wrong often enough you get so confused you're never ever going to get it right.

They've all come here to decide my future. Not what I want, but what will be best. The second daughter has briefed me. 'We have to be realistic. And reasonable. It's no good setting your heart on something that can't be provided.' It didn't seem all that long ago I was saying stuff like that to her. She was a child full of longing and discontent.

She has been here with me for quite a few days and is growing impatient. She wilts and paces, and fans the air that barely warms me. Her name — I knew it would come — is Sarah. She has a home of her own, and a woman who lives there with her. They're a couple. The woman is called Janine. No, she's not — Janine is my other daughter's name; Sarah's friend is called something else. It could be Jackie. I have the feeling this Jackie woman doesn't like me, but that may be wrong, I don't know her well. Their place is a few hours' drive from here and Sarah usually comes on her own.

Now she wants to be back in her home. And I want that for her — she has a life to get on with.

So, I hope, do I.

Twenty-four-hour care is what can't be provided. It seems I've turned into an infant needing constant supervision, and those who could be trusted with my care are already occupied with homes and lives and jobs. Twenty-four-hour care is what rest-homes are there for.

I'm not recovering fast enough for their liking — those neurons are still a bit flibbertigib — and they don't believe I will ever again be capable of living alone. No need for them to say this aloud: it's there in their faces. And they may be right. Age is against me. Who do I know, of my age, who has recovered from even the smallest stroke?

But then, who do I know, of my age, who's still alive? Old Ronnie Whatsit, two years ahead of me at school, and in the paper for making a hundred, grinning away like the mad old turkey he always was.

That's it — just Ronnie.

Check list of parts. Teeth in. Hearing aid in and on. Glasses on. Stick in hand. We could all sit around in the rest-home lounge and talk about bodily malfunction, that being the only thing we're certain to have in common. Comparing our medical and surgical milestones — the knee, the hip, the stroke, the turn, the heart attack, the medication-induced coma. An acceptable risk, that last one, since it's tablets that keep us going: a daily army of tiny mechanics despatched to oil the rusting parts.

First, to the loo. I admit to having been caught short a time or two in recent days. The mortification lingers.

How many others would have to share my toilet? If I'm not paying it won't be anywhere fancy, you can bet. Could be the place by the football grounds. I only went there the once — who was I visiting? There were two old dears who couldn't shut up, and others with that faraway look that I took with a shudder to be evidence of cranial vacuum. Now, thanks to my friend, I'll choose to believe they were happily absorbed in their private parade of memories.

Interned or at large, we are refugees in a country taken over by our children and our children's children. Old dogs unable to come to grips with new and alien cultural tricks.

Turn around, bend down and wipe the seat. Drips may be held against you. Hope that the sound of flushing will serve as an excuse for your very delayed entrance; even the young can have slothful bowels. Wash hands thoroughly to show that you have retained a knowledge of basic hygiene. Begin, at last, the journey to the living room.

I have my words prepared. I want to stay here. I believe I can manage on my own. And if I don't manage — if something goes wrong — well, that's a risk I have chosen to take.

It seems they have given up waiting and started without me. As I inch towards the open door a man is speaking. It's not my son's voice, it's some other man I don't know, with a slippery yet gravelly way of speaking. He says, 'Power of attorney was documented and signed back when we set up the trust, so there's no problem there. And, while you may be tempted to look for stop-gap solutions, I do think that, given your mum's magnificent age, this is really the time to face up to the inevitable.'

'That's how we see it.' I think that was my daughter-in-law.

I would need, at my magnificent age, to digest all this, but there is no time for I have now reached the doorway. As I crab into the room there's a hush, then they're all talking at once in silly encouraging voices. Here she is, they say. The woman herself... Making an entrance ... Way to go, Mum.

They watch me limp and shuffle to my chair and I think they're holding their breath as if I'm taking my very first steps. And for a moment it feels as if I'm no taller than the arm of the chair I'm heading for and they are circled above and leaning forward in their seats, poised to catch me. But I do not fall. I reach the chair and steady myself on its arm while I lean over to hook my stick on the edge of the little high-legged table. Then I manoeuvre myself around and prepare to sit down. This is where an extra hand makes all the difference, though I have managed it on my own once or twice.

None of them moves to help me so I know that this has been planned.

Bugger you, I think, and I drop myself backwards into the chair and land at an angle, when it could have been a simple, dignified lowering. My son's patience is running out. He clears his throat and begins to speak while I am still struggling to realign my scrawny buttocks and straighten my spine.

'I need to say that Janine says sorry she can't be here, and she'll be happy to support whatever decision we come to about . . . the future and ensuring that Mum gets all the care she needs.'

Janine, who's sitting beside the friendly woman from Social . . . Something who came around just the other day, looks grumpy, and I think she's about to point out her brother's mistake. Instead she mutters about people who think their lives are too important to take time out from. Then she glares at her brother and sister-in-law and says, distinctly, 'Like, how come I've been the only one?'

And my daughter-in-law turns to my son and hisses, 'See? I told you it'd be like this.'

My son drops his head into his hands with his fingers over his ears, and the other man, who looks like someone I used to know, says, 'I think we need to leave the past behind us here and focus on Mother's future. I believe that is what we're here for?'

I'm finally straight and comfortable and now no one's talking. I look around at their faces — my son, my daughter-in law, my youngest daughter, the friendly woman, the man and another woman, quite young and dressed for a day at the office. She's the only one who meets my eyes, and she gives me a little smile.

Some day will they come back to this moment, remembering every detail? The square of sunlight on the carpet, the moth-flutter sound of a hand mower across the street, my torturous journey from doorway to chair?

I'm wondering if they are waiting for me to speak. But this is not a waiting kind of silence; it is heavy and grey, a foreboding silence, giving notice of how things will be. Nothing I say will make it different.

My daughter Janine gets up from her chair and threads her way through to my kitchen alcove. As she passes me she bends to press the top button of my blouse back into its buttonhole. 'You trying the old cleavage routine?' she says, close to my ear.

We smile at each other and her eyes break my heart.

'Thank you, Janine love,' I whisper. I'm about to protest that I'd checked and rechecked my buttons and they'd all been done up, but she's gone.

In the kitchen she runs a tap full throttle and clatters my cupboard doors. My guests exchange looks but still no one's speaking.

In a voice louder than necessary my daughter says, 'In the end it's all about money. Let's at least be honest here.'

My son pretends we're still back at the point where I sat down. His calm face insists there has been no eloquent silence, no angry words. He sends me a smile. 'You're the one we're here for, Mum, so I think we ought to hear from you first. We all know the situation so . . . well, give us your wish-list.'

But whatever it was I was going to say has gone from my head and all that's left is an aching, childish sense of everything being unfair.

'You were my babies,' I announce. They look at me, then sneakily at each other. They're embarrassed on my behalf, and I realise I'm not making sense. Most of these people were not my babies; I may not even know them. And one of my babies is missing, and the other two wish they were anywhere but here with their useless, maudlin mother. They have no idea what I'm trying to say and even if I went on to explain they wouldn't understand. My daughters have had no children and my son and his wife sent theirs off to . . . one of those places where they look after the little ones.

'Yes, Mum, we were your babies.' He's humouring me in the voice he used on my grandchildren when they were young.

I don't reply. I can't; tears are tumbling from my eyes and sliding down beneath my glasses. So I can still cry. I look down to see a single drop fall onto my blouse, spreading darkness. The buttons are all done up.

'Jesus.' It's my daughter again. 'Can we please just get this over with!'

Sarah. Her name is Sarah Ellen. The other one who lives in . . . could it be London? She is Janine.

Owen Marshall

Patrick and the Killer

'AND HOW ARE YOU ANYWAY?' said Uncle Blick when they met without design at the airport.

'Not so bad, not so bad,' said Patrick's father, who was dying of prostate cancer at the time. Afterwards Patrick asked his father why he didn't tell the truth. 'None of his bloody business,' his father said. 'He's always been a snooping sort of bastard.' Blick came to the funeral three months later, though Patrick put it down to a sense of family solidarity rather than callous curiosity.

'He went down so quickly,' said Uncle Blick sombrely at the chapel. 'I met him at the airport only weeks ago and he was fine, then wham. There's no way of knowing, is there, and he was three years younger than me.'

'We appreciate you coming,' said Patrick.

'Wham, just like that,' and Uncle Blick's face contorted slightly as if he felt the impact.

Patrick was unsettled by his father's death. He felt grief, of course, but also it forced him to evaluate his own life. He was thirty-eight, unmarried, and with a polytechnic diploma in small business administration. Unfortunately he didn't have a business of any size to administer. He worked as a salesman for Globus Aluminium Mouldings, and usually pronounced the name of the metal in the American way, because he thought it sounded more classy. In an endeavour to improve his circumstances not long after his father died, he asked GAM for a raise in salary and a better company car. Both requests were refused, and the manager said that in fact things weren't that good, and they'd have to let him go with a redundancy of just a week's salary for each year he'd been with them. 'It's something I hate to do,' said the manager. 'It's a hell of a thing, I know. To be honest, Patrick, we've had to consider as priority those with dependants. You'll appreciate that, I know.'

To save a little face with family and friends, Patrick told them he'd resigned because he wanted to live in a bigger place with more opportunities. He moved to Wellington and rented a rundown bach at Eastbourne in which the sound and smell of the sea were always present. The owner intended bulldozing it and building a new place on the valuable section, but in the meantime, because the lease was only month by month, the rent was reasonable. Someone had gathered shells onto the small frontage over the years, and it resembled a giant child's sandpit. Someone had painted a green and blue parrot on the roughcast by the low back door, and the single bedroom smelled of stale sweat as well as the sea.

Within the first week, Patrick had a choice of two jobs: one was handling freight at the airport, the other was in a Johnsonville video store. He took the latter because it was closer to Eastbourne, and also because he was fond of films and videos. The guy who interviewed him said the staff were entitled to fifty per cent reduction on hire, but in practice if you took stuff home at lock-up time and had it back when you came to work, no one bothered about it. Just keeping your fingers out of the till was the main thing, he said.

Two of them were on at a time and Patrick was surprised how busy it kept them. Issues and returns were only part of it. He spent a lot of time sorting out those titles that were to be put out for cheap sale because of excessive wear, or because they were no longer in demand. There were thousands of videos and DVDs and a special computer program to keep track of them. There was a screened section at the back of the shop that held the porno stock, and Patrick soon noticed how many of the customers would add a highbrow art movie to their stack of porn, as if that made the average content morally acceptable. It wasn't a career, of course, and Patrick intended to find something with better prospects within a few months.

All that changed the day he met the killer at the petrol station in Petone. Twenty dollars' worth of 91 unleaded, and he wanted a paper as well. It was a cold Sunday morning in August, and the light rain shoaled in with the wind from the sea.

Afterwards Patrick wanted a piss, and he went past the two aisles and into the lavatory that had a small black cut-out of a man on the door. That's where the killer was, although Patrick didn't know his identity at the time. The killer wore a black beanie, black jeans, leather boots and a grubby, blue windbreaker. He was smoking and looking reflectively at the roof as he pissed onto the stainless steel back of the urinal. Patrick took up his stance at the far end of the grating. Sometimes he'd noticed that men preferred to go into a cubicle if there was even one other person at the urinal, and that seemed oddly prudish to him.

The killer washed his hands briefly, and balled a paper towel.

'It's a real shit day out there, mate, isn't it? Bloody wind and bloody rain and bloody Sunday.' He was a thin, undersized man with a face like a chisel and a small goatee beard. He worked the zipper of his jacket up and down, and then left it in the same position as before.

'Nasty day all right,' said Patrick. He took his turn at the basin as the killer stepped aside to check his teeth in the mirror.

'I suppose a joker just has to keep on keeping on, eh, mate.'

'That's about the size of it, I'd say,' said Patrick.

So they came out of the lavatory together, and Patrick was only a step or two behind as they went past the aisles towards the counter and the door. Afterwards, Patrick would say that he noticed there was no one behind the counter, and had an uneasy feeling, but it wasn't true. What he did notice were the three policemen standing around the killer's car by the pumps, and he had a glimpse of others going around the back of the shop. 'Ah, fuck it, no,' said the killer, in a tone of both weariness and anger, and he reached to the back of his jeans and pulled out a knife with a straight blade. He waited until Patrick drew level, then he took him by the shoulder. 'What we do, see, is walk right on by so everyone's okay,' he said.

'What?' said Patrick.

'A hostage like, mate. And you and I walk right by the cops so you don't get hurt.'

'It won't work,' said Patrick. 'It's like stuff on video, and that never works in real life. Only cocks up things worse.' He didn't believe that on such a drab day anything of moment could happen.

For just an instant the killer looked highly brassed off, and Patrick half expected a blow, but then his companion said, 'You're right: course you are. Bugger,' and he dropped the knife and sprinted for the door. He was pretty speedy, even in boots, and he made the doorway before the police could intercept him, and hared away across the forecourt, leading with his narrow chin and goatee. A car of police reinforcements was coming out from the city, though, and they spilled out eagerly and brought him down. Whatever he'd done, Patrick still felt a certain sympathy to see the poorly dressed, skinny guy borne down by so many. There was something of an augury in it, perhaps, because Patrick's own life hadn't been going that well.

The police showed some special interest in Patrick at first, but after the counter and forecourt men said he'd arrived separately from the killer they eased up, even letting him walk up close enough to the captive still on the ground to see the small grey stones caught in the matrix of the wet soles of his boots, and his thin, hairy wrists in the handcuffs. The killer lay passively, with one cheek pressed on the glistening road and his eyes half closed. It reminded Patrick of the way chooks are when you hang them by the legs. A sergeant said the killer's name was Geoffrey Madden Wenn.

A journalist arrived when Patrick and the two garage men were still giving information to the police, and he said he wanted to talk about what had happened. Then a TV crew came and were disappointed that the killer had been taken away. Patrick spoke briefly to them as well. It was the security camera footage, however, which showed on the news the next day, that created the surge of interest. It caught Geoffrey Wenn gripping Patrick by the shoulder and holding up the knife, and although Patrick's words to the killer couldn't be heard, the trick of the camera was to make it seem that Patrick was full of composure rather than bafflement, and that his insouciant advice had put Wenn to flight.

So both the print and television journalists sensed the possibility of one of those passing, but profitable, instant celebrity creations so much a part of their trade. The security camera film was replayed in many contexts, and the revelation that Patrick and Geoffrey Wenn had talked together in the lavatory before the latter's arrest provided further ramifications. 'In Lieu of Danger' was the punning headline in one Sunday paper; 'Killer's Philosophy in WC' was the banner of another.

It wasn't that Patrick set out to tell any lies, or even to take advantage of fortuitous circumstance: he was just an ordinary guy unaccustomed to being sought out, unaccustomed to flattery, or being the centre of attraction. The attention of women journalists in particular he found strangely gratifying, and he was drawn into specious elaboration, exaggeration and conjecture by their open interest and familiarity. The brief conversation between Patrick and the killer in the men's room was spun out because of the intensity of interest into an exchange of some depth and significance. 'I think he was oppressed by the dismal day and the sort of life he had,' said Patrick. 'He wanted to talk, and said that Sundays were always a bummer for him. He was determined not to give in to despair, however. He told me that you needed to be resilient: to keep on keeping on. I got the impression, too, he was a lonely, troubled guy. I don't know all the things he's done, of course, and there was definitely threat and anger in him, but there was something of reaching out as well — some plea, I reckon.'

What Geoffrey Wenn had done was run over a man who had discovered his cannabis plot in the bush behind the Butterfly Track: come down on him in his yellow Holden ute, the prosecution said, and run over him full tilt. The defence lawyer said the dead man was a known drug dealer who had threatened to take over Wenn's plot. The prosecution said the victim was a reformed man, innocently taking exercise on his doctor's orders.

It was a high-profile case, partly because the defence lawyer hinted that they could name some well-known Wellington personalities with links to the growing of marijuana. The publicity kept Patrick's name in the news also, and there were benefits in that. Globus Aluminium Mouldings had its head office in Wellington, and were keen to have Patrick back on the staff after his heroism. The CEO himself called Patrick in, and said that the regional manager who had sacked him had shown a regrettable lack of judgement. Patrick was offered the situation of deputy to the national sales manager, who was due for retirement within a year or so, and the position carried with it a new six-cylinder car and mortgage availability for house purchase. The CEO also said that they hoped to structure a new advertising campaign around Patrick, which would stress the reliability and value of GAM products.

Patrick took the job. He was a reasonable salesman and understood that he'd got a lucky break which could be the making of him if he worked hard. As the CEO realised, the publicity of the Wenn case was a definite advantage in attracting business. People liked the association with him, which gave them a talking point with their fellows and families. 'You know that guy who talked down the murderer in the Petone service station?' they might say. 'I had him in giving a quote for the new conservatory range frames today. He's GAM's chief salesman here. Seemed a decent bloke and we had quite a chat. No way was he going to back down at all even if the bastard did have a knife, he told me. Said he'd twigged right from the start there was something odd about him.'

Sonia Tonkisse was the accountant at GAM. She was a year older than Patrick, better qualified and with an equable temperament, which is very attractive in a woman. She was good looking, too, in that way that emphasises grooming rather than obvious points of appeal. Patrick liked her, and rather to his surprise Sonia favoured him too. They began going out together and getting to know each other in the rather measured sort of way that suited both of them. Patrick was still regaining confidence after his GAM dismissal, and Sonia was as scrupulous with life's decisions as she was with GAM's accounts.

Patrick bought a house in Seatoun: a double-storeyed roughcast-over-brick home with a glimpse of the sea. The price was a good deal more than he'd planned to spend, but he went along with Sonia's advice. Best to take advantage of the firm's low mortgage rates, she said, and the place was bound to appreciate considerably in that area and with that construction. She had contacts in the real estate business, and also there was the tacit understanding that she and Patrick might in time live there together.

Two women's magazines ran features on the couple. The cover photograph of the first showed Patrick standing at the bottom of the front steps and Sonia two steps up, leaning informally on his shoulder. The shot was nicely framed by the arched entrance, and the article stressed both Patrick's record of heroism and the romance he'd found since. The second cover showed the two of them framed by the lounge window and with the sea just visible. 'Killer confrontation forgotten' was the caption, by which the magazine hoped to keep the incident alive in the public mind.

Neither prosecution nor defence called Patrick at the trial, and Geoffrey Wenn received a sentence of fifteen years' imprisonment. The trial stirred up public interest once more, but it subsided more rapidly the second time: new trepidations and monsters soon filled the media and the national consciousness. Patrick, however, found the incident hard to put out of his mind. The image of the killer face down on the wet road: the sordidness and loneliness of that slight man borne down by the righteous supremacy of the police. Patrick had benefitted from a random meeting with him, and felt obscurely under some obligation because of it. It occurred to him that maybe he should visit Wenn in prison. The idea came back more strongly on the day the GAM CEO called him into the office to congratulate him on orders, and confirm the expectation of Patrick's promotion after the retirement of the national sales manager. 'And Felicity and I would like you to be our guest on a yachting trip next weekend. Time we all got to know each other better. We're asking Sonia, of course, and a few friends we'd like you both to meet. I like to think of our management team as a family. We'll probably sail across to the Sounds and do a bit of blue cod fishing. Sheer heaven.' The CEO came from behind his desk and lingered at the door with Patrick a while to show the possibility of a new relationship. 'All work and no play, you know,' he said. The CEO's personal assistant in the outer office looked up and smiled at them both warmly.

Even the weather mirrored Patrick's fortune: calm and bright. He resolved to visit the killer in prison, aware of how their lives had diverged so sharply since that rainy day at the petrol station in Petone. He found, however, that this wasn't a simple matter. Geoffrey Wenn had been sent to Paremoremo prison in Auckland, and prison visits were initiated by the prisoners themselves, not visitors, and as well there was a whole sequence of applications, approvals, booking times and identifications required. Also Sonia wasn't in favour of his renewing contact. 'Nothing that he did was intended to favour you,' she said. 'He killed somebody, right, and wouldn't have hesitated to kill you. Best to keep away from someone like that, and you don't want people thinking you've any sympathy for a murderer.'

'I suppose his life's hell,' said Patrick.

'And so it should be,' she said.

Patrick didn't mention his intention to Sonia again, but when the GAM CEO asked him to attend a sales conference at Titirangi, he wrote to the killer, who put the bureaucracy in motion. Patrick described his visit as being based on non-religious, yet compassionate, grounds.

Visits were allowed only in the weekends, so on the Saturday following his conference, Patrick drove to Albany and Paremoremo. He expected to be sitting before one of those glassed-in booths he saw on TV crime shows, but the visiting room was open and reminded him of his home-town polytechnic where he'd done his trade exams. Small, cheap tables beyond squinting distance of each other, and tubular chairs. There was one warder seated by the door, and two others wandered listlessly among the groups, or stood intent before the one window.

Patrick didn't at first recognise Wenn. He no longer had any sort of beard, and, although still scrawny, he'd lost the hard edge of freedom, had already slackened with apathy. He didn't regard Patrick with any apparent anticipation. He sat well back in the hard chair, with his knees apart, and, after a glance at Patrick, seemed more interested in people at other tables in the visiting room. He caught the eye of a fellow prisoner talking to a hard-faced woman in jeans, and gave the thumbs up sign. Wenn made no attempt to start a conversation with Patrick, neither did he show any eagerness for his visitor to begin one. What need of hurry, what possibility of good news, could there be for a killer serving a long term? No doubt he'd had the odd Bible-basher call on him before.

'I brought you some cigarettes and biscuits,' said Patrick, 'but the staff took them to check, and said you'd get them later. Do you remember I was in the petrol station when the cops came to get you?' said Patrick.

'Yeah.'

'We came out of the lavatory together, and then you made a break for it when you saw the police.'

'That's right. Yeah, I remember.' But the recollection didn't cause him any excitement, or surprise. He remained well settled on the chair, and with his hands on his splayed knees. He sucked his teeth. 'You were in the paper and that,' he said. Patrick realised that their meeting that day meant nothing to the killer: nothing had come from it to benefit him, nothing to make it noteworthy in a day he wished to forget. For Patrick it had been a lucky strike with a string of consequences to his advantage, but for Geoffrey Wenn, Patrick was just a guy he had pissed next to before being arrested.

'Anyway,' said Patrick, 'I just thought maybe a visitor would be something of a break for you, and they tell me cigarettes are always useful in here.'

'Yeah,' said Wenn. He seemed to be waiting for Patrick to come to the point of the visit, to start talking about the capacity Jesus had for forgiveness, or reveal a programme of reading skills supported by the local Association of University Women. Yet Patrick had no further explanation for being there than he'd already given, and felt awkward.

'Can't be much of a life,' he said fatuously, and the killer didn't bother to reply, just let the bottom of his thin face twist a little.

Conversations at most other tables were equally desultory, and prisoners and visitors glanced around often as words failed them. In a way it reminded Patrick of visiting his father in hospital, where he'd been given an even more severe sentence. Only the woman in jeans seemed to be talking against the clock, on and on about her money troubles. Patrick heard snatches to do with back rent, hire purchase goods, Sally Army parcels, repossession of a free-standing hotpot, and the inability to afford a school camp for one of the kids. 'It's the kids, though, isn't it?' she said, not lowering her voice at all, oblivious to listeners in the intensity of her focus. 'I mean, okay, we've fucked up, but I can hardly stand what it does to the kids. You know?' The man had no hair, and his skull bones made uneasy conjunction. He nodded affirmatively, as if she had suggested a treat. 'You know how Shane is,' she said, and he nodded again. 'Sometimes at night I stand outside the little bugger's door, and I hear him crying in his sleep.'

Patrick tried to focus on the killer's face so that something to say would come to him, and the woman's life would recede. He felt that he was in some bog of existence and would be sucked under if he stayed longer. He wanted out. 'Am I allowed to give you money?' he asked Wenn. 'Just a few bucks I've got on me?'

'Stuff it up your arse maybe,' said the killer. He leant back a little more, and grinned at his bald-domed mate.

Patrick didn't know how to respond to such animosity. 'I suppose I'd better be going and start home,' he said. The killer showed no interest in where that home might be. He remained seated as Patrick stood up and began to leave. When Patrick glanced back from the door, Geoffrey Wenn was still seated, his arms folded, and his attention on the bald man and his woman visitor.

In the carpark a large woman struggled to get out of her small car beside Patrick's. She seemed winded by the effort, and stood puffing for a while, her small mouth with dolly pink lipstick open wide. 'They don't think of us, do they?' she said. 'Oh no, no, they don't think what it does to the family, do they? Punish one, punish all: that's what they reckon, don't they? What show have we got, eh? NO show at bloody all, that's what, isn't it?' It was another chorus to that of the hard-faced woman in the visiting room. She swayed off towards the prison buildings.

Patrick decided there was no need to mention the visit to Sonia: that there was no one to thank for what had happened to him over recent months. It was just the play of indifferent circumstances: sometimes supporting you above your fellows, sometimes pulling you down. As he drove he concentrated on a projected new range of aluminium struts for caravan and campervan awnings, and occupied himself by going over the specifications in his head. He'd always had a knack with figures, and found it reassuring to let them form and disassemble in those predictable patterns quite free of emotion, or any augury.

Carl Nixon

Rocking Horse Road

LUCY ASHER'S MURDER HUNG OVER the Christmas of '81. It drifted over those days like acrid smoke from a neighbour's bonfire, lingering right through February and March until the terrible events of early autumn blew it out to sea. The beach, the sand dunes where we gathered, the school pool and the cracked tennis court, even our homes, our own bedrooms (normally such citadels!) were all permeated by it. Over those thirteen unforgettable weeks of our awkward adolescence we sucked Lucy's murder down into our lungs until it travelled on into our blood, where it has remained.

The Spit is as far south in the suburb of New Brighton as you can go without getting your feet wet. A long finger of bone-dry sand. The only thing separating the cold water of the southern Pacific from the swollen estuary formed by the meeting of the Avon and Heathcote rivers. Down the middle of the Spit, like a single dark vein, runs Rocking Horse Road.

December 21st, 1981. It was a Sunday and four days before Christmas, 7.30 in the morning. The sky was clear and the sand already warm to the touch. It promised to be a scorcher. It was Pete Marshall who found her naked body at the foot of the sand dunes in the reserve that marked the end of Rocking Horse Road. As we could all tell you later, she was lying close to the sun-faded sign warning people about tidal rips and swimming near the deep channel that connects the estuary to the ocean and marks the end of the Spit. It was obvious, though, right from the very beginning, that neither of these mundane dangers had killed Lucy.

Her head rested just below the high-tide mark where the darker waterlogged sand met the dunes with their covering of tussocks and scraggling lupins. She was face down, arms and legs slightly out from her body — 'splayed like a starfish' was how one reporter (inaccurately) described her in on the front page of the following morning's *Press*. One leg was further down the beach than the other, extended as though she had paused in the act of dipping her toes in the ocean to test the temperature.

The dunes extended a fair way back towards the road from the beach and were criss-crossed with paths both official and improvised. Pete ran the most direct way, sticking to the sandy ridges, leaping hollows, crashing though lupins, until he arrived panting like a dog at Jase Harbidge's door. Jase's dad was Senior Sergeant Bill Harbidge, who in a few minutes would himself be running over the dunes, wearing faded shorts, his shoelaces lashing his ankles, and a white shirt snatched from the clothesline flapping open around him.

'Like a big white albatross' is how Pete described him years later. 'I remember him bounding down the face of the last dune and it seemed to me that he might take off. I guess I was pretty freaked out.'

The night before, there had been an unusually high tide. Not a storm, just a very high tide with larger-than-normal waves. Big swells barrelled across the Pacific before rising up and breaking, one after another after another against the beach. Each one was ushered in by a stiff easterly wind. It's easy, in retrospect, to anoint events with a significance they don't have at the time, but in the days immediately following the discovery of Lucy's body several of us recalled lying in our beds that night and listening to the waves rolling in to the beach, eating away at the dunes that were the only defence our parents' homes had against the ocean. The wavesound was a dull background roar that we had grown up with but, nevertheless, could not entirely shut out. We could hear it from our homes and over the teacher's voice as we sat at our school desks. The waves underscored our shouts as we played in the sandy, grassless grounds of South Brighton High School. That night, though, the sound seemed, to more than one of us, to have deepened and become mournful, like an endless train going by in the darkness, cursed to be always passing, never gone.

Standing in the Harbidges' doorway, Pete told Bill Harbidge that he'd been down on the beach at 7.30 in the morning walking his dog. It wasn't a very convincing story — Pete's family didn't own a dog, for a start. Later that day, in the official interview conducted at the main police station in the city, Pete changed his tune. Not that anybody official noticed. Pete was not being treated as a suspect. We have a copy of the police report (Exhibit 2). For the record, Pete claimed that he was down on the beach that morning jogging to get fit for the rugby season. At least his revised version of events bore some scrutiny. Pete did play for the Brighton Club's under-sixteen team, although, of course, nobody began training that early. It is doubtful whether even an All Black would have been out pounding the dunes at 7.30 in the morning four days before Christmas.

Years later, Pete confessed that he'd been in the dunes retrieving a copy of *Playboy* he'd pilfered from his older brother, Tony Marshall.

Pete had hidden the magazine, along with half a block of milk chocolate stolen from the local dairy and some suntan cream, in a metal tackle-box he'd buried in a natural amphitheatre in the dunes. The place was surrounded by tall lupins and almost impossible for the uninitiated to find unless they stumbled right onto it. Pete and some of our other friends used it as a meeting place, though that morning he'd been alone.

So why had he gone up to the top of the dunes? When finally asked (this was about ten years later when he was in his mid-twenties), Pete said he didn't know. He just wanted to look. At the waves? At the risen sun? At the first surfers, who, like dark seals, were paddling out to sea up the beach by the surfclub? A shrug. Just to look, apparently.

So there's Pete, fifteen, his head full of airbrushed fantasy, walking to the top of the dunes, the sand already warm to his touch. And looking down at the deserted beach.

'What did you think she was doing?' (This is from the official police interview now.)

'I thought she was sunbathing.'

'At 7.30 in the morning?'

And then Pete had said something to the interviewing officer that showed more insight than most people gave him credit for. 'When you're fifteen and you see a naked girl lying on the beach you stop thinking that clearly. I thought she was sunbathing.'

Lucy was lying, slightly on her side, facing away from him. (Actually, her right arm and shoulder were partially buried in the sand but Pete couldn't see that yet.) All he could see from his vantage point were her tanned legs, the swell of her hips and then the rollercoaster dip down to her waist. And yes, the split and roll of her buttocks, which until that time Pete had never seen on a real live woman (and still hadn't — technically). And her back. Lucy was a swimmer and a lifesaver and had a broad, lightly freckled back, but Pete still did not know who it was he was looking at.

And here we might depart from all the interview notes and reports to speculate. To Pete Marshall she must have looked like all his dreams come true. An anonymous naked woman there on the beach in the stark morning light; a page from one of his brother's magazines brought to life for his own gratification. That idea cannot have been far from his mind (Pete was fifteen, remember). Or, just possibly, he imagined something even more exotic. If, in those first heady moments, Pete Marshall thought of mermaids or banished daughters of Atlantis, he never let on. Certainly not to the police. Not to us.

Pete told us it was only when he got closer that he saw the woman's left arm was strangely mottled. Closer still and he could see that her skin seemed flabby and ill-fitting across her broad swimmer's shoulders. Her hair was matted and there was a small piece of driftwood, like a bleached fingerbone, tangled up in it. (Lucy Asher had been in the water about twelve hours before she was washed up, according to the coroner's report. Exhibit 5.) Pete told the police that when he got even closer he could also see there was something strange about the angle of her head against the sand.

There is one photograph taken by the police photographer (Exhibit 7) where you can see a footprint in the sand almost in contact with her outstretched hand. The hand is lying palm upwards, the fingers slightly curled as though she had been cupping a ball which, sometime during the night, the covetous ocean had prised from her grasp. The footprint is slightly below the body, on the water side, almost touching her little finger. It is from a Converse shoe. The type with a canvas upper like a boot that used to come in blue and red with a white star on the side over the ankle. It was the type of shoe we all wore in those days.

All Pete ever said, though, was that he got close enough to see that it was Lucy Asher and that she was wearing a necklace of bruises. A parting gift from whoever had strangled her in the night and then tossed her body into the deep water of the channel.

And that's when, according to Pete, he 'freaked out, man' and turned and ran back through the dunes to get Jase Harbidge's dad, who was soon to came flying over the sand like a great white bird.

Lucy Asher went to South Brighton High School along with the rest of us, although she was older, seventeen, and had technically finished school three weeks before. Her parents owned the local dairy and Lucy was their only child. She often worked behind the counter after school and during weekends and we had seen her almost daily, although we paid her no more attention than the deepening lines on our parents' faces or the colour of the houses we had grown up in. Before her murder Lucy Asher was as unheralded and as ubiquitous on the Spit as the sand.

In the days after her body was found the papers were full of the story. Reporters roamed up and down the beach like stray dogs. They stopped us on the road to ask if we had known Lucy and what type of girl she was. Occasionally we would see our own words in the paper attributed to 'a close friend' or 'longtime classmate of Lucy's'. Words uttered in passing looked awkward in black and white and seldom matched what we thought we had said. Certainly the words never came close to describing the Lucy we had seen every day at school and in the dairy.

There was one photograph that the *Press* and the *Evening Star* favoured. It was taken the summer before she died: Lucy standing outside the surfclub holding a small trophy she has won for beach racing at the provincial championships. You can see her from the waist up. She is wearing the red one-piece togs she competed in. In the photograph she is tanned and smiling and holding the small silver trophy out towards the camera with both hands as though offering it up as a gift to the photographer. Her hair is light brown, bleached lighter than it was in winter. (We found out later that she squeezed lemon juice into her hair before bed each night in an effort to lighten it.) She had brown eyes and a wide, almost American mouth.

We still have the trophy, although it was soon to be broken and has never been fixed. About a month after Lucy died the trophy turned up on the street in the Ashers' rubbish. It was sitting on top of the bag and was found by Tug Gardiner, who had a paper round that included the Ashers' place. The trophy is actually meant to be awarded for running but whoever bought it for the surfclub must have thought it looked right enough for the under-seventeen girls' beach racing: a silver girl finishing a race, head dipping forward, arms flung backward. The finishing tape is draped across her chest. The trophy hadn't been significant enough to be engraved with a name (or possibly there hadn't been time) but there was no one else it could have belonged to except Lucy, and of course it matches the one in the photograph perfectly.

All things considered, it's a very good photo of Lucy. We like to think that in different circumstances she would have been happy for it to be printed so widely.

The stories the reporters wrote in those first days only confirmed what we already knew. Lucy had been strangled and her body dumped in the ocean. On Christmas Eve a police spokesman announced, in veiled terms, on the *Six O'Clock News*, that the motivation for the attack was being treated as sexual. That caused the story to briefly surge back towards the front of the next edition of the papers on the 26th. But, as Grant Webb bluntly put it, 'She was naked, wasn't she? Of course it was sexual! He screwed her, then he killed her.' He was right. You didn't have to be Sherlock Holmes to work that one out. We all knew it from the start. Lucy's murder oozed sex.

There were ten detectives assigned to the case and that number had swelled to fifteen by mid-January. There was pressure on the police to solve the case. Non-domestic murders were still unusual back in the early eighties and the seemingly random killing of an attractive young woman quickened the national pulse and caused widespread outrage. And of course there was the fact that, like Marilyn Monroe, she was found naked. That didn't hurt newspaper sales either. The papers soon started calling the murderer 'The Christmas Killer'.

It helped us that Jase Harbidge's dad was a cop. We got first-hand information we wouldn't have otherwise been privy to. Mrs Harbidge had run off with the local butcher six months before so there was just Jase and his dad at home that summer. In '81 Christmas dinner was macaroni cheese, which the two of them ate sitting in front of the television. Bill Harbidge reclined on his chair and downed beers with a steady rhythm. He had been drinking a lot of beer since his wife left. Jase told us that the drinking made him talk about his work, and not just the Asher case. Murders, rapes, gang shootings and music teachers interfering with schoolboy saxophonists — the whole works, cases dating back through twenty years in the force, were all trotted out by Bill Harbidge from his possie on the La-Z-Boy.

The Queen was giving her Christmas message when Jase's dad told him that whoever killed Lucy was smart to dump her body in the ocean. The water flushed away all traces of the killer: no bodily fluids, (by which he meant semen) and left no fingerprints. Jase's dad also told him, and Jase told us, that Lucy wasn't dead when she went in the water, although the person who strangled her probably thought she was. Lucy Asher was just unconscious. There was water in her lungs. Technically she had drowned.

Even from the inward-looking world of fifteen we realised that the Christmas of '81 must have been a pretty strange time for Jase Harbidge.

We gathered in Jim Turner's garage to hear these details. Jim's dad didn't own a car and he kept an uneven pool table out there. We would drift in during the late mornings and play doubles and talk about Lucy. The garage was also used for storing sheep manure, which Jim's father made him dig into the vegetable garden every autumn. The garage always had an odour of sheepshit and wool, a smell we eventually came to like. There was a dart board hanging behind the side door and a bench-press with heavy metal plates which we used to test our manliness while we were waiting for our turn on the pool table.

Al Penny took to cutting articles out of the paper and sticking them up on the unclad wall with drawing pins, next to the photo of Lucy. We read them over and over until our talk became smattered with reporters' phrases. It was not uncommon to hear Pete or Jim or Roy Moynahan refer to the 'profoundly shocked community' or the police's 'growing frustration'.

The talk, however, was not just of how Lucy died. In fact, as the days passed, that became a minor part of our conversations. It was in the Turners' garage that we constructed our memories of Lucy's life.

It began when Roy Moynahan recalled seeing Lucy cut her lip, several years before — she would have been only fourteen or fifteen — while drinking from the tap in front of the school library. We would have been in our first year at high school. Some boys had been pushing and Lucy's face had been shunted forward into the silver tap. Roy told us that he had seen blood flowing freely down Lucy's chin but that she had not cried. For a day or two there was dry blood smeared on the edge of the tap before someone washed it away.

Another of us offered up the story of how he had dropped some carefully drawn maps from his Social Studies folder in the playground where the easterly wind had greedily snatched them away. It had been Lucy Asher and a friend who had helped him get them back.

Lucy Asher riding her bike to school on a rainy day with the sky as low as a parking building's concrete ceiling. In memory, the hem of her dress was soaked dark by the water coming up off the road in a hissing arc.

Lucy raising her hand to tell the teacher she had 'women's trouble' and would have to go home early. The way the boys in her class had sniggered behind their hands. (This was a received memory; one that came to us through Tony Marshall, who had been in Lucy's class. It was not as authentic or trustworthy as our own memories but was added to our store nonetheless.)

Lucy Asher coming second in the intermediate girls beach-racing three years before and the feelings that had stirred in us, new at the time, when we witnessed the way Lucy, and several of the other girls, had begun to fill out their red togs. Over the long winter months, while cocooned inside the heavy layers of their school uniforms, the girls had metamorphosed into seemingly different creatures.

Lucy, glimpsed from a car window, standing among a group of friends at the bus stop on a Friday afternoon. (We speculated that she was on her way into town to see a movie.)

Lucy putting up posters of her lost cat, Marmalade, on lampposts up and down Rocking Horse Road. A reward of five dollars was offered.

Lucy Asher playing hockey on a Saturday morning in the sea mist that sometimes covered the whole of New Brighton during spring and autumn. Lucy ghosting up the right wing with the ball. Now seen. Now lost in the shifting walls of mist. Eventually the game had been called off because the sea mist showed no sign of clearing and it was considered dangerous to carry on.

Between Christmas and New Year we met in Jim Turner's garage and, amid the cicada-click of pool balls and the clang of the metal weights being slid home, with the smell of sheep manure in our nostrils, we gifted these and many more memories and half memories to each other. Perversely, the weather outside was the best it had been all summer. The sky was blue and cloudless. The temperatures soared up into the thirties.

Lucy, like all of us, had lived on the Spit her whole life and there was a rich store of small encounters and sightings from which we could draw. It was true that individually none of us could recall that much of her. Being three years older than us she had moved outside our sphere, but collectively we had enough to grasp onto her life, to truthfully answer, yes, we had known Lucy Asher.

Matt Templeton was our emissary to Sarah Fogarty, solely because he had five older sisters; he was well versed in the high rituals of young women. He had breathed in their incense. Matt found Sarah at the school tennis courts. She was alone and hitting a ball against the concrete practice wall. When she first came to South Brighton High School in the fourth form (her family had moved up from Geraldine) Sarah had been a champion tennis player. She had regularly beaten girls three years older but gradually, for reasons known only to herself, had given the sport away and now played only for fun.

All the boys at SBHS were habitually wary of Sarah. She had a pervasive aura of disdain for all things masculine and had been known to hit boys who annoyed her hard enough to deaden arms. We all agreed that she had been an unlikely best friend for Lucy Asher.

When Matt found her, Sarah was hitting the ball forehand with the ferocity of her previous match-winning line drives. The ball slammed into the wall at almost the same spot every time. It was just before eleven in the morning, twenty-eight degrees and cloudless.

'Well?' she said, when it was at last clear that Matt was not going away. He told us that she spoke without looking over at him.

'I wanted to talk to you about Lucy.'

'No shit.' Another reason boys were wary of her was that Sarah had the disconcerting ability to out-swear even the toughest boys. 'That's all anybody fucking talks about these days. Can't you see I'm trying to practise here?'

'We were wondering if you knew who killed her.'

As investigative work goes it was pretty crude stuff, but at least the question made Sarah stop hitting the tennis ball. It bounced back off the wall and rolled across the ground past Matt's feet, coming to rest at the foot of the spindly umpire's chair. Sarah looked at Matt for the first time. He told us later that she had the sunken bruised eyes of a losing boxer. According to Matt Templeton, Sarah looked as though she had hadn't slept for a year.

'If I knew who fucking killed her I'd tell the police.'

Matt didn't comment. Being at the bottom of an entirely feminine pecking order had taught him how to maintain an almost monastic silence. Sarah walked over to retrieve her ball. She had to pass close to where Matt was standing and he tensed up, waiting for her to plant her knuckles into his arm. But Sarah simply picked up the ball and went back to hitting it against the wall.

Thump. Thump. Thump. Interspersed with the twanging music of the strings.

Matt waited for a long time but she didn't say anything else. It was clear to him that Sarah could go on hitting the ball all day.

Matt was outside the tall wire fence and walking away when Sarah called out to him. 'Hey, shithead.' He turned back and saw that she was standing by the fence, her raquet hanging loose in one hand. Even from a distance and through the air's shimmer he could see Sarah's cavernous eyes. They made him shiver, even in the heat.

'She was seeing some guy but she wouldn't tell me who.' And then she turned away, leaving Matt feeling as shaken as he would have been if Sarah had hit him after all.

The news that Lucy Asher was seeing someone caused a wave of consternation to wash through Jim Turner's garage. 'Seeing someone', and all that it implied, tarnished those memories of Lucy Asher we had assembled and now guarded jealously. Other images came unbidden and unwelcome. Grant Webb openly asked about the possibility of Lucy having 'done it' but was quickly hissed down and retreated into sullen silence. The idea was anathema to the Lucy we had breathed life into during the hot pungent days.

By consensus we decided that if Lucy had a boyfriend then it must have been someone who took her to the movies a couple of times, maybe held her hand — certainly nothing more.

The only first-hand report we had from inside the Ashers' house was from Roy Moynahan. Roy's mother and Mrs Asher had belonged to the same Plunket group and Mrs Moynahan insisted that Roy and his eight-year-old sister accompany her on Boxing Day to pay their respects to the Ashers.

The Ashers' dairy was on one corner of Rocking Horse Road and Tern Street. It was a pretty standard Summerhill stone house but Mr Asher had built an extension on the front, right out to the footpath, with large glass windows covered in advertising, and a door into the shop with a harsh buzzer. Although most people in the area used the dairy, even at fifteen we knew that there wasn't a lot of profit to be made selling ten-cent mixtures, newspapers, bottles of milk, bread and ice-creams in the summer.'

Roy's mother had to lift the police tape to get to the back door. The yellow tape was wrapped around the whole of the back porch, giving the impression that the house was a giant present left unopened from the day before. Police had been swarming around the house since Lucy's body was found. When the Moynahans arrived, though, the police seemed to be on their lunch break. Only one remained: a skinny man in his early twenties who hovered outside the door and seemed uncomfortable in his stiff blue shirt and tie. He asked them the purpose of their visit and recorded Mrs Moynahan's name in a black notebook.

Roy admitted that it was hard for him to get an accurate impression of the inside of the Ashers' house because of the flowers. They covered every flat surface. There were so many flowers that Mrs Asher had given up putting them in vases. Huge bunches lay on their sides on tables and on the arms of chairs, even on the floor, all of them withering in the heat. Roy and his sister and his mother had to move flowers to the side so that they could sit on the couch in a small lounge at the back of the house. Mrs Asher sat opposite them, stiff-backed, and passed muffins. She wore a new black skirt and a white shirt buttoned at the collar and Roy said her long hair was pulled back so tightly from her face that she had a permanent expression of open-eyed amazement. 'She was like one of those people in that movie about the alien body-snatchers. All still and scary.'

No one had air conditioning in those days and Roy was wearing his Sunday jacket. The sweat was running in rivulets down his back. His younger sister sat next to him and sniffed. Emma Moynahan had a summer cold but Roy suspected Mrs Asher thought the little girl was sniffling out of sadness, grieving at the loss of Lucy.

The only showing Lucy's father made was in the photographs hung on the wall behind where Mrs Asher sat. Portraits mostly, the head-and-shoulders type they take at schools every year at the same time as they take the group photos of each class. There were also snapshots deemed good enough to be blown up and put in a frame.

Lucy on a rocking horse aged about three or four.

Lucy grinning at the camera without one of her front teeth.

Lucy with one or other of her parents: with her dad on the beach with a small black and white dog; her mum and Lucy on the footpath outside the dairy.

Roy could see only one photograph where all three Ashers were together — a formal portrait taken in a park greener than anything the Spit could provide. He guessed that it had been taken in the Botanic Gardens, and quite recently, probably last spring. They were all standing beneath a large tree. Mr Asher, tall and thin, looked stiff and unlike himself in a suit and tie. Mrs Asher stood on his right and did her best to smile. Lucy sat on a park bench in front of her parents, ankles crossed, arms folded in her lap. Each parent had a protective hand on one of Lucy's shoulders and all of them were staring earnestly into the camera.

Apart from the dying flowers and the photographs, the other thing Roy mentioned was the Ashers' Christmas tree. It took up one whole corner of the lounge, the top pressing hard against the stuccoed ceiling so that there was no room for an angel or even a Christmas star. As if to make up for this lapse, each branch was sagging under the weight of the decorations. It was clear to Roy that all the family's presents, including Lucy's, were still beneath it, unopened. By surreptitiously turning his head sideways Roy could read Lucy's name on at least two of the small cards sitting on the top of the presents, like pipi shells, mouths partly open.

Roy reported back to us that he sat on the couch, sweating in the heat, listening to his sister sniffing and his mother and Mrs Asher talk about things apart from Lucy for as long as he could stand it. At last he asked to use the bathroom. Mrs Asher directed him through a door into a long, narrow hallway. The toilet was at the far end but Roy nosed around until he found the door to Lucy's bedroom. The door was partly open but more police tape was strung across it. Ducking low, Roy passed inside.

We can only imagine how Roy must have felt standing there in Lucy's room. Beside him, Lucy's bed was unmade, either left that way by Lucy or by the police during their search, Roy did not know. Roy had no older sisters and Lucy's room was a foreign world to him, as exotic and steamy as the jungles of Borneo. There were posters on the wall of Sting and Adam and the Ants and a dresser littered with mysterious tubes and bottles. Roy told us that the smell of lavender soap hung in the air almost thick enough to see. When pressed for further details he remembered a bunch of dried roses hanging upside down from the ceiling above the dresser. There were, he claimed, also other darker smells he could not identify.

Through the walls he could hear the brittle voice of Mrs Asher talking to his mother in the lounge. As he looked around he noticed patches of light grey dust on the dresser and the windowsills and on the headboard of the bed, as though a large moth had blundered down and flapped around desperately in agitated circles before taking to the air again. It took Roy a while to realise that it was the dust police used to look for fingerprints.

Using only his fingernails for leverage, Roy opened Lucy's

wardrobe. He imagined Lucy standing where he now stood, selecting the dress she would later be murdered in, holding it up in front of the full-length mirror hung on the inside of the door. (Would she have chosen a different one if she had known? A stupid question in many ways, but the type of thing we used to debate for hours.) Roy later said it made him feel humble to just be there, looking at her clothes, breathing in the same scented air as Lucy breathed.

At last, reluctantly, Roy took one final look around Lucy's room. His mother and Mrs Asher would miss him soon. Easing the door shut behind him, Roy went to find the loo — which by then he really did need to use.

Mrs Asher had told him that the toilet was at the end of the hall. There were two doors at the far end and the first one he opened turned out to be a cupboard. Jackets and umbrellas hung from hooks on the wall and several suitcases were pushed to the back. Lying next to them and half covered by a fallen raincoat was Lucy's bag. Roy recognised it straight away. It was a canvas duffel bag with two strings that Lucy used to hook one arm through so that it dangled from her shoulder.

Roy picked up the bag and felt that it was full. Inside was a can of Coke, a box of sanitary napkins (which made him uncomfortable), two French textbooks and a thick book on photography with a naked black woman on the front. At the very bottom of the bag was a small blue notebook with a soft cover. It was held together by a yellow ribbon. On the cover it said: LUCY A. PRIVATE! The letters had been so deeply overwritten in black pen that the words could, if necessary, be read with only your fingertips.

Roy put everything else back in Lucy's bag and returned it to the cupboard, carefully covering it in the same way as when he found it. Lifting up the back of his jacket he slipped the book down between his shirt and his belt, into the small of his back, where it did not leave a bulge and where it was held tight.

Lucy Asher's diary lay on the pool table, lit only by the beam from Jim Turner's torch. The circle of light surrounding it shook slightly; whether Jim's hand was unsteady from excitement or from the strain of keeping the torch still was impossible to tell. It was ten o'clock at night and dark outside, although heat still simmered up from the tarseal of Rocking Horse Road. The fug of the estuary at low tide was stronger than it had been all summer. The smell came from the dark heavy mud, over which armies of crabs scuttled, but also from the bloom of sea lettuce, lime green and decaying, which that summer threatened to choke even the deepest channels. As we stood in the garage we could hear the low waves on the beach side of the Spit mutter against the shore. Aslan, the black Alsatian at No. 67, had barked himself hoarse earlier than usual that night and was sending out rasping coughs into the world outside his gate.

We stood around the table in silence. Several of us were wearing clothes over our pyjamas. Al Penny wore tartan slippers belonging to his father. Tug Gardiner had on a sweatshirt with a hood, which for some reason he had pulled up over his head, but we were in too serious a mood to question him. The news of Roy's find had travelled from one of us to the other; from house to house like a moth in the night. We had feigned sleepiness and gone to our rooms, only to slip away through back doors and open windows. The moon was unaccounted for as we slipped through the tepid darkness. We were the furtive noises in the night.

It was Pete Marshall who broke the spell. He carefully lifted the book off the green felt. Perhaps because he had been the one who found Lucy's body, Pete felt he had a special right, or possibly an obligation. The ribbon resisted him but at last succumbed to his fumbling and he opened the cover to the first page of the book of Lucy Asher. Jim held the torch higher so that the narrow beam of light spilled over Pete's shoulder and onto the first page.

From that day on, although we all handled the book and read its contents, only Pete ever read aloud. By being the first to intone Lucy's words to us he became, in a sense, her voice. He read well right from that first night. Pete instinctively knew not to try to imitate a young woman's voice, nor to insert dramatic emphasis where he thought it might be warranted. He kept his voice neutral, clear and slow, which allowed us to hear within it Lucy's own. All the drama we needed was there in the words.

The diary started on Lucy's seventeenth birthday, May 29th, seven months before she died. There was an inscription on the inside cover — To Lucyloo from Dad. To the uninitiated the details might have seemed mundane, even trivial, but we were fifteen and in the grip of something huge and powerful that held us tightly, even jealously. All that summer shook us awake in the morning and laid us down in our beds at night. It muttered from the dark corners of our rooms as we tossed and turned in the heat. It is enough to say that we hung on every word Pete read.

May 29: Mum won't let me go out with Sarah and Megan tonight!!! She says I have to stay here for a FAMILY DINNER! Sarah says Mum still treats me like a baby because I'm an only child. She's allowed out because she has three older brothers and her parents are too tired to care. If only my parents were Catholics too and not boring old Presbyterians who are allowed to use a rubber. Worse luck me.

June 2. Bought the latest Bowie album. It's great. David's hair looks great. Still too cold to swim. Can't wait for weather to get warmer. Read in the Woman's Weekly that lemon juice in your hair makes it lighter. Have been doing it every night but not sure if it's working. Mum wanted to know where all the lemons were going. Have to be more careful about what I pinch from the shop.

Lucy did not write in her diary every day. Many pages were tantalisingly blank or contained nothing but absent-minded scrawls, swirling labyrinths from which there was no way in or out. (Pete held these out in the gloom for us to peer at.) Some days she only wrote a couple of words. 'Weather crap' was a typical entry (August 21st).

The first reference to SJ was on June 13th.

Met SJ in town today. He was shopping for a shirt. Really weird to see him doing something so normal. I saw him before he saw me. I almost kept on walking but soooo glad I didn't. He asked if I'd like to have tea with him at the Ballantyne's tea room. Almost said no but he's really easy to talk to. Keep thinking about him. He has really nice teeth.

June 20: SJ smiled at me today but didn't stop to talk because he was walking with some others.

July 16: Some little twerp spilled chocolate milk in the shop the other day and most of it must have gone under the fridge. Just my luck it was a cold day and all the heaters were on. Smells DISGUSTING! Mum blames me for not cleaning it up properly.

August 7: School holidays. Haven't seen SJ for days and days. Feeling sad and lonely which is silly because we hardly ever talk anyway. Think he might have gone away with his family. Mum really being a pain. Might kill myself [and in differently coloured pen] *THAT WAS A JOKE! HA HA*

The batteries in Jim's torch were fading fast. As Pete read, the light dimmed until the book was almost indistinguishable from the darkness in the garage. Pete's voice stayed clear and steady but he leaned further and further forward so that by the last few pages he seemed to be about to devour the diary.

> *September 14: Played tennis with Sarah today. She thrashed me — as usual. Feel bad about not telling her what's been going on but SJ has made me promise not to say a word. He's right that people wouldn't understand about our friendship. Taking the bus into town to meet him again today. Think Mum might be getting suspicious about all the time I'm taking off from the shop. Had a big fight about it. Think she's been nosing around in my room. Will take this diary to school from now on. Too dangerous to leave it here.*
>
> *September 28: SJ invited me back to his house tonight after softball practice. Of course we had to go separately. It wasn't like how I imagined it. I thought he'd have heaps of books and stuff like that but he's hardly got any. HE KISSED ME!!!!!! About time. I liked it, apart from the way he got a bit rough at the end before I said I had to go. Good that I did leave and not just for the obvious reason. Mum freaked out anyway when I got home because she said anything could have happened to me biking home in the dark. Had another big argument so I'm writing this in my room instead of having dinner. Had some poached eggs at SJ's anyway but Mum doesn't know that. Hope she thinks I'm starving. P.S. Kissing S was not at all like kissing Phil. Don't know if I should go back.*

And then Lucy seemed to lose interest in the diary. October and November were mostly blank. The last entry was on December 15, six days before she was murdered. It was a list of Christmas presents to buy for her family and friends. SJ was not mentioned. Only two were crossed off: a book called *The Painted Years* for her dad and lavender soap for her Nana.

It took Pete just under an hour to read the whole diary aloud. His last words hung in the air and then drifted away through the cracks in the garage walls. We stood in the quarter-light of the dying torch and listened to Aslan coughing. No one moved to switch on the overhead light. We did not want to see one another's faces — to see written there our own feelings, which we did not have the experience to pin down with names. We were uncertain whether men could even speak to one another about such things. We just stood there lost in our thoughts. In that way our emotions were stillborn in the darkness — unnamed and unembraced.

    Eventually three white candles were rummaged up from a box in the corner. They were placed in old tin cans, where they were solemnly lit. The diary was carefully arranged so that it sat propped up on the workbench immediately below the photo of Lucy. By that time the photo had been slipped into an old gilded frame someone had brought along. The three flames danced in the cross-draughts and in the ebb and flow of our breaths. The flickering light reflected off the glass in front of the photo and off Lucy's trophy so that the running girl seemed to move with a liquid grace, dipping even lower as she crossed the finishing line, and then springing forward and up in triumph.

    It is impossible to say when the first of us slipped out of the garage and it has never been established who was the last. Jim Turner reported that from his room he could see the candles flickering through the cracks in the garage walls almost up until dawn. Each of us knew when our time came to leave — to say goodnight to Lucy and to slip silently away. Tug Gardiner was still in his dark cowl. Al Penny's overlarge slippers flip-flopped on the concrete path.

    It would be safe to say that none of us slept that night. How could we? We lay on our beds, on top of our summer sheets, wrapped only in the torrid smell of rotting sea lettuce coming up off the estuary. Who among us did not stare into the hollow space above his bed and, with the white noise of the waves whispering suggestions in his ear, try to put a face to the initials SJ?

During the sweltering weeks of January, people took to leaving objects near where Lucy's body had been found. At first they simply placed their offerings on the sand, but high tides and the easterly wind soon carried them away, so the danger sign became a natural shrine. It was above the high-tide mark and protected from the wind by a dip in the dunes. We never saw anyone coming or going. Bunches of daffodils and lilies miraculously sprang out of the dry sand at the base of the pole before wilting away in an afternoon. Notes and letters, weighted down with painted rocks, would appear overnight. A small brown teddy bear, and later a pink rabbit, lived there for most of January and half of February before moving on.

    On New Year's Eve a black and white photograph was carefully tied to the pole with a yellow ribbon. It was a picture we had not seen before. Lucy, sitting on a couch, wearing a summer dress that showed a lot of her legs. She was relaxed and smiling, looking out boldly at the photographer over the top of heart-rimmed sunglasses. The photo made us anxious. Lucy looked older than we remembered her, more confident and womanly than our memories of her allowed. We were suspicious and jealous of whoever had taken the photo and wondered how long would be a decent interval before we could shift it to our files (Exhibit 14).

But mostly they left poems. It seemed to us that everyone who had ever known Lucy became a poet that summer. They attached poems to the sign with drawing pins and twine but they always blew free. It was not uncommon to find a poem tumbling along the road in the wind or crucified in the branches of a lupin. White poems flew like seagulls against the blue summer sky. They were to be found tossing in the wave foam or bobbing like Moses' cradle in the reeds at the edge of the estuary. More often than not, the words had sunfaded into nothing or slipped away into the water like fry, but sometimes they could be read.

The consensus among us was that the poems were written by girls. 'i's were dotted with broken hearts. 'Lucy' rhymed with 'mercy'. Those legible poems we did retrieve we felt obliged to take back to the sign. We pinned them back up or weighted them down with rocks so that they would not blow away again soon.

We spent January going over and over all aspects of Lucy's life, hoping to shed light on the identity of SJ. There was one person we knew with those initials who lived in the area, Steven Jones, but he was nine years old, and what we called in those days a mongol, so he was immediately excluded from our list of murder suspects. There were three other Stephens in the South Brighton area and at least another dozen boys whose names started with a twist and a hiss. But we knew we were clutching at straws. It wasn't proof of anything to be called Stephen or Stuart, Jamieson or Johnstone.

School had been back for a month before we discovered who SJ was. By then the days were not as hot but, even so, the classrooms' top windows regularly had to be cranked open to let in a breeze. We slumped at our desks in our grey shirts, unable to focus. The papers reported that the police were following several lines of enquiry but there was little progress. The number of detectives on the case had been scaled back. Our own lack of progress in identifying SJ made us torpid. The teachers tried to install in us a belief in the importance of the sixth-form year but we were becalmed and unable to concentrate.

It was Matt Templeton who worked it out. On the first Friday of February Matt had arrived late at school; assembly was already under way. He told us later that he was waiting at the back of the hall, ready to merge into the exiting crowd, as though he had been there all the time, when he saw a car pull into the teachers' parking area. Matt slipped further back so that he was hidden by the trunks of two cabbage trees growing next to the rubbish skip.

Mr Jenson remained in his car slumped over the wheel as though he had been shot by a sniper. He was a young English teacher in only his second year of teaching. Matt had never been taught by him. The new teachers were generally broken in with the younger kids, third- and fourth-formers, with maybe one seventh-form class as a consolation. Mr Jenson remained in his car for a long time. When he eventually got out, he wiped at his eyes with the sleeves of his white shirt, took a deep breath and began the walk towards the staffroom. It was only as Matt watched him go that he remembered that Mr Jenson's first name was Simon.

We tried to discover all that we could about SJ. He was twenty-three years old and unmarried and had moved north from Dunedin at the beginning of '81. His voice carried a hint of southern burr, the 'r's in Shakespeare and pentameter rolling like a sea-swell into the end of his sentences. He rented a two-bedroom cottage at the head of Rocking Horse Road, only a few minutes' walk from the Ashers' dairy. It was an old bach, barely more than four rooms and a tin roof, with the edges of the garden plots marked out with hundreds of whitewashed rocks. The bach sat on a quarter-acre section which, at the rear, was only distinguishable from the dunes by two stands of sagging wire.

Enquiries revealed that SJ was well liked by his students, especially by the girls, who considered him handsome. Collectively, we felt uncomfortable about judging his physical attractiveness. SJ was tallish. His eyes were brown. His hair was dark and slightly longer than was normal for a teacher. But we were reluctant to draw any conclusions from the parts of the man we could observe. Only Matt Templeton with his five older sisters was unequivocal in his assessment. 'Sure, girls would go ga-ga for him.'

Boys who had been taught by SJ simple reported him to be 'okay'. We discovered, though, that between the girls in his classes petty rivalries and jealousies darted like ball lightning. Not that he seemed to do anything to fan the girls' interest, nor did he appear to show favour. Even Martha Ferguson, the plainest of the plain, had been gifted an occasional smile and an encouraging word. She was a member of the photography club that SJ ran after school every Wednesday. All but one of the members were girls and the one boy who did belong was a seventh-former with an undisguised interest in theatre who was regularly referred to as 'the poofter'.

In our interview with Martha she described SJ as 'different' since school had come back. In what way? we asked, anticipating a revelation. Her plain, round face gazed earnestly up at us and her mouth gaped like a deep-sea fish in a rock pool. 'It's like,' she said at last, and sighed, 'like he's gone away and now all that's left is his shell.'

At every opportunity we trailed through the school behind SJ, down the corridors and over the parched school grounds. We were like blowflies behind a shit-stained dog. Our eyes crawled all over him.

February rolled over into March and the afternoon meetings in Jim Turner's garage became tense. SJ had done nothing incriminating or even unpredictable for three weeks. Apart from his damning initials and the few private minutes Matt had witnessed (plus a plain girl's opinion that he was 'different') we had nothing.

One faction, led by Roy Moynahan, wanted to make an anonymous call to the police, telling them of SJ's identity. There was a special phone number being advertised in the paper and on the radio for people with information. (It must be said that Al Penny and a couple of others had wanted to hand the diary over right away but had been out-voted.) Surprisingly, Jase Harbidge was the most vocal among us against both ideas. Jase argued that the best we could count on from the police was that they would interview SJ. 'If he's covered his tracks and he's a good liar he'll walk away, no worries. It happens all the time.' (It is also worth noting that Jase's confidence in the police had been shaken. His father had not returned to work after Christmas. Bill Harbidge was officially on sick leave but we all knew he now seldom moved from his spot in front of the television and cracked open his first beer with breakfast.)

It was Jase and Pete Marshall who took it upon themselves to break into SJ's house. They arranged to meet in the vacant section next door at a time they knew SJ would be teaching his fourth-form English class. Pete later told us they left their bikes in the waist-high grass, dry as hay, and entered SJ's section through broken boards in the fence behind the garden shed with its two-stroke mower. The back door to the house was locked but Jase wrapped a whitewashed stone from the garden in an old rugby sock he had brought along for the purpose and broke the lower pane of glass in the door. He reached in and flicked a latch and suddenly, against both their expectations, they were in.

Pete, reporting to some of us privately, said that Jase immediately began to pull drawers out and empty the contents onto the lino. 'He seemed really mad. Just went nuts. I didn't think it was a good idea to try and stop him.' Knives and forks and spoons monsooned down, along with whisks and corkscrews and an eggbeater. Soon the kitchen floor was flooded with cutlery.

Jase and Pete did not know what they were looking for and Pete admitted that it very quickly did not matter. In a later interview he confessed to personally hurling a bag of flour against the kitchen wall so that it exploded in a white cloud. All the food was pulled from the cupboards. Packets lay scattered around. Dried macaroni and cornflakes crackled beneath their shoes like brittle shells in the silvery water.

When they were finished in the kitchen they moved on. SJ's bedroom was quickly turned upside down. His surprisingly small collection of clothes was tossed around the room and some of it ripped. The sheets on his bed were roughly stripped off and the mattress tipped from the wire base so that it lay drunkenly, blocking the door.

The second bedroom had been converted into a darkroom. The windows were blacked out with sheets of black polythene taped down at the edges, and a long trestle table against the wall was covered with plastic bottles of developer and fixer. SJ even had an enlarger, tall and spidery, where images could be manipulated.

The packet of photographs was sitting in plain view. It was Jase who picked it up. Even years later, Pete remembered hearing him gasp as though he had been sucker-punched in the stomach.

Even by today's standards the pictures of Lucy were pornographic.

The photographs awaited us in the Turners' garage, fanned out on the pool table. It is not an exaggeration to say that we were appalled; our faith was shaken. We could not match the Lucy we knew with this brazen doppelganger spread in front of us.

The pictures had obviously been taken on several different occasions. In some, Lucy's hair was tied back with a ribbon, in others she wore unbecoming makeup. Most of us had seen her naked before, on the beach, from behind the police tape in the half-hour before the forensics people screened her off, but that was the type of nudity we associated with children, with sisters and mothers. There was an innocence to Lucy in death that these photographs called a lie.

There was now no doubt in our minds that SJ had murdered Lucy. We agreed that she must have seen the huge mistake she was making involving herself with someone who would do this to her. She must have tried to call it off. In a fit of demonic rage he had strangled her. It was obvious. Wasn't it also likely — more than likely, probable — that he had manipulated her (blackmailed her!) into posing for these photographs? Of course it was. What other explanation could there be?

No one suggested we call the police.

Pete Marshall was openly weeping as he carried the photographs out onto the Turners' back lawn. We all watched in silence as he placed the pile in the middle of the grass. Roy Moynahan had a box of matches in his pocket along with his Marlboros. The photos caught easily and curled up from the outside in. The chemicals made the flames flare orange and yellow. The grass was tinder-dry but short. Even so, the brown stubble caught and the flames spread out from the central pyre. It was only when they threatened to take hold in the old nectarine tree that we moved to stamp them down.

By the time we had put out the grass fire the photographs had been consumed, rendered down into single layers of ash. Some of the translucent layers lifted off in the breeze and rose above us into the empty sky. Al Penny, quite recently, recalled seeing Lucy's face, rising up, cleansed by the flames, smiling down at him. 'She was so beautiful.'

We agreed to meet at 9.30 that evening. By then it would be dark. Nothing was said about what we would do but there was an unspoken knowledge. We went to our homes and had dinner with our families as though nothing were wrong. If we were more surly or distracted than usual, no one bothered to comment. Our families were used to our secrets and our sullen silences, which they mostly labelled adolescence and shrugged off.

When we met again that evening we avoided the pools of light from the street-lights near SJ's house. Jase Harbidge was carrying his father's five-iron. He had been the first to arrive and tapped the head of the club with a metallic watch-tick against the footpath as he waited. We came singly and in pairs, converging on SJ's house out of the surrounding darkness. A strong wind had come up off the ocean and behind the dunes white waves stampeded into the beach. Some of us came through the sandhills, slipping down paths we had worn bare ourselves during daylight. Tug Gardiner's hood was back up. Jim Turner had blacked out his face with shoe polish so that the whites of his eyes showed bright in what little light there was. Both Al Penny and Matt Templeton wore balaclavas and Matt carried a softball bat. Pete Marshall bore Lucy's silver trophy through the night like a talisman.

SJ had gone to bed early and the only light came from a naked bulb above the front door. It was mild Roy who surprised us all by throwing the first of the whitewashed stones that ringed the garden. The stone arched through the darkness. We watched its progress as it travelled through the air and then carried on through the bedroom window. The shatter of glass. A pause and then the bedroom lit up. We could clearly see SJ. He peered out through the jagged pane, but as more stones began to hit the house his head darted back and the light in the bedroom went off.

Some of the stones bounced off the weatherboards; others found their mark and more glass shattered and fell. The stones that went high landed on the tin roof and roared and growled as they rolled back down.

And then SJ was standing on his front step. He had pulled on a T-shirt but was still wearing boxer shorts. He was lit from above so that we could not see his eyes, only dark sea-caves where his eyes should have been, inside which, we were certain, lurked a black soul. He shouted garbled angry threats into the darkness but we knew he could not see us or, if he could, we were only darker shadows in the night.

Who threw that first stone? We don't know. (Even if we did, we wouldn't tell, even to this day.) All we will say is that it was a good throw, hard and accurate. The rock struck SJ on the forehead just above his left eyebrow. A communal sigh of satisfaction came from our mouths. There was immediately blood and SJ clutched at his head and staggered forward. This involuntary movement took him down the single step and out of the light from the bulb above the door. Perhaps if we had been able to see him more clearly what happened next would have been avoided. But then again, probably not.

More stones flew, striking him on the body. Nobody was holding back and we were not kids any more. At fifteen, all the power in your arm is there and your eyesight is sharp. Very few missed their mark. SJ staggered again and fell, and tried to regain his feet. White stones flew in like tracer in the night.

We closed in on him, forming a wide semi-circle in the darkness. A large stone struck his left knee and he cried out and fell. He did not try to get up this time but simply curled into a ball and took all that we had to give. By then he had stopped shouting and if he was moaning we could not hear it above the rushing sound in our ears.

When the stones close to us ran out we threw whatever was at hand. The golf club helicoptered through the air into his body. Someone threw a potted geranium that fell short, the pot shattering. In the end we resorted to snatching up the very earth, the sandy soil, darting forward, yelling and hurling it in our rage. The silver trophy was the last. It pierced the darkness, striking SJ on the shoulder where he lay, still now. The silver girl broke as she rebounded back, the metal separating from the plinth where it was only glued, and both parts lay on the ground.

We stood panting, all our anger at last exorcised. Nobody spoke. There was only the sound of the waves and the strong wind in the lupins.

The tin of lawnmower petrol from the garden shed, once spilled over the floor of the darkroom, would have welcomed a match as a natural progression. It must have gone up with a pleasing whoosh. We stood, surprised and then elated, as the black polythene covering the darkroom window melted away and the long flames licked the cool outside air. The flames quickly reached out and up into the roof and then they were flickering through the broken glass of the other bedroom. Flames stalked the house, moving quickly from room to room. We soon felt the heat on our bodies and had to move back. SJ lay still, light and dark flickering across him.

We stood watching the fire for a long time. It was only when the first siren sounded, still far away, thin and whiney like a mosquito in the night, that we came out of our trance and, one by one, turned and walked away into the darkness of Rocking Horse Road.

For the record, we did not kill SJ. He suffered a severe concussion and needed twenty-three stitches on his head (medical report, Exhibit 18). His left wrist was broken, probably by the impact of the golf club, and he had extensive bruising to his back and legs, which had taken the brunt of the stones as he lay on the ground.

SJ spent a week in hospital, during which time he was twice interviewed by the police. The first interview was in regard to the attack on him. SJ must have recognised at least one of us because the police moved quickly. We were all picked up. We were questioned separately and made to give formal statements.

On the second occasion, as a result of what we had to tell them, the police wanted to talk to SJ about the murder of Lucy Asher. They quickly found out that during the weekend Lucy had been killed, SJ had been staying with his parents in Dunedin. He had been best man at his brother's wedding and more than sixty witnesses could vouch for him on the night Lucy was murdered.

So, SJ had committed no crime, not in a strict legal sense. Lucy Asher had been of age. SJ was only guilty of an indiscretion and a betrayal of trust. He declined to press charges against the 'unidentified youths' who had assaulted him (*Press*, Feb. 19, 1982, Exhibit 26), probably out of fear of what would be reported in the papers about him if the case went to trial. Despite all the interviews — and we told them everything — the police were never able to establish which of us threw the first stone or who set fire to the house. Prosecutions require specific evidence and collectively we were hazy on all but the most esoteric details.

The day he got out of hospital SJ packed his car with what little he had salvaged from the gutted shell of the house and left South

Brighton High School and the Spit forever. All we now know is that he moved to Australia. Until a few years ago, when we last checked up, he was married with three kids and living in Adelaide, where he worked for Rank-Xerox as some type of manager.

All that was twenty-five years ago and in another century. Most of us still live in New Brighton and occasionally a few will get together for a beer. Inevitably the conversation comes around to the case, but casually, as though that weren't the whole point.

Lucy Asher's murder has never been officially solved. The police still have DNA evidence taken from under Lucy' nails, but in the early eighties a DNA database was undreamed of. Even now, when DNA matching has solved several almost forgotten crimes, the sample from the Asher case has never been linked to anyone. Tug Gardiner is now a detective and lives up in Wellington. He keeps us informed if there is a case that shows any similarities to Lucy's, or if a likely suspect turns up.

It would be fair to say that none of us has ever got over Lucy Asher. She was our first true love and, in some sense, our last. Of course we do not say that to one another in so many words but all of our lives are littered with troubled relationships with women. After all, what real woman can compete? Break-ups and divorces seem to be par for the course. More often than not, the houses where we meet are the homes of single men whose kids visit at the weekend or whose new, often younger, girlfriend resents our presence. We joke about it after a few beers and our conversations are filled with self-mocking asides, but beneath the laughter you can feel the undertow of tension and sadness.

The unspoken truth is that we are all still searching for something. Not just for Lucy's murderer but for a moment in time when we served a higher purpose and a greater good. You could say that we are haunted by what happened back then. There are no rattling chains or shimmering visions. Just our memories of a long, hot summer and the ghost of a broad-shouldered girl who swims in our blood and looks unlikely ever to leave.

Vincent O'Sullivan

Mrs Bennett and the Bears

THE FIRST TIME HE TRIED to phone there was difficulty getting through. Ten minutes later the line was clear as glass. Jackie picked up the phone and shrieked, 'Edward!' She raised her hand to hush the women at the table behind her, on the other side of the two bottles and the plates with their scattered shells. 'Have we had a night, believe me!' Jackie said.

'Who's there?' Edward asked her.

'Your sisters,' Jackie said, 'who else!', and Shirl called over his wife's shoulder, 'Ask him how the little Nip ladies are!'

Edward was fifty-six. It still surprised him that he was in Japan at all. The director had come through into the smallest of the three divisional offices and said, 'We have to send somebody up there, and I'm damned if I want to face that lot again. Intestines of sea-slugs for breakfast. Not on your nelly.' He turned to Lucy, the administrative assistant, who sat a few feet from Edward's desk. She laughed and knew exactly what the director meant. 'Emetics aren't in it,' she said. 'So I've heard.' So Edward had said all right, he'd go then, it was about time he took one of these information jaunts. Making it sound casual. In fact he had felt — not his word, true, but one that Jackie had used on his behalf — he had felt more than a tad excited at the prospect. A conference in Sapporo on the care of the aged may not sound quite the most exciting assignment, but Japan, after all . . .

He would not have admitted it to a soul, not even to Jackie, but when he thought of the place it was pretty much what his father would have thought. Which meant, seeing Dad had never been closer to the war than training on Motutapu, it was a view based almost entirely on the movies. The deck of an aircraft carrier far below with a pilot's face smooth as butter, a white scarf fluttering from his throat as he tilts and aims dead centre . . . A sword flashing down above a bowed neck . . . Less nasty things, of course. Olympic gymnasts arcing back from the rings, rice rolled in seaweed, a woman with her face whitened with flour. Yes, he was glad he said he would go. Jackie and his sisters thought it an absolute scream, Edward off to Nippon at his age when he'd hardly been out of the North Island! Shirl, who always talked to him as though he were on the end of a distant telephone call in any case, now clinked the bottles behind his wife's head and called down the thousands of kilometres, 'Tell him just listen to what he's missing!'

Edward put down the receiver and stood at the window, fifteen storeys high above the long artificial lake. Scullers in bright jackets sliced the dark water, their wakes spreading out and intersecting. It was his first time away from home for years. And if what he now felt was loneliness, then that was all right too. But it was a strange feeling. Then he stepped back to the window, startled. A large wide-winged bird, a hawk it must be, swept in to within feet of the plate-glass he stood at. It was the air currents, he supposed — the warmth from the huge hotel that towered where natural cold should be, and the birds rode the comfort of it. Or perhaps that had nothing to do with it. He turned and went to the sofa in the most luxurious room he had ever spent a night in. They told you that, didn't they, that Japan was luxury? Billy Collett in Policy had said to him before he came up, 'I've been there three times and I don't pretend to know the first thing about the buggers. But they do know what a hotel is. You'll see that soon enough.'

He sat and took off the new shoes he had bought for the conference. He had not liked it when he phoned just now. He had not liked hearing his sisters — Bernice who was married and Shirl who was divorced — both trying so hard to show what fun they were having. Perhaps they were. Perhaps they were as happy as he and Jackie were most of the time. He had been elated all day, and the phone call made him feel so flat. Visiting the hospital especially, now that was something. The quality of the place, so much finer than anything he knew at home. He had taken careful notes. The young caregivers who trained for two years and wore long blue aprons as they moved cheerfully among the aged patients — their good humour and dedication that so struck him. The few old people who tried to speak to him and shook his hand. The large impressionist prints on the walls, the cages of bright singing birds. He had talked with a physio from Christchurch, brought up here for a year to work with local staff. The young woman told him not everywhere was like this, of course, but there was nothing back home to touch it either.

He returned to the window and placed his forehead on the cold glass. The air outside was grey; lights twinkled in moving streams on a distant motorway. Another of the large birds swept in. It levelled out and hovered so close to the glass that the darker markings of the feathers stood out as clear as writing. Then the bird tilted and flowed down towards the sheet of now blackened water.

The phone shrilled on the bedside table. Mr Tanaka said he would be in the foyer tomorrow morning at eight o'clock; would Edward be so good as to meet him there, promptly? Seeing it was their free day. Mr Tanaka was youngish, handsome, connected with a string of hospitals. He had given a paper on financing care for the aged. He referred to flow-charts and the economies of several countries. He said, 'What we do for them today we do for ourselves tomorrow.' He would drive Edward to the country to see the bears. And Mrs Bennett, he said. She had been a student with him and now lived in Sydney — perhaps Edward met her already? He said he thought so. A tallish woman with high-piled hair, she must be the one Mr Tanaka meant.

He was quite wrong. Mrs Keiko Bennett was — well, dumpy, Jackie would have called her. Her hair was short, with a shiny fringe across a roundish, middle-aged face. She spoke English and once had an Australian husband. She smiled when they shook hands. She was the first Japanese he had met in two days who did not bow and make him feel the awkwardness of his body.

Mr Tanaka sat in the front seat, next to the driver. Edward and Keiko — she asked him to call her that — sat in the back. We are like a bridal party, Edward thought, these white antimacassar things across the seats, the lacy fringes, the white gloves the driver wore. Keiko broke the ice. She said, 'I have never seen the bears either.' Mr Tanaka told them the animals they were going to see were called higuma. For all other bears there was a different word. This was only for those in Hokkaido, which were almost the biggest in the world.

It surprised Edward that he did not feel awkward with her, not in the least. Women, as Jackie sometimes teased him, were hardly his thing, were they? 'Forty before he tried one!' she said once to Bernice. And Bernice had slapped her hand and said, 'That's my big brother you're talking about, you wicked widow!' Later Edward told her, 'I wish you wouldn't joke like that.' It made him look, well, stupid, didn't it? Then Jackie lifted her cashmere sweater and crushed him in against her breasts and tousled his hair and told him there, if they couldn't joke among themselves, the family, then who could they joke with? She had held him so tight her nails hurt his shoulders. She called out, 'My God!' and when she got her breath back she said, 'Doesn't that tell you something, now, doesn't it?'

Mr Tanaka said a friend of his was once playing golf not far from the hot springs where they would park the car, and take the funicular several hundred metres into the densely wooded hills. His friend was teeing off when a cry went up along the links. A bear had come out of the woods and ambled along the course. Players ran in all directions, tossing their American clubs and their expensive Italian leather bags all over the greens.

Keiko laughed for the first time and Edward thought, how good that sounds when she laughs. Her face was lit with the thought of it — the running golfers, their dignity dropped as quickly as their number eights, and the slow, lumbering, casual beast. Her teeth were even and small; she looked ten years younger when she laughed. Edward was laughing too. She held his glance when he looked across at her. And then he remembered she was Japanese, and how foreign she was, after all. How foreign their whole excursion was. But there was a warmth between them.

It was two hours later, after they had eaten buckwheat noodles off heated black tiles, and Mr Tanaka had dropped them at the funicular, whose small red cabin gently swayed them away from the dock and out over the steeply ascending forest. Keiko pointed to where the sun broke from the afternoon rainclouds and the distant sea flashed out its great sheet of foil. 'See that, Edward?' she said to him. And when they were through the gates of the park she said, 'Here, hold your hands like a cup.' She poured the round toasted pellets from the bag she had just bought. She tilted the bag and steadied his own hands with one finger. It was as natural as a mother doing it to a child. But her touch surprised him, and pleased him greatly, and she smiled when he looked at her.

They walked in silence to the parapet and she said, 'Ah!' as she looked over. 'You think so too?'

'Yes,' Edward said, 'yes.' He did not catch what word she had actually said. But yes to whatever it was, for when he looked down and saw the bears he felt the catch in his breath. They were magnificent and poised and huge. Directly beneath him one hoisted itself up from where it rested on all fours. It rose and expanded and its sheer presence came up to him with the rough, tangy stench of the pit. It held up a soft black paw beneath the sheathed curve of its claws, a kind of benign, slow, imploring wave as he threw pellets down to it, then the quick easy movement of the massive head as it snapped at the flying scraps of food. There were dozens of them in the huge concrete pit. 'See the necks,' Keiko said. Her hand lifted, then fell back beside his own on the iron rail in front of them. She meant the wounds slashed in long red trenches on the shoulders and chests of several of the bears. 'They fight because of the space.'

They watched for almost an hour. Edward said, 'I feel like a child, watching these.'

'They would kill you like that,' Keiko said. Again her hand raised slightly and fell back to the iron bar. 'They are very beautiful and they would kill you like that.' And they laughed together, although there was no particular reason to. Then she looked at her watch and said, 'The Japanese are never late.' And as if to place herself a little to one side, she smiled at Edward and told him, 'I have been in Sydney now for as long as I was Japanese.'

Mr Tanaka's driver asked if they would like to sit in the car or walk a little while they waited for their host to return from one of his hospitals down the road.

'We'll walk,' Keiko said. They walked for ten minutes, passing beyond the public buildings to a small park and a few trees. The first drops of rain were sudden and big as coins. The downpour pinged off car roofs and hissed on the open ground. Edward put on the light raincoat he had carried all afternoon. 'Mr Tanaka will drive down this way,' Keiko said. 'He's bound to.'

Edward held open the sides of his raincoat in what he knew must seem a comic enough gesture. He said, 'I'm afraid there's nowhere else.' The woman stood in close against him. She put her hands just above his own and drew the coat as best she could in front of both of them. The rain ran behind Edward's glasses and inside his collar. He could smell the rain on Keiko's hair. She stood close against him, her head beneath his chin. She laughed and her hair moved against his throat and she said, 'We must look very strange.' It was only a minute. The black car eased down the street towards them. The driver's white-gloved hand rose and beckoned them to the kerb. That was all there was. They had stood in the pelting rain, their bodies close, as at ease, Edward thought, as he had ever been with anyone. 'Thank you,' Keiko said. Then they scrambled into the car.

Keiko rubbed her face and her hands with a towel Mr Tanaka handed back to her. She then ran her fingers though her hair and held the towel towards Edward. Mr Tanaka and the driver were highly amused. As they dropped Edward back at his hotel Keiko touched his hand and said to him, 'Next time an umbrella!' He stood at the hotel entrance and raised his hand. She waved back from the other side of the rain-dotted window. She was leaving the conference early, to visit a sister at Kyushu. She kept her hand flat on the window until the car turned into the main road.

Edward sat in the huge lobby, where a man in a white suit played a grand piano on a dais between ten-metre artificial palms. High above, in the fifteen-storey atrium, life-size models beneath brightly coloured hang-gliders swooped forever in the same place. He ordered a brandy and watched the capsule-shaped lift, beaded with tiny lights, run up and down the enclosed wall of the hotel. He knew Jackie would phone his room as arranged at six o'clock, but he preferred to sit down here.

He knew it was love, and knew it was absurd even to use the word. He knew that in a day, in two days, this elation would pass, and he would never know it again. Never. She had felt it too. Pressed against him. Laughing. Knowing as well as he did that it was a splinter of time that never should have occurred, a pure gift. He took a mouthful of brandy and held it without swallowing, prolonging the pleasure of its taste.

Twenty minutes later he signalled to the waiter for another drink. He smiled at the young man in a strange operatic uniform who carefully set the balloon glass on a coaster. Edward would have liked to joke with him, but he knew he did not have the knack for that kind of easy rapport. He thought how he would tell Jackie about the conference, about the marvellous geriatric baths he had seen yesterday, for example, whose sides rose from slots in the floor to the level of a metal stretcher wheeled above them, the bath literally coming to the patient. He could hear himself saying it: 'Geriatric care we've never dreamed of at home.' And Bernice rolling her eyes and Shirl passing another glass of pinot all round and Jackie joking, 'You don't have to be so interesting, pet.'

Of course he would never see Keiko again. That seemed not to matter. Her hair wet and scented, he was not sure with what, beneath his chin, her hands resting on his where she held the sides of his coat together. They would never know about that. He would not even tell them about the bears that rose up as tall as in stories, their questing muzzles lifted, their eyes small as currants. There was no sadness in his thinking: This is the last secret I shall have in my life. He picked up the glass and looked again, up to the vast shadowy atrium, to the figures on the hang-gliders like high stalled hawks.

Jo Randerson

The Sheep, the Shepherd

ON A TUESDAY IN 2004, at the end of the month of May, a middle-aged man arrived at Charles de Gaulle Airport in Paris, which is the capital city of France. He had just flown in from Helsinki, which is in Finland, and was on his way home to Christchurch, a small city with smog problems in a southern country called New Zealand. Here two teenage boy-children were eagerly anticipating their father's return, as was his wife Elizabeth. The man's name was Edward or Eddy, which rhymes with steady: an interesting point to remember.

When Edward's plane SN 923 landed in France, he took his hand luggage, his coat and his bottle of duty-free vodka. He disembarked with the other passengers, chatting politely to the hostesses with what little French he knew. (Hot/cold, many/few, yes/no.) He passed successfully through the little routine known as 'customs'. And there he stood, now officially in France, and he glanced around at the anxious lines of overburdened passengers cramming their way onto already-full flights. A low-bickering couple walked past: she had forgotten to pack his loafers; he was understandably annoyed. Announcements advised travellers to clutch their possessions at all times. A TV played in a nearby lounge; some soldiers, some place, some people getting killed. And suddenly Edward felt very tired. Very, very tired indeed.

He watched the departures boards flicking over: Beograd, Johannesburg, Amsterdam, Bombay. He thought of all the places he had been, and all the places he had yet to go. He witnessed time — which he had previously experienced as a long, infinite continuum — suddenly fold in on itself, condensing into one single and complete moment; he suddenly perceived the world as a dirty grey ball floating in space, and saw himself as the tiniest and most indistinct of specks on it. And something inside him made a sigh; something inside him near his heart made a very deep sigh and the tiniest particle in his brain changed position ever so slightly, and that was it.

At this moment, it would be fair to say that his thoughts were not of his wife, Elizabeth. Nor his family, nor his job, nor any of the lesser details that concerned him as a man. His thoughts were entirely connected with his real self, his deeper self, and the tumultuous chaos he had unleashed within his head.

In a moment he had left the airport, left the baggage hall far behind, and had slithered off into the gulf of great unknowing. Down into the endless caves of withering time, where all that has ever been (and all that wished it had) rushes around itself in a mad and filthy haze, this way and that — a terrifying place to be, and groundless; faces fly past in the fog, people you once met or wished you hadn't; parents, grandparents, children who could one day call you Daddy; the boy you could have been if you had looked the other way: all potential outcomes, all possible turns of events and twists of fate rear their hideous heads and lurch their grotesque leers at you, calling your name so gently, then spitting with venomous sneers as you approach; they barrage you with your deepest regrets, howling with laughter at the mistakes you have made, kindly replaying the bad times over and over for their own frightful delight. A malformed young deer hobbles towards you with the face of your first best friend, killed at fifteen in a bloody car crash, whispering, 'If only you'd married her . . . you shouldn't have said that to him . . . if only you'd been a girl . . . '; wise and ugly old hands reach out to young ones now passing, forcing all they have seen into the untouched and hopeful young hearts, clouding clear eyes, staring deep into their souls trying to crush in the weight of the centuries, 'Mind out! Mind out! It is all not as it seems. Remember me now, remember — these few words will get you to the gates of heaven. Don't forget us: we died for you! Stay strong, feel the fight, tell the truth but it's sometimes better to lie; hold your ground, stand firm, laugh at the devil but don't answer him back, LISTEN NOW, boy, IT'S IMPORTANT,' but you're lost and away, with your mother's face as it died, and the sound of your father's heart breaking, you are gasping for air, you leap for the surface, desperately scrabbling for footholds, greeting yourself on the way back down — the you of a minute ago that is, and you're chasing the light: you grab after your foot, just ahead of you, reach down a hand to another self down below, yelling, 'Stop! If we all just stand still we can all catch up with each other,' but it's too late as you see yourself ahead, urging your flailing figure on, reminding itself to be strong, stand firm, to speak what is true, fight for what is just, and to never, ever look back.

Have you ever felt like this? Perhaps you can relate to our poor friend's predicament. For that is the state our Edward was thrust into, there in old Charles de Gaulle Airport. And he stood, in the centre of the baggage hall, for just under eight minutes with chaos around him, chaos inside him, but standing utterly still.

When they did the airport rounds that night, he was sitting on a bench. His bags had gone; he had no coat, no bottle of duty-free vodka. He held his head in his hands and was breathing the breath of a very old man.

A security guard asked him (in English, which was his guess as to the man's origin) if he required assistance. Was he seeking accommodation? Did he need a ride somewhere? Edward said nothing, but looked up at the guard with eyes that were described later as 'bottomless pools of despair, empty but full of a thousand separate fears competing for attention'.

Other airport personnel were called in. There were a number of whispered conversations, a number of questions asked. The man would respond to nothing. He was handed a cup of tea. It sat beside him, cooling in the chilly, conditioned air.

So how should anyone deal with this man? No one had any strong opinions on the best way forward. He didn't seem to have suspicious motives — he just seemed to be a little lost. Somebody said something about a sheep, and something about a shepherd. Everyone nodded. Eventually they wrapped a blanket around him, and said he could stay the night if he promised to go in the morning. It seemed the only reasonable solution.

The security guard agreed to keep an eye on him during his shift, in case there was any funny business. Besides, there was something about Edward that unnerved him a little: his eyes were pricking at some long-forgotten experience; it 'struck a chord' (as he was to remark later) but he couldn't exactly say why. Through the night the men sat quietly, watching the light fade and then grow again, and in the morning there was an invisible thread between them. A dark sorrow hidden deep within each man had glimpsed its reflection in the other, leaned over and gently embraced itself.

A day passed. Edward remained. No one was happy with the situation, but there was no obvious precedent to be followed, no right path to be taken. The rules clearly disallowed any such circumstance. There were to be no vagrants in the complex at any time — there are staff and there are passengers; there are personnel and there are travellers; there are fixed points and then variants. There is no such thing as a fixed variant. There is no such thing as a constant temperature, it is always either rising or falling. He should either be coming or going, not hanging around in the middle, unsure. It's like being in a battle without choosing a side! 'You're for or against, otherwise you're just wasting time,' as the Airport Information Desk liked to say.

Yet Edward posed no immediate threat of any kind and

although he was not technically right there, he was not exactly wrong in any way either. He had a nice suit — that is, it was clear he meant no harm — so it wasn't fair to apply the usual rules. He was a temporarily stalled traveller, a little point moving around the map that was simply taking a breather. If you didn't look at it too hard, perhaps the point would just start moving again, just like an unwatched pot. And so everyone averted their eyes a little, and hoped something would happen. Some people were praying, and some just imagined they were.

And Edward stayed.

Days slowly passed, as days always do. And everyone wanted something to be done, but no one knew what, so no one did anything. Every few days a small man with a lot of badges would come through and wave his arms about, saying, '. . . cannot be tolerated . . . immediate cessation . . .' and other such phrases, and everyone would nod and agree and promise, yet somehow Edward would still seem to be there the next day, sleeping in the captains' lounge, showering in the travellers' toilets and dressing in anything they could salvage from the lost property bin.

And he was starting to make a number of friends! Alongside the security guard, whose name was Jean-Marc, the American-Style Donut girls had also grown rather fond of this peculiar and out-of-place man. Suzanne caught him eating a stale Chocolate Royale from the trash and marched him immediately over to her cart, insisting he devour as many fresh donuts as his mouth could handle. Every morning she would beckon him over, dodge his gentle protestations and slide him a brown paper bag jam-packed with all his favourites. He didn't so much like the ornamental ones, he explained in his pigeon French mime: the bits got stuck in his teeth. Suzanne was delighted to make someone happy. It soon became the highlight of her day.

In return, he would take out the trash for her, to the waste area in sector four. He was always very courteous, holding the large plastic doors open for the little French men who whizzed around on their motorised carts. Sometimes they would give him a ride around the terminals, his ecstatic grin more than enough incentive to stretch the airport rules a little.

And when he wasn't around, the staff delighted in speculating as to his history. Where had he come from? The current most popular story was that he had been a high-ranking business executive who had made a major slip-up, costing his company millions. He had been dismissed in Paris but couldn't face going home to tell his family, and was thus stranded in Charles de Gaulle until his courage returned.

The ex-army man at the KLM Help Desk thought he was a hobo who had attacked a rich businessman, stolen his clothes and was now attempting to sneak his way into the upper-class world by feigning amnesia. This was not a popular explanation, although the ex-army man was very persuasive. But most agreed Edward was far too gentle and honest to be hiding anything, and besides, the confusion in his eyes was real. They had all seen him grasping desperately for a foothold in reality, anything to get himself going again. Sometimes he seemed to almost connect: his eyes would flicker as if he had found something that was almost-maybe-just-nearly enough to break through, the tiniest start, a beginning, of anything — but then it would fade and the haze would cloud over again, a quilt of unknowing, safeguarding the delicate neurological interactions taking place in that particular soul from external interference.

Suzanne from American-Style Donuts believed Edward had been travelling in a hire car with his daughter, escorting her to the French university she had just won a scholarship to. They had rounded a corner and bang! Straight into a truck. The girl died on impact. Edward remained unharmed. And now, unable to bear the grief and the guilt, he was having some sort of internal breakdown. And his wife had died years before, so he was all alone. Considering this possibility, she would always slip an extra donut into his bag, jelly-filled — Edward's favourite.

In reality, his story was much simpler than any of this, as Jean-Marc, the security guard, was beginning to understand.

Every night, at about three, after he completed his rounds, he would sit next to Edward in the baggage hall, sharing tea and the occasional stale donut. They mainly just sat, or strolled quietly around the conveyor belts, but every once in a while Edward would speak. Always the same thing.

'Lost,' he would say. 'Completely lost.' And then he would sigh, seven times, eight times. Seven or eight times. His eyes would flick around the room.

Jean-Marc would light up a cigarette. Take a slow drag. 'Lost? From where?' he would ask. 'What are you looking for?'

There would be three or four more sighs. Then: 'It's like this. This is what it is like. In my life I have been presented with many walls. And when I have reached them, I have climbed them. Wherever I can, I have continued. Boundaries that I had previously considered uncrossable, I have crossed. Time and time again I have reached the bottom of the abyss and said, 'There is no further.' And then I have noticed a light. Distant, yet distinct. And so I have pursued it, and it has yielded to me. And then I reach another bottom, another final depth. And so I accept this final limit; I accept that finally, this time, here is an end at last, I have finally reached an irreconcilable pass. I can go no further. And so I have waited for rescue.

'And then, from the corner of my eye, I have suddenly glimpsed another light, or fancied I have. Just when I thought I had finally reached the bottom! And it is with such exquisite pain that this new, dim and increasingly singular ray asserts itself, and of course I must pursue it! What choice do I have? And so I pursue this light, this new light, and sure enough, once again there is another depth, and another light, another depth, another light, and so on. And I accept this, although it tires me, this searching and finding, closing and opening, filling and emptying. Questions come, then answers, which lead to more questions. This has been the pattern of the days, and I reconcile myself to them.

'But now, this one. I cannot get through this one! There is what I see of the world, what I observe of it — the news. Then there is what I know of myself and what is in my head, and some sort of . . . vision, a possibility. And I am trying to make these two realities coincide, to marry them. I am trying to wed these realities. Daily, each minute, every second I try to bind them, to join them together as I know is the only way, and I CAN'T. I can't! Even to sit beside each other. I am trying, and trying, and trying, and I am simply unable.'

He pauses for a minute, sighing and shaking.

'I mean, what is this place? What is this? What is this that we have come to . . . this . . . men with guns? These bombs, prisoners? These weapons of mass destruction? What kind of room, this room, this . . . What cave have we stumbled into? They send the young ones out to die? To kill? In whose name? For the sake of peace? What name is there for this lunacy? And how, where . . . where can be the way out of this mansion? Oh, the path is getting narrower and narrower — it will come to an end! I can feel it closing around me and I can't, I can't . . .'

The words fail. Jean-Marc draws on his cigarette.

Edward turns to him and looks hard into his face. Everything he is saying is coming out through his eyes.

Jean-Marc nods. 'Yes, yes, yes. I understand: this war, these wars, this endless fighting. I feel it too. In one's head it is so simple, yet . . . where is the shepherd to guide us? What should we do, what can we . . . and then, of course, nothing, and one thinks: this world — do I really want a part of it? This . . . yes, yes. I understand.'

Edward nods, and something inside them keeps talking, but there are no more words. And here they sit, with the conveyor belts turning around them, and there are no more bags. And no one knows how long Edward will be here, or who can help him, or if he can help himself. There is a plane somewhere, perhaps, that could take him where he needs to go, if he could somehow get himself onto it. And, again, the shepherd and the sheep, because in a small country at the bottom of the world a woman and two small boys lie awake each night, praying that God will return their daddy to them. Praying that there is a God. Praying that something, somewhere — sanity, karma, fate, the universe — something will help this lost little sheep return home because it is one of those times where the one that is lost needs more help than the ninety-nine others who all know where they are. And the shepherd knows this as well. So surely: where is he? Where is this shepherd who is long talked about, long promised and for whom we wait yet who never seems to appear?

Tina Shaw

Julia

JULIA MADE A LIST. A list of self-improvements, to take effect from when she got to the island. *Exercise. Sightseeing. Reading. Cut back the booze. No more bastards.* These were things that Julia felt were entirely possible to achieve. Other people did them and lived normal lives. So could she: it could happen.

She'd gone to the island to make a fresh start. To shift sticks and start over. Some place nobody knew her, some place she could be a different person and live a different kind of life. Well, okay, not entirely different. You still had the same kind of job (working reception in a hotel) and you were still hanging out with the same kinds of people (other hospitality workers), but hey, they were different people, and this was a completely different place. It could work out. Julia had the idea it might work.

That was what she'd been thinking about on the plane, thinking long and hard, on the way over to Norfolk Island. If the old life didn't work, then you needed to make up a new one, from scratch. Approaching Norfuk Ailen (she said the words under her breath, face close to the window), she saw scimitar beaches, rolling green and the dark dots of pine trees: this had to be paradise. A complete change of scene, yeah.

And she was going to clean up her act, try some new things. There was a bunch of stuff she hadn't done before that might help her to become a better kind of person — you just had to stick with it, not give up.

Exercise.

As soon as she was settled, she got hold of a bike and went out every day. Biking around the island, usually early in the morning before her shift started, puffing up and down hills, salty wind in her face and lips dusted with salt, stopping to look at views of the sea, glittery and sharp through pine trees, hurting your eyes, the sea dashing white onto dark rocks; sheep on the hillsides and often on the road, shaggy horses too, also left to wander; horns tooting as vehicles went by, men hanging out of windows, dirt-spattered utes. There were places with names like Rooty Hill Road, Ball Bay, Buck's Point, which made her think of men she'd known back in Sydney, men before Brian. Except she was trying not to think about Brian (*no more bastards*), looking out instead for Helen Reddy, who was supposed to live on the island. Even though Julia had no idea what Helen Reddy looked like, and she was probably an old sheila by now. Not that that helped. The island was dotted with old sheilas.

The views were nice, but she couldn't say she enjoyed the biking. It was damned hard work. At least she was getting fit. It made her feel virtuous (a new feeling). If she could just cut back on the ciggies, she'd be doing really good.

Sightseeing.

Julia drank on the boat to calm her nerves.

The water was all dark, jagged little swells. Hardly waves. More a pitted surface you might cut yourself on. And it was cold, even though the sun was out. The boat, a sightseeing ferry, headed out of the enclosed harbour and rounded the point. Out there, the ocean rolled huge and endless: best not to look that way. Julia looked instead at the rocky coast slipping past, the rolling green hills and secret sandy bays.

She watched the honeymoon couple. Australian. The new wife was young, in shorts and sandals, and got her guy to pose at the bow so she could get some of the island in behind. 'That's it, baby,' she cooed. He grinned in dark glasses, ginger-haired and obese. Julia, watching from her perch at the bar, couldn't understand the attraction. Surely the girl could've landed a better guy than that. She hated couples who called each other names like sweetie-pie, honeybun, sugar. It made her sick.

She ordered another Bundy and Coke, the mirror behind the barman showing an attractive young woman with long dark hair. She tied it back when she was working, but she wasn't working now. No, she was sightseeing. She was taking in the sights, as they say. She knocked back the drink and lit a cigarette. The girl in the mirror looked a little grim, but Julia just smiled at the barman and ignored her.

Reading.

She'd never had much time before for reading, couldn't see the point. But over here there was so much more time (amazing how *much* time) — as long as she didn't go down to the pub too often. She spent long evenings alone in her motel unit, reading books. There was a library in the town, a one-room wooden building presided over by a woman in gumboots who'd glared at Julia. As if she didn't belong in a library. Huh. She knew about libraries. She'd even managed to get out three books. Two bodice-rippers, and one that had a picture on the cover of a naked woman being mugged by a thunderbolt. Julia didn't know what that one was about, but grabbed it anyway.

So she'd read, while the night ticked on like a clock. Then she'd have to go outside for a break, have a ciggie and look at the stars in the black sky. So many stars, like you never saw back in Sydney. The thing about reading was that it made her tired, sapped her energy, turned her brain to jelly. It wasn't like going down to the pub and having a laugh with some mates, then going clubbing and dancing till 2 am. But she stuck with the reading for at least a week, even though she was still on the first book. She was determined to make a difference in her life. And who knows, maybe she'd meet a guy she could talk to about this book, with its stories about gods, heroes and monsters.

One story was about a woman who got zapped by great god Zeus; another one was about a chick who'd turned herself into a horse to get away from this bloke who was after her, but then he'd turned himself into a horse as well and fucked her anyway. Another story was about some sheilas who'd gone crazy and thought they were cows. They were mooing and carrying on until some bloke had 'cured' them (yeah, Julia thought cynically, that'd be about right). And Medusa (even Julia had heard that story before), with snakes for hair and how she could turn a bloke to stone. Not bad, that one. She could've done with that kind of hairdo!

Yet mostly these stories puzzled Julia.

She read these things with the book held out at arm's length, as if it might contaminate her. The stories bugged her, and made her want to drink and get wasted. Some of the people in the book got into her dreams. A woman burning until she was just a heap of ashes, cows being chased by a demonic horse with red eyes. Julia would wake up gagging, while outside the night was so quiet it was like being in the country (she *was* in the bloody country), except for the lonely sussuration of the sea. And the sheer lack of noise freaked her out as well. Julia clicking on the bedside lamp and sitting on the edge of the bed, holding her bony elbows and telling herself to get a grip.

So when Red asked her out for a drink, she went.

Maybe she had one too many. Ended up on the dance floor with some other guy, then there was another guy — she couldn't remember next morning what exactly had taken place, couldn't remember any names, but it was a good night out. A cracker.

Except for the next morning, at the hotel, when she'd bumped into Red coming out of the bar. He glared at her, practically growling for her to get out of his way. Hey, was that deserved? *I don't think so.* Bloody inbred islanders.

So she didn't go out with him again. There were plenty of

others wanting to take her out — dancing, for a meal, a ride on a motorbike, or for a picnic on a secluded beach. See yorlye mai. See you all later!

'What you running from, girl?'

Did Inez actually say that? Julia frowned, thinking maybe the girl had said something else.

They were in Julia's motel unit, lounging on the furball-textured seventies couch. Inez stroked Julia's hair, which was so smooth and glossy, unlike her own thick, frizzy mass. Inez kept asking her nosy questions, but Julia didn't want to talk about the past, so instead offered to straighten Inez's hair for her, using the tongs, but Inez said she couldn't be bothered with getting a nyuu luuk. Julia shrugged: suit yourself. *Just trying to make some improvements. Maybe you could get a guy if your hair looked a bit less like a pot scrubber.* Sometimes she thought things like that but then the words popped out of her mouth before she could stop them. She didn't mean anything by it. It was just the drink talking.

Inez stopped stroking Julia's smooth glossy hair and averted her face. Her gaze fell on the book lying on the floor. She picked it up and idly flicked some pages. 'Whaa dis book? Have some funny piktures inside.'

Julia wrinkled her nose. 'Old stories,' she said, taking the book from Inez. 'This sheila here, she's real mean. She's got snakes instead of hair and if a man looks straight at her, he gets turned into stone.'

Inez shrieked with laughter. 'I don beleef eet. How she do eet?'

'How should I know? It's just a story. Estole. It's not real, or anything.' Julia threw down the book. 'You must have stories like that here, maybe that your granny's told you?'

Inez thought for a few seconds, her brown eyes resting on the white concrete block wall. 'I remember one story.' In her sing-song voice she told Julia about the fish trap, which the Big Man set to catch unwary souls, luring them out into the lagoon by calling their name. 'That's why, if you not be careful, mebbe you get caught in daa trep. Then you don get out, not ever. That's why, you must be very careful not go down to the water alone. Must always have some other person with you, so they can pull you away quick if the Big Man calls out your name. He a kind of monster.'

Julia lit a cigarette. 'What's this trap thing look like?'

Inez shrugged. 'Nobody know. Only person who see this trep, they not come back.'

'Jeez, what a load of bull crap.' Julia waggled her fingers at Inez.

'Who's afraid of the Bogeyman?' she moaned.

Inez smiled, showing the gap between her front teeth, her gaze sliding back to the book in her lap. 'Yeh. Who afraid? Jest some story.'

Julia stood up, tugging at her skirt. 'Let's go down to the bar. Maybe we'll find a different kind of Big Man down there, eh?'

Anyway, she was not running away. No, she was making a new life for herself — big difference. It just happened to be a world away from Sydney, that's all. Julia wrinkled her nose as she watched the local girls, flowers behind their ears, chatting on 'main street'; she held her nose going past the pig pen down the road from her motel; she stared back at the tour buses of overweight, elderly tourists doing the island circuit; she deliberately looked away from the rugged hui-hui men unloading the fishing boats at the wharf; she stopped her ears against the local band playing eighties covers; she glared with dismay at the dismal little restaurants with their puke-pink tablecloths and the bars shutting up shop at nine o'clock on a weekday evening. The word 'rustic' sprang to mind.

Whatever had brought her to this godforsaken hole?

Brian, of course.

That doctor back in Sydney who she'd got the Aropax off, he said she should talk to somebody. What was to talk about? The bastard broke her jaw. End of story.

Would anybody blame her for amusing herself with the locals? What else was a girl to do? And they loved it. It saved one or two of them from having to fuck their cousins, or their sisters.

Brian had said he would love her for always. *Baby, oh baby.* Coming home from the workshop at the end of the day, grime beneath his fingernails, pushing her up against the wall (the way men seemed to like pushing her up against walls, against benches, fridges, the walls of shower cubicles), lifting her, legs locked around his hips, and carrying her to the bedroom. *Baby, baby.* Laughing and drinking Bundy late into the night, after her shift at the hotel, drinking with their buddies, downtown, uptown, whatever. On their first anniversary they took a dinner cruise out on the harbour as the sun was sinking, then they hit the town. The heat of a Sydney summer's night: like a plastic bag had been tied down over the entire city. So hot you were afraid to strike a match in case it started a fire. Down a flight of stairs, down into darkness and the sounds of a Portuguese dance band, Julia in a short flippy skirt, and she couldn't help it if other men looked at her, they always did, that was how she'd met Brian, he'd been watching her from the edge of a dance floor, the way other men looked, admiring, and she *liked* to play up to it, it didn't *mean* anything. But Brian, back home, pulled her out of the taxi, both of them off their faces, and the tail lights of the taxi barely rounding the corner and winking out of sight when he'd punched her. Sent her flying out onto the moon of buffalo grass. She lay still, aware of the prickly feel of the grass pressed into her cheek as she kept thinking she should get up, but hurting too much. Lying there, looking up at the pale orangey cloud cover and the sagging fronds of the palm tree and a sense of clarity washing over her like a premonition: *you have to get out*. She lay there, looking up from that new angle at the pink stucco front of their rental place. There was a concrete flamingo by the front door that used to make her laugh, but now she couldn't see the joke. It was time to move on.

Cut back the booze. That was a hard one.

Cause just when you thought you were doing all right, that you were on top of things, then you woke up one morning after a kooky dream (a crazed cow writhing with snakes and galloping across a coastal headland) and you were in a bad mood all day. Work didn't help. You got one too many picky customers, you got some prick who patted your butt, you dropped something and made a mess, you started feeling so shitty you wanted to scream, or hit something. There was nothing else for it but to start drinking, early, as soon as you knocked off work, to try and make the scratchy bad feeling go away. But it didn't go away. It went deeper, got meaner. So you drank more (even though you weren't supposed to drink too much on the medication). Then, if you were lucky, you reached a place where you didn't feel so bad. Where you could put things into perspective. Where things didn't look so stink any more. You reached a certain plateau of hope.

The light of a big moon was flooding the hills as Julia, holding Spider's clammy hand, staggered along behind him down the track to the beach. He'd brought a blanket, so they laid that on the sand and flopped down onto it. It had been a long day at the hotel, and she'd been on her feet for most of it. She kicked off her shoes and lay back, stretching her tanned legs, pushing her arms above her head.

Spider, smelling of fish, was on her in a flash.

'Gerroff,' she shouted, sitting up. Then more gently: 'Jeez, man, can't a girl relax a bit first?'

'Sure, Julia, sorry about that.'

He popped the bottle of sparkling shiraz. Dark bubbles fizzed out, but Spider quickly sucked up the spilling wine. They took turns drinking straight from the bottle. They were on the second bottle when Julia jumped to her feet.

'This is great!' she exclaimed to the night.

Here she was, on a beautiful beach on a warm summer's night, not a soul in sight, and it was, yeah, like paradise. The moon's reflection gleamed on the oily, swelling surface of the sea. A soft, tropical breeze muttered through the black pines on the cliff above the beach. Then Julia had to feel the warm night air on her skin — right there and then. Forgetting all about Spider, she started taking off her clothes, that stale hotel uniform. She fumbled at the blouse buttons and unzipped the skirt, tugging it off and kicking it across the grey sand. She ran stumbling down to the water, arms out, and started spinning naked on the sand, pale froth at her feet, laughing into the night. Screaming out the Patti Smith version of 'Gloria', the way she and Brian used to sing it: *'Ju-lia, J-U-L-I-A-A, Juuu-lia—'*

Then she was wobbling in her spin, salty hair plastered across her face. But Spider was there, catching her just before she fell, his big hands on her slim waist. She pushed him away — she wanted to *dance*, for chrissake. She didn't want to—

But he picked her up anyway, as if she weighed nothing, and carried her back to the blanket: his trophy.

With her head hanging over his arm, looking back, Julia glimpsed something out in the water. She squinted, seeing double. She blinked, but the image had gone. Nah, couldn't be. She hiccupped, then giggled. Bloody fish trap! What a joke. There was no such thing as monsters. She might as well have snakes for hair.

Julia lay on the rug while Spider loomed darkly over her, a big chunky shadow, unzipping his jeans. And a crazy notion popped into her head. She touched her hand to her hair, just in case, thinking there might be snakes. But there were no snakes — of course! — nothing there to turn a man to stone, nothing to stop the desperate tide of ill-luck, no weapon of myth to save Julia, only her salt-flecked hair, and an impotent gesture, the way you'd touch a table or a doorframe for luck, the way, jokingly, you'd touch your head.

Alice Tawhai

Something Will Change

She lay very still in the half dark. Snow lay behind her, mimicking her position. His breath sighed over her shoulder as the darkness thinned, like the breeze of the ocean, sighing over a swell. She knew what he looked like without even turning her head.

He had coffee skin and Milo eyes, and black hair cropped close to his head, number one style. Snow wasn't his real name, but the joke was that when he was six, his mother had taken him to audition for the part of the new Milky Bar Kid on the ad for Nestlé white chocolate bars. She'd heard it was worth something, and she'd thought that maybe it wouldn't matter, him being dark.

So there he was, surrounded by little blond boys with fair, fair skin and silver cap-guns, and the man in charge had come up to him and said, 'Sorry, Snowy, you're not quite what we're looking for.' He'd got a free chocolate bar, in a creamy-coloured wrapper, with a picture of the original Milky Bar Kid on the front: wearing spurs, blue jeans and a red and white checked shirt. When he opened the bar there was a raised imprint of the Milky Bar Kid on the chocolate. He was more impressed with this than anything, and not at all disappointed with his morning.

The name Snow stuck, and by the time he realised that it was a joke, and people were laughing at him, not with him, he didn't care, because it was part of him. These days he often covered his brown chocolate eyes with white contact lenses, making his eyes look like hard chips of ice, startling against his black lashes and the colour of his skin.

They made him look cold and absent, as if he were backing away from her and keeping her distant. He couldn't keep them in for too long, because they irritated his eyes. She was glad that he wasn't wearing them now, even though his eyes were still closed.

She looked at herself in the mirror. It was early, and there was still greyness in the light inside the bedroom, and a smokiness about her reflection. Her silvery-blonde hair was pixie-cut, and it usually took on the sheen of whatever she was near. On this occasion there wasn't much light and the colour was pure. Down the side of her face — she was never sure if it was her left or her right side, because mirrors always confused her — a strawberry birthmark ran from the outer corner of her eye to the outer corner of her lip.

Snow often told her that she looked as if she'd fallen asleep at the kitchen table, with her cheek resting in a puddle of strawberry jam. This didn't bother her, but she did feel old and worn. The lines on her face were deeper than they should have been at thirty-six, and the smudges under her eyes were darker. She knew the cause. A half-finished glass of bourbon was still on the dressing table in front of her. Next to it, an ashtray overflowing with cigarette butts was mirrored back alongside her own image.

There was a silence about the hour that was somehow eerie. Even the birds are weary this morning, she thought. Maybe they had a hard night too. She lit a cigarette, and because the ashtray was full, she flicked the ash into her son's small silver christening cup. It was engraved with a stork, a calendar, a clock and a pair of scales to represent his name, his date and time of birth, and his baby weight.

Waste of time, she thought bitterly. He wanted to live with his bloody father. And if anyone was ever hopeless with kids, it was him. The truth was that her son had hated Snow, and had resented being corrected and disciplined by a man who was not his own dad.

The problem with Snow was that he always had to be right. There were never two ways of doing things, there was only his way. He had to do everything perfectly: follow recipes exactly, have all the gear for everything, read up on the correct procedure.

He did all the cooking, because he couldn't stand the way she'd throw in a pinch or a handful of something. He had a set of measuring cups and a set of measuring spoons, and every grain of salt was accounted for.

Her parents liked him because he cooked. They'd stopped on their way through last week, and stayed for a drink. The fire was roaring in the sitting room, and Snow had filled her mother's blunt-cut crystal glass with home-made bourbon, while her dad watched TV without the sound. 'What's happening? What's happening?' he'd ask every now and then, but nobody else was watching, so they ignored him. Sometimes he'd suddenly cackle, certain that he'd figured it out.

She'd been with Snow for years now — just the two of them for most of that time, just the two of them since her son had left.

The china cabinets in the sitting room were filled with the kind of treasures that can't co-exist with people who have children. Stuffed ducks, woodpigeons and tui that Snow had carefully stitched up himself. China teapots in the shape of cabbage leaves, silk fans and a collection of knives. In the corner of the room was the only known fully preserved moa, also the product of Snow's taxidermy. It was brown and fading, but its feathers had a slightly violet sheen under the light. It had been found down south, in the subantarctic islands, in a deep shadowy cave under permanent ice. It had been given to Snow by a friend of his, someone who'd been on that trip. That was the sort of person Snow knew.

Snow didn't like stereos. He still had a record player, and the needle was kept scrupulously clean. He chose the music, putting on some Tom Petty while her mum poured bourbon into everyone's glasses as if she was running a bath.

Snow got out his little burner to have some spots. He was not the sort of man to get his precious kitchen knives blackened on an element. He had a special way of spotting, which involved sucking through glass tubes so as not to waste smoke. Later, he lit a joint and offered it to her mum. 'This is good shit,' he told her. 'Best you can get.'

She knew he was showing off, because he'd grown it himself. He had a hydroponic outfit under the house, and he was a major supplier around the North Island. Her mother declined, waving her glass with a shaky hand. 'This is enough for me and dad,' she declared. Her father nodded from the corner, surrounded by the haze from his tobacco, trying to work his Ventolin inhaler with his left hand and keep one eye on the TV.

Snow woke up, and she clicked back into the present. Her cigarette had nearly burnt down to her fingers. 'Don't smoke in the bloody bedroom,' he said. 'How many times do I have to tell you? Every time I turn around, there's another fucking ashtray to empty.' She didn't say anything, just stubbed out the cigarette and looked backwards at him through the glass without turning around.

'Too good to speak to me now, are you?' he asked. 'Too fucking good? Are you too fucking beautiful, sitting there, looking at yourself in the mirror?' She chose not to reply, because she knew from experience that whatever she said would be wrong. She was always wrong, whatever she offered. It was always Snow who was right.

'Get the fuck out of here, before I get pissed off,' he said, and she got up quickly, thankful that he'd been too lazy to hit her.

'Take his ring off,' her sister had said one afternoon, a long time ago, as they'd sat drinking some ales at the kitchen table. 'Those are diamonds. It must be bloody worth something, and he's just a shit. Don't think I don't know what goes on in this house.'

But she didn't take his ring off. 'What is it?' asked her sister.

'Are you too scared to leave? Because you can come to me.'

She thought of the fear of staying, knowing that at any moment Snow might get angry with her for not replacing the sugar in the sugar bowl after she had taken a teaspoonful, or for leaving the back porch light on after she went to bed. She thought of the bruises under her silver hair, and the times when she had believed that her skull must be cracked with little zigzag lines. The constant alertness, the racing in the pit of her heart: that was the fear of staying, not of leaving.

'I love him,' she told her sister. Her sister had snorted. 'How can you love someone who treats you like that?' But she couldn't explain it. Snow loved her. Why else would he take such an interest in everything she did, and make sure that she did everything just right? She loved him. Why else would she stay, even after one of his punches had left her deaf in one ear? It was a deep, deep love, and that was why other people sometimes didn't see it.

'One day, something will change, and you'll be out of here,' said her sister. But nothing had changed, and her sister had given up now, content just to bitch about Snow on the phone.

She went outside, wanting to put some distance between herself and Snow for a while. The long, frosty grass by the shed was like snap-frozen candyfloss, sitting in a chiller, waiting to be thawed and eaten. Even the shorter grass was sharply defined, blade by icy blade, like hair on the hard-packed dirt. It reminded her of when she and Snow had first got together, before she had become wary. She would lie behind him in bed, her warm breath on his back, her lips touching the fine hairs that grew there, brushing across them without grazing his skin and wondering if he could feel a touch so light.

The sun was a burning white circle in the mist, surrounded by a golden-white halo: an angel that it hurt her eyes to look at. Darker sky was gathering at the low horizon across the valley, threatening to take over the brightness. It was very quiet, and the silence was overwhelming, and still eerie. Nothing moved in the trees, and the wind had dropped down to complete stillness.

Last night there had been a gale, and she and Snow had made love in their shadowy bed, her sitting on top of him like the mast of a boat tossed around by passion and the roar of the wind outside. Her moaning was the creaking and groaning of the timbers, echoing the gale whipping furiously around the corners of the house outside.

She wondered whether the mist would clear today. Sometimes it just hung around in the valley, and the house was like an island above the sea that it created, and she was marooned.

Apart from the silence, everything seemed to be as usual. Later, Snow came stomping inside, all rarked up. 'The fucking dog's gapped it!' he said. 'I let the back of my ute down to untie the bitch, and the minute the leash was unknotted she took off, dragging it behind her. Bloody nearly bowled me off the tray. I'll get the fucking stick onto her when she gets back.'

'She can't have gone far,' she said, drawing her breath in tightly. 'Normally Ayla never leaves your side.'

'Hrmph,' he said, stomping off, her second escape of the day. It was mid-afternoon, and time, she thought, for another drink. She put a country music album on Snow's record player, being very careful with the needle. Her bourbon sloshed from one side of her glass to the other, spilling onto her hand.

Then the house shook, as if God had it by the scruff of the neck and was trying hard to shake some sense into it. The needle made a graunching sound as it skated across the record. She knew she'd be in trouble for that. The things in the china cabinets tilted forward, and some of them smashed against the glass. The cabinets themselves began to topple over. She felt as if she were walking up hill, towards the wall.

The moa slid past her as if it were on wheels, its black eyes looking enquiring as it elegantly nodded its head up and down, greeting her as it glided past.

When the heaving stopped, and she found her feet again, she went and stood outside on the grass, where she thought it would be safer. Further down, to her right, a power pylon had caught fire. A haze of malevolent green swept upwards from the cross-bars and into the dark grey sky, which threatened to turn black with rain. It glowed like something spiritual, and angry electricity crackled and sparked down the lines crossing the valley.

Below the pylon the ground had slipped and the dirt was exposed like moist chocolate cake ripped apart by greedy hands. The air was filled with the insistent hum of leaking power. She could still hear echoes of the song she'd been listening to inside, before the quake started. '. . . and the Wichita line man is still on the line . . .' It sounded lonely and faraway.

She shook herself. No, it was a dog howling in the distance. She wondered if it was Ayla. To her left she could see Bottomless Pit Lake, steel grey on the far side like the sky, but silver on the near side, like a mirror lying in the dark, brooding grass.

She remembered what her sister had said. 'One day, something will change.' She tried to notice if there had been an earthquake in her heart: a sliding apart, with new cracks forming.

She saw Snow coming up the metal road, and remembered that he'd been out looking for Ayla. He was holding his left arm awkwardly by his side. Maybe he'd fallen when the ground shook. When he got closer she saw that he had his contacts in. Perhaps it was because his eyes were white, but she thought he looked a little bit scared. Everything inside the house was crushed and broken and scattered and mixed up. But he was still the same, and she was still the same too. She hoped he wasn't hurt. She loved him.

Fay Weldon

Exit, Pursued by Taxman, or, Shakespeare's *Winter's Tale* Brought up to Date

A SAD TALE'S BEST FOR winter, Shakespeare said, adding that the red blood reigns in the winter's pale, and it was certainly true that year: the Christmas Leo and I broke up for the first time. We were snowed in, there was a power cut that went on for days, and Leo got it into his head that Polix and I were having an affair. Red rage, black heart and cold fingers, while the snow flakes fell and whited everything else except his jealousy, and envy.

You notice I wrote 'for the first time'. It was a tumultuous marriage. You could perhaps compare it to that of D. H. Lawrence and Frieda, who having sought out a cottage in distant Zennor, the better to pursue peace and solitude, then rent the Cornish air with marital discord and terrified visiting friends with the violence of their midnight brawling — only to startle them by being sweet and gay (in the old sense of the word) by breakfast time, no doubt after sex.

Leo and I went to Scotland, not Cornwall, but the principle was the same. The writer, the artist, needs peace to create. Cut yourself off from the world, from the conveniences and lures of civilisation, build an ivory tower in a world in which ivory is banned, and live in it. Once in it, of course, the artist sets about his own destruction by summoning friends.

Talk about lust, love and revenge amongst the writers! I, by the way, am Hermione, Leo's wife, the one whose unstoppable stage play, *Perdita* — the film just out, the musical on its way, the opera following, merchandising and spin-offs on sale in all appropriate outlets — is currently filling screens and theatres worldwide. I am not as young as I used to be: in fact I got my senior citizen's rail-card only this month. I applied for it not because I expected ever to use public transport again — I can snap my fingers and summon the helicopter — but because I feel society owes me something. In fact a great deal. Society gave me a rough time in earlier years: a twelve-year prison sentence on false evidence provided by one's husband is no small thing. I was the victim of a great injustice.

But picture Leo and me back in 1985, before my troubles began, when we were still lovey-dovey — so long as I did exactly as he suggested, Baby Max only three months old, holed up in Bohemia Lodge in Midlothian. It was more of a castle than a lodge: all mid-Victorian turrets and battlements, sprites and goblins and no central heating. A benighted age as well as a benighted place. No mobile phones, no Internet, no Broadband: just a telephone way out in the servants' quarters of the west wing, an uneasy electricity supply and a post box a mile away where damp heather met icy swamp. How we lived then! No servants, of course, to fill up the wing: just dusty, frozen rooms, and only me to sweep them.

We hadn't enjoyed our family solitude for more than three weeks when Leo decided he must ask Polix up to Scotland to join us. It made sense. The two men were working in tandem on the script for *Red at Night*. Remember that project? The award-winning TV series on BBC1? It ran for three years, was repeated every Christmas for another five and then the audience lost interest. It fell from view and public favour. These days co-authorship is easy enough — the click of a mouse sends ideas and documents hurtling through space — then it was a matter of finding envelopes, stamps, and walking a mile to the letterbox. But winter was closing in, and even Leo could see that Baby Max came home blue with cold when I returned from 'doing the post'. I didn't drive, and Baby Max couldn't be left behind in case he cried and disturbed the genius at work. Leo liked to work in peace and quiet so peace and quiet was what we most certainly had. But he just hadn't reckoned on snowstorms and power cuts, and no hot water, and the baby crying and, frankly, not much conversation. Women with small babies do not make great conversationalists.

So now there was Leo, Max and Polix for me to look after. Not that Polix was much trouble. He always helped clear up after meals, and drove the five miles to the shops twice a week, so the shopping could be brought back in the car and not wheeled in the pram. He was a gentle, pleasant, thoughtful man, younger than Leo, quite slight and small, with blond hair tied back in a pigtail. I did not realise at the time the extent of his ambition, his determination to make it in the scripting world. It had always been my own ambition to be a writer. But once we were married Leo said there was only room for one writer in the house and he was obviously the one. He was the genius, I was the muse — and that was the way things were and were going to stay.

The men drank and wrote, and drank and wrote, and smoked a certain amount of spliff and I carried logs for the fire and mended fuses, and fed the baby and washed the nappies. Leo didn't approve of domestic machinery so I did them by hand. Leo really hadn't much good to say about the modern world. And I cooked. I was not born to cook, and it showed. There were still a few leeks in the kitchen garden; I'd wash them and free them of slugs and grit as best I could but cleaning vegetables in cold water in winter is never fun, and though Polix ate valiantly Leo would make terrible faces. But our lovemaking was the more intense and noisy because of the other male in the house. See what I have, that you haven't!

I had hoped that when *Red at Night* was nearing completion, and talks with the director were to begin, that we could all decamp down south to civilisation, but for some reason Leo decided to bring Camillo to him, not Leo go to Camillo. Camillo was small and smart and all charm, like a mischievous elf, and as gay as all get-out.

I realise I haven't told you much about Leo: he looms so large in my mind I can scarcely separate him out from myself. Let me just say he is built on a massive scale, to suit his massive intellect and ego. He is like some great bear wandering through the literary undergrowth, trampling all around. A lesser man than he could be dismissed as an obsessive compulsive, but since he'd won the Booker Prize and a couple of screenplay Oscars, Leo was known as a creative genius, a perfectionist and a national treasure. Let me make it clear: I loved and still love Leo. I'm just one of those tenacious, old-fashioned women who weather the storms of marriage for love. Frankly, Leo was just very, very good in bed. Boho Lodge boasted fourteen bedrooms, all vast, all barely furnished, and we had already broken the rusty coiled-spring bedsteads in six of them.

Then nothing would do but that Antigonus, who was to play the lead, was asked up as well. He was well built and good-looking in a clean-cut kind of way and did his own stunts. More, he was married to my best friend Paulina, which meant she'd come along as well. Sensibly, she never let him out of her sight. And that was good: she was a bold, red-haired actress, noisy, talented and kind; at last, another woman, someone to talk to, someone to help cope with Boho Lodge. I walked all the way to the post to send a letter warning them to bring their woollies. But now we were to be six, plus one baby.

There were ancient sheets in ancient cupboards: they needed washing but how could I ever dry them? I aired them and shook them and put them on such beds as were still unbroken. I found mouldy blankets and scraped off the worst of the green. Max developed croup and the doctor was called and suggested a warmer house, but Leo said he didn't feel the cold and Max took after him. Max got better. He too was in the habit of obedience. And up they all came in Camillo's Mercedes, the boot packed with wine and whisky.

And then the snow began. It came first in great, white, slow flakes from a dull sky, and then changed its nature: it became small and mean and a wind got up and we were in a blizzard, whited out. The gale would lift the snow from one field and plonk it down in another. The drifts were immense, the roads impassable.

Max, Polix, Camillo and Antigonus — and now Paulina too, for Leo wrote in a part for her, at Antigonus' insistence — scarcely registered the force and power of the blizzard, or its inconvenience. What better place was there to be but here, amongst friends; cold? who cared? Whisky inured them to it. I was breastfeeding so could not indulge. I began to feel left out, nothing but the drudge. *Red at Night* occupied their thoughts, their dreams: ideas flew between them like hummingbirds, bright and swift. Never had so much creativity gone into what was, frankly, a rather trite thriller. I knew: I'd read it while Leo slept, massive snores shaking ancient roof timbers. Leo was an uneven writer, and not good at judging his own work. This was not his best.

The great snow, the great row. They go together in my mind. On the night in question Leo came into my bedroom after midnight, very drunk. The last climactic scenes had been written: celebratory champagne had been added to whisky. He found me in my woolly dressing gown, hair loose, bent over the first twenty pages of a manuscript. I had been secretly writing. Worse, Polix was bent over too, whispering into my ear. I did not know which was the worse crime: secret writing or an apparent assignation with a man. I told Leo I was asking Polix's advice about the opening pages of a stage play I was writing. Its name was *Perdita*. I was not believed. Leo's reaction was extreme.

He gave me a blow concomitant with his size — I am quite a little thing — and accused me of having it off with Polix. Under his nose, behind his back, his co-writer, he might have known. His rage was magnificent. I was quite flattered. He cared after all. Polix, the self-serving creep, cowered and apologised, I squealed — Leo had broken my eardrum — Max woke up and screamed, Camillo and Antigonus came running. Paulina wisely kept to the safety of her room and the company of poltergeists.

Then Leo snatched up the manuscript of *Perdita* and ordered Camillo to take it— the entire first act, as it happened, not just the opening pages — and burn it, and Camillo, the miserable toe-rag, went off to do so. Leo, one hand wound around my hair and the other massive paw keeping both hands behind my back, led me to the dying log fire and I had to watch while flames devoured my creation. There was only the one copy. All these men and none of then did a thing to save me, so intent as were they on getting *Red at Night* off the ground. The fever of creativity devours common sense as easily as flames devour paper.

Oh, the red blood reigned in the winter's pale, all right. Worse was to come. Leo laid about him with an axe. He could have been Jack Nicholson in *The Shining*. Doors splintered, sideboards split; we dodged, he chased. It was me he was after but no one was safe. We hid in the pantry. Then Polix, Camillo, Antigonus and I decided our best bet was just to get out of there until Leo sobered up, and to take the *Red at Night* scripts with us in case in his madness he burned them too. Brave Paulina offered to stay behind to look after Baby Max. It was too cold for him out there in the night: his croup was returning.

We took the Mercedes. We had no snow chains. At first I thought that it was hopeless but the thaw had just begun. We pushed our way through slush. Polix was driving; I was in the passenger seat. All except me had been drinking. Then, like a wraith, a child came out of the snow and ran into the road. Polix braked and the car spun into the child. I heard the bump. I knew he was killed. The skid ended suddenly in a tree.

When I regained consciousness I was in the driving seat, and the police were all around. There was no sign of Polix, Camillo or Antigonus — they had scarpered. They had taken the scripts and left me to take the rap. I swore to the police that I had been the passenger but it suited them to believe I was the driver. The fact that I had never taken a driving test did not mean I could not drive. Leo was a power in these parts.

And it was Leo who swore in court that I had been at the steering wheel, and alone in the car. I don't think he did it to punish me for having slept with Polix — we had been having an affair, actually, but how was Leo to know that? I could see Leo's reasoning. 'Either I lose my co-writer, my director and my lead — or I lose my wife. It had better be my wife.' In the great world of the arts, wives and mothers are expendable. It is their duty to sacrifice themselves in the name of literature.

Now I'm not going to bore you with prison details. Prison is not nice. It is depressing and boring. It is demoralising. Worse for a woman than for a man. Friends and family shun you. To cause death by drunken driving is to be a pariah. My friend Paulina was the only visitor I had during all those years. But the authorities were sympathetic — gave me pen and paper and allowed me to write. Leo might have destroyed the first act of my play but he could not destroy *Perdita*. I knew every word by heart.

Meanwhile *Red at Night* went from strength to strength. Leo, Camillo and Paulina's husband Antigonus were the nation's darlings, thriving at my expense. My name was not mentioned in Bohemia

Lodge: little Max grew up among its towers and battlements, its goblins and sprites, knowing nothing of his mother.

And as for me: I wrote and wrote, in between slopping out and de-lousing, and in five years had the complete manuscript. So long as no financial gain accrued to me I was allowed to send written work out of the prison. And so I sent my darling *Perdita*, child of my creativity, to face the perils of the outside world.

I sent her where I thought she would be safe: to Paulina. Now Paulina's marriage to Antigonus was on the rocks — fame and fortune had not dealt kindly with the great actor: he had taken to drink, drugs and whoring as the weak-minded will when faced with too much opportunity. He was on the verge of bankruptcy. Leo was bailing him out. Paulina showed Leo my play, thinking it would impress him, hoping it would make him relent and forgive me.

'See,' said innocent Paulina, 'how hard Hermione works, how much she suffers. Is this not a creative genius in chains crying to be free?' It was the worst thing she could have done. Leo cunningly sent the play off to Antigonus, behind Paulina's back, with a view to him playing the lead, but knowing full well he would simply put it in his in-tray and forget all about it. Which was what happened. So there the manuscript mouldered, unseen and forgotten.

Leo had the courtesy to send me a little note. 'Well done, darling. Paulina showed me. *Perdita* is a lovely piece of work. You always said you needed peace and quiet to write, and now you have it! Be happy.'

I suppose I am lucky Leo did not burn the manuscript. Sending it to Antigonus was the next best thing, and saved him from guilt.

Another Christmas: the red blood reigning in the winter's pale. This too I do not think about too much. A month to go before I was free. Little Max, daring to ask his father if I was dead, was told it was worse than that: I was in prison for murdering a little boy. Leo had been drinking that day: the blind rages were under control by doctor's prescription, but medication and alcohol combined to blur his judgement. The poor child ran out into the snowstorm, and in cruel repetition of that incident long ago, was knocked down and killed by a hit-and-run driver.

I was allowed to the funeral, in handcuffs. They were all there — Leo, Polix, Camillo, Antigonus — in their Armani suits and black ties, smooth and sauve, crocodile tears flowing, paparazzi clicking and popping. They had just signed up for the fifth triumphant series of *Red at Night*.

The vicar quoted Shakespeare at the graveside as the little coffin was lowered:

> *'What's gone and what's past help*
> *Should be past grief.'*

I didn't agree with that at all. Nothing is past grief.

Now I was out of prison, alone, without funds. Family and friends had cut me off. This is the plight of the female prisoner. There is precious little funding for their rehabilitation: the lion's share goes to the men. I went on the streets for a time. I was homeless, my son was dead, *Perdita* languishing forgotten: I could comfort myself in my heart that I was a better writer than Leo would ever be, but the knowledge didn't stop the paddling palms and pinching fingers that were now a feature of my life. Many of us have patches in our lives we are not proud of: this was one of mine.

But *Perdita*, my other child, had a life of its own. If art is the fruit of suffering, and I believe it is — and I had most certainly suffered — it was bound to come to something. None other than Polix's son Florizel came across the work, lying neglected, abandoned and unread on a shelf. Young Florizel, training at RADA, was doing work experience with Antigonus, archiving his press-cuttings and reviews: a dusty job and, as it was to prove, a distressing one.

Antigonus had neglected to pay his VAT bill; he had simply failed to open envelopes or respond to their threats.. The bailiffs broke into the house to reclaim Her Majesty's debt, as they are entitled to do, and, pursuing him with their writs, found him finally in the attics, hanged by the neck, still swinging. Poor Antigonus, out of the plot. Exit, pursued by VATman.

And Florizel read the play, loved it, and wanted to play the lead. He knew it would make his fame and fortune and so it did. He took *Perdita* to his father, Polix, who recognised the work as mine, Hermione's, from so long ago, and went with it to Camillo. The passing years had worked their soothing magic upon even such ruthless men as they — or perhaps it simply was that with the death of Antigonus *Red at Night* had died as well. They had nothing to lose. Now, in *Perdita*, they could see a new future.

Their minions searched the back alleys of the city and I was found, washed, coiffed, restored, made much of. No-one apologised: they expected me to be grateful. And so, such is the nature of women, I was.

Leo was kept uninformed: he was holed up in Bohemia Lodge writing his autobiography, *The Sadness of Fame*. Central heating had been installed. *Perdita* went on in a nice little theatre in Newbury, Berkshire, called the Water Mill, and the critics loved it. It transferred to the West End. Overnight I was famous, applauded, my time had come. Leo turned up, of course he did — well, his time was over and he knew it. I was of the new world, he of the old. He was prepared to bask in my glory, it paid so well. He wanted me back, to comfort him in his old age, and today's Leo is much comforted by Viagra.

And do you know, I went back? I forgave him. Because after all it was all for art and as Shakespeare said, when we write we go to undreamed waters, unknown shores, and must expect to. Writing is a dangerous business.

And by the way, Camillo married the widowed Paulina. Leo told him to.

Peter Wells

Little Joker Sings

THEY MET EACH NIGHT BY unspoken appointment. It was like so much about their meeting — words unsaid. It was as if vocabulary were numb between them, or certain words were deleted. But this did not stop them meeting by the third lifeboat portside at dusk. Harry, who was practical, had untied the canvas lacings. Jim brought his lifesaver, which he placed as thoughtfully as a cushion on a sofa. There were many men sleeping on deck at that time. The war was over, discipline was slack. It was so hot below decks it was almost unbearable. The *Orion* was moving through the tropics, taking the troops home.

Harry met Jim every night inside the lifeboat and there they made love. Nothing much was said — what was said was whispered. Yet their meetings had about them something intense, something crucial. Time was being snatched away from them. They smelt it inside their mouths, up in the high point of their nostrils — it was in the prism of sweat on their fingerpads as their hands roamed again and again over the other's back or as one man buried his tongue deep inside the other's mouth, as if trying to excavate something in there, hook out something — something final and elemental, something that would endure.

They had met, perhaps fittingly, at the New Zealand Club in Cairo. They were in different battalions and had ended up on a truck together going back to camp after the trams had stopped. In the dark the men, all peacefully drunk, had entertained themselves by singing. They had shared the songs they knew in common — 'Wish me luck (as you wave me goodbye)', 'Bless 'Em All', 'Run Rabbit, Run'. It was then that Jim had piped up and, without saying anything, sung 'Lili Marlene'. He sang it with such trenchant melancholy, with such an undertow of fierce longing, that all the other men fell silent when he finished. They listened to the roar of the wheels, looked out at the disappearing light. The dust out the back door spangled like a phantom. Then some joker farted and the other men groaned and laughed. It allowed them all to escape the pincer of emotion. In the gloom of the truck Harry had not been able to see who had sung 'Lili'. He felt angry for some reason at the joker who had farted. He wanted to thump him.

When they were dumped outside the garrison he had looked around, searching for the man who had sung so beautifully. But all his eyes saw was a group of Kiwi soldiers. To a degree they all looked the same, just as they did in the showers — sunburnt, faces blunt, bodies pupa-white where the sun did not penetrate. He turned to the joker beside him, a little chap, and said, 'Whoever sung that bloody "Lili Marlene" belongs in the fucking Kiwi Concert Party.'

The little chap had smirked. Harry wanted to bash him hard. But then the little chap said 'C'est moi.' Harry had no idea what it meant. Something raw in his face made the little chap say quickly, in a low voice, 'My name is James Henshaw. Most people call me Jim. It was me who sang earlier.'

In the strange clarity of desert night Harry had surprised himself by looking all over Jim's face intensely. Jim was not particularly remarkable-looking. But what he had — beyond a prominent nose that looked like it might have been broken, a broad shield of a forehead, as if to deflect aggression — was an inner liveliness, something silvery, fast. His eyes looked liquid. His body was muscular as an acrobat's. Harry had been taken aback by a fierce erection springing up inside his shorts. This had taken him so unawares that he grew flustered. His throat felt dry. He separated himself quickly from the little man (who anyway showed no particular interest in him). They parted company and that appeared to be the end of it.

One week later, at the New Zealand Club, Harry surprised himself when, three sheets to the wind, he found himself searching. It took him some while to realise he was searching for 'the little joker', as he called him to himself. He was drunk, he knew that. He told himself he wanted to hear the little joker sing the song. That was what he said. But the little joker was nowhere to be seen. Harry, remembering back to the fierceness of his erection on that moonlit night, had told himself — argued with himself, really — that he was missing his wife, naturally, and missing the comfort of women. He had not gone, like other men, to the brothels in the Berka. He was keeping himself clean for Joan.

It was getting late and all around him at the club the other jokers were disappearing out the door, looking for fun. Only the losers were left behind — the barflies, the nearly psychotic. Harry was wandering down the hall, drawn to the intoxicating noise of Cairo by night. It was then that Jim walked past him quickly. He was carrying a bag of something. He didn't look at Harry, which cut Harry to the quick. Harry found himself following him. He walked behind him silently for a while. He was surprised to find himself looking at Jim's neck. Like all soldiers' necks it was deeply tanned, but there was a feathery shape of hair at his nape as neat in its shape, Harry told himself, as a duck's arse. The little joker's hair was a kind of fairy gold (these words shaped themselves in Harry's head). The little joker was ugly as sin but incredibly fascinating.

He grabbed hold of Jim too roughly, by the shoulder, and pulled him around. Jim looked pale. He wasn't exactly frightened. In fact Harry got the distinct impression that Jim, although a little joker, could look after himself.

'What the fuck—' Jim said.

Harry said, 'It's me . . .' leaving a poignant space for Jim to fill in.

'And who's himself when he's at home?' Jim said.

'You know.' Harry felt his face redden. He was suddenly as bashful as a boy at his first dance. He was eloquently aware that he did not know the steps. 'We met — truck — you sang "Lili".' This is when Harry surprised himself. 'I loved your voice,' he said.

He fashioned this statement as an axeman attacks a block of wood.

Something in his gaze held Jim's. Jim wanted to say (and would have, if the bloke had been different), 'My voice?' using a questioning irony. But he could see this man was sweating it out. There was a sheen of moistness on his shaved upper lip. Jim knew desire when he saw it. The man could not stop looking at him — or rather into him. Jim, who had been going to deliver some linen-silk he had bought (at 18/6d a yard) to a nurse he knew, instantly changed his plans. He was mercurial like that.

'Hang on a tick,' he said to Harry, winking at him. 'Yours truly will be right back.'

Later Harry would say he could never rely on Jim for anything. Jim would correct him. 'I think, darling, you can rely on me for one thing.' Harry would say, 'Don't use those women's words, Jim. I don't like it.' Jim would say, during lovemaking, 'But you like this?' sliding his hands up the inside of Harry's thighs — 'You like this?' cupping Harry's balls tenderly in the hollow of his palm — 'You like this?' gently running the veldt of his tongue over the glistening head of Harry's cock.

The little joker pretty soon had complete mastery over Harry who was saving himself for Joan. But Harry knew, instantly, from the way he had developed this terrible longing to be with Jim, that something had changed in him. He had never felt like this about a man before. That is, not precisely like this. He had had intense friendships with men, but that was mateship. Mateship was a kind of marriage, but without the marriage bed. His relationship with Jim was fuller this way — it was with the marriage bed.

Harry did not like to think of their first time together. In fact, up until Cassino, he had not really allowed himself to think of the little joker much at all. Except as some kind of convenience. Jim was a sexual and (he had to admit to himself as time went on) emotional convenience. Their lovemaking, which could be brisk and emotionless as a chat between two jokers at the waterpump, at times became more floriferous. Harry surprised himself by becoming almost womanly in his wants. He wanted to be loved — to be made love to. He had begun to feel, as the war went on, that he was developing some kind of emotional numbness. He felt a vast distance between himself as he was now and as he had been when he was a farmer in Wellsford. He saw the war as a long process of attrition, the point of which had been to separate the old Harry from the current Harry. Unnaturally talkative at times, he was given to being a silent, bitter drunk. He felt nothing. He saw only corpses in his dreams. He awoke shouting. He was like many of the other men, so nobody took too much notice. They all spent a lot of energy on being drunk.

  He began to be involved in fights. One of these — though he would never tell Jim this — was over what one of the men said about Jim. The man said Jim was 'obliging as a gharry'. Harry had seen red. Harry had gone berserk. Harry had ended up in solitary for over a week. When he came out, he thought all the blokes would know he was mad about a fairy called Jim. But by that time it was El Alamein, and what did his being mad about a fairy called Jim matter then?

Harry never allowed himself to get 'spoony' or 'soft', as he called it, about 'the gharry', as he came to call Jim in his head. He decided he'd made a mistake about the whole thing. The war was fucking him up in his head. He decided he would join the other blokes next time they went to a brothel. He felt sure Joan would understand this. (Though when he saw himself trying to fashion the sentences that would explain, first Jim, then this visit to the brothel, he found he could not actually say the words. He woke up, sweating in a nightmare.) But when he lined up in a queue — some men joking laconically, others mute with desire, prefiguring in their heads what they would soon do — he found he couldn't go through with it. He peeled off, saying he was going off to get up a bit of Dutch courage. Instead he went in search of Jim. He knew he was likely to be at the New Zealand Club. He found him in the kitchen.

Something in his face made Jim go white. 'What's up, Harry? I haven't seen you for ages,' he said. But Harry said nothing to him; pulled him into a storeroom. He leaned his back against the door. He whispered, his voice harsh and crackling. Jim felt the cold spittle land on the innermost recess of his ear. What Harry said was, 'Jim, mate. Do me a favour.'

The rest did not need words.

Harry wanted to forget. Harry didn't want to remember. Nothing was said during this encounter. But Harry listened to the moans and cries, at first smothered, then, in time, naked, angry, begging or, most shockingly of all, moans of submission. When he realised they were coming from his own mouth, he gave in to this moment of self-recognition. He did not care. He was 12,000 miles away from Harry Gatman of No. 3 Road, Wellsford RD. He needed to escape.

For a man so ordinarily manly, nothing suspect or pansy about him, it was peculiar. That's the strange thing, the others said — with a fairy like Jim, everybody knows what's what. It's what turns your stomach, or doesn't, depending on your point of view. When a man has seen a lot he keeps silent, hugs its impossibilities, what can never be said.

Joan started to say in her letters that she suspected one of the Kiwi nurses was choosing her presents. There was the silver-thread bangle inset with turquoise scarabs, which would have suited a sultry Hedy La Marr. And the pale blue silk pyjamas that matched Joan's eyes perfectly — the fabric, she said, 'definitely showed a woman's eye'. Harry blustered in his letters, saying he had asked 'advice' from 'one of the nurses who is a real hard case'. Indeed there was a woman like this, but it was actually Jim who did all the shopping. Harry had never known a man to spend so long looking at a scarf.

They went to the outdoor movies and once, when a sandstorm swept in, they held hands — fiercely — in the dark. Another time they spent hours at night at a skating rink, Jim doing show-off circles. Harry stood gripping the side, aching, waiting for the moment he would spend alone with Jim. It was all about sex and it wasn't.

Sometimes Harry felt he'd almost go insane if he didn't get to spend time with Jim. Not that he ever really conceded that he and Jim were, as it were, together. They were just knocking about. One day Jim took Harry into the hospital at Maadi — he knew one of the nurses — and he X-rayed Harry's heart for him. He showed Harry the X-ray, which he held gazing down at this theorum of darkness, at the shadowy shape of his organ.

They made love wherever they could — mostly standing up,

in cupboards, in storerooms, in rooms where the smell of the last occupants was still in the air. They made love in the desert, when it seemed as if they were at the beginning of time and its end. They never once used the word 'love'.

It was after Cassino, when Harry took some shrapnel and was laid up in hospital, that he began to feel the shape, as it were, of his love for Jim. It was in Jim's absence that his real shape took form. He conceived a real anxiety that Jim was wounded or, worse, dead. There was a surfeit of horror at that time. There was a whole ward of men, Harry knew, asleep day after day after day, men who were given drugs so they might sleep off whatever had happened to them, or not happened to them, or what they had feared. Sometimes he heard a man screaming. There were hurried footsteps, the sounds of a struggle, silence. It was worse than what you heard on a battlefield. There were men without legs, without arms, without eyes. Without faces.

Where was Jim?

It was during this time that Jim actually came to take form. There was his body, which, Harry came to realise almost with shock, he knew intimately. And then there was the aspect of Jim that Harry loved most of all — the sound of his voice. Oddly enough, this was the most intangible thing about Jim, yet it was located inside the mystery of his body. It was as if, in their lovemaking, Harry was always trying to dig inwards, to unearth the source of this mystery — what happened when Jim sang 'Lili Marlene'.

Harry also thought quite separately about his wife, and of Wellsford with its main street running along the back of a hill. Some nights he found himself going up the main street, remembering each shop. He found, when he did this, that he got into conversations with people he met. Farmers, neighbours. But this dream, which was very peaceful and kind, would change later in the night or early morning. He awoke hearing 'Lili Marlene' — he listened acutely to Jim's voice — and found he had an iron hard-on, and all around him — men. He began to pull himself off. He sank beneath a sea of erotic memory to do with Jim.

It was not unusual for men to toss off. God knows, they needed some relief. For the first eight months of the sex they had together, Harry had told himself it was just a further progression of tossing off. It was like the sex adolescent boys had together. It was functional, intense because it carried the freight of so much unexplored feeling — but it was meaningless. Once over, it had fulfilled its purpose.

But Harry realised now that his need for Jim was something

deeper and closer to love. He did not approach this word, however. That would be being unfaithful to Joan, whom he loved quite separately. Joan, after all, would be the mother of his children. He had two nephews — Keith who was five and Roger who was three. He and Joan looked after them at times. He carried their photo inside his wallet. The three of them sat on the grass in the back yard. There was a chicken coop in the background. Nearby there was a row of silverbeet. Joan had a wooden peg in her hand. She was looking into the sun, but also up at Harry, who was holding the camera. She had that look he knew so well, both trusting but also faintly worried that he might get it all wrong.

When Harry needed to be reminded of what it was all about, he got out the photo and studied it. But most of the time he was happy just to know it was there. It was like a key a kind relation leaves out. You could always let yourself back inside when you needed to.

He cleaned himself off quickly. He would sleep now.

They ran into each other in Trieste, at the tail end of the war. Trieste had been liberated only two days before: the stand-off between Tito's partisans and the New Zealand troops had suddenly been resolved. The city was a minefield of strange deaths — Germans who would surrender only to New Zealanders — the crack of gunfire from upper balconies — a body hanging by the feet at the end of an arcade — and the peculiar white light of the Adriatic, calming and almost phosphorescent. Suddenly it was an open city. Everybody was out celebrating. Italian flags hung from every balcony and the streets were full.

And there, in the crowds, was Jim.

Harry was surprised because it was as if Jim's body were outlined in a darker silhouette — as if Jim were somehow cut from a different film and laid over all the other people pushing along, talking, laughing. Harry noticed how Jim's short legs gave him a fast, almost paddling way of walking, how he every so often skipped forward a few steps. But all Harry felt was a burst of pure, incandescent joy.

He was alive.

He went up to him and said, in an ordinary enough voice, 'G'day mate.' Jim was with a flock of nurses and pansies. Harry saw that. The men all looked at Harry and some of them leaned together and smiled. They were part of the Kiwi Concert Party, Jim said later. Jim walked a little slower, and Harry walked slower still. Gradually the others moved ahead — they were off to a café called San Marco. Jim called out to them that he'd catch up with them later. One of the nurses called something back and the others all laughed. Harry did not like that. He felt angry for some reason. He couldn't understand the blackness of his own emotions. He felt betrayed — by the fact that Jim seemed quite careless about Harry's love. He didn't seem to realise that Harry had missed him, had thought about him endlessly, had worried about him.

Here was Jim, thinner it was true, but with no wounds, just his old self, smiling, laughing — liquid.

How many cocks . . .

But this sentence never came out.

In broad daylight Jim grabbed Harry's body and thrust it hard against his own — it was like two shields clashing. Then he took Harry's face and, 'in the continental manner', Harry told himself in a dazed voice, Jim kissed Harry on the side of one cheek — a loud, warm, popping kiss — then the other cheek. It got worse — or better. Quite casually, as if he were to the European manner born, Jim laced his arm through Harry's and began to walk along. Harry felt the most abject terror he had felt since he left home. It was worse than when the white line of a torpedo had come straight towards their ship on the way over. Worse even than when he got wounded. He wanted to remove his arm but Jim wouldn't allow it. And gradually he realised nothing was happening or going wrong. Other men — Europeans, it was true — were walking along arm in arm. There were even youths, quite manly youths, he saw, walking along with one small finger laced around each other's. Nobody gave a tinkers.

'It's the end of the war, Harry,' Jim kept saying. 'The world's going to change. It's all going to be different now!'

Then they turned a corner and ran into a flock of other Anzacs — they were all drunk, belligerent. Harry felt his body stiffen but Jim, by quickly mimicking a slightly drunken walk, managed to get past. One of the stragglers called out in a sentimental voice, 'And have another one for me, mate.'

When they got past Jim whispered into Harry's ear, 'Shall we have another one for him, mate?' Harry had stopped still. They were near an alley. Effortlessly Jim walked him into velvet darkness and found a closed doorway. Jim pressed his body into Harry's, then took Harry's face between his two hands and kissed him — tenderly, lightly, delicately — all over his face, ending finally on Harry's cracked lips. Harry felt defenceless. He felt broken down by the long moan of need for this strange little coot. He wanted to be taken. He wanted to be reduced. He wanted. He did not speak. He parted his lips and all that came out was a strange, almost bleating moan. The word he said — and it was a word he said over and over again during what followed — was 'mate'.

The hours were dropping off them. The hours were disappearing. After Port Tewfik they had to turn their watches forward half an hour. After Aden they lost an hour every night at midnight. Their lovemaking during these final hours was more intense: as if each man wanted to engrave as deeply as possible, imprint as much as possible, the other on the retina of memory. They had meals together, they slept together, they washed together. They walked the deck together. When Jim sang in the nightly concerts Harry sat at the back of the crowd and ached with the importance of his connection to Jim. They played cards together. And each night at dusk they crept into the number three lifeboat and made love.

But then the ship entered the Australian Bight. By now time was slipping away fast, being ripped off them like a bandage. It was a cold wind that felt around their faces. The sea was a misty grey, the waves white-tipped, heaving. Men became sick again, just as they had when they had first left New Zealand, but now it was as if everything were happening in swift reverse.

They were given New Zealand currency, ration books, telegram forms. Harry telegrammed to Joan: 'Home at last stop expected arrival 15 Dec Wgt stop love — your Harry.' Stop. He had thought a long time about the words 'your Harry'. He did not sleep with Jim after this moment. He explained to Jim as well as he could that he was keeping himself now for Joan. Jim was quiet after this. They then immediately broke the new rule and made love. This making of love was slow, wettened with tears. When they lay together, slicked and sweaty, Jim looked up once, winked and said, 'I'll wait for you by the barrack gate.' It was Harry who cried like a baby. It was Jim who held Harry in his arms, consoled him.

> This was the parting of the ways
>
> Harry went home to Wellsford
> putting on the clothes of the farmer
> husband and father
> only to be caught off balance
> remembering
> the sweet loss, the pierce of the arrow
> and how he had joyfully bled.
>
> they never said a word.
>
> they were home.

Many years later
they would find each other
at the pub
six o'clock swill
surrounded by many men
hectic in their fight
to remember and forget

back to back
they bumped into
the past

the vast gap
a blink
mote in the eye
'blasted thing,
stuck in there,
making a bloke weep'

they made love
in an alley
watched by a cat
curious to their keening
gasps and sobs

don't ever leave me
said Harry to Jim
don't
ever
leave me
replied Jim.

So, in rare visits to town,
they kept up
their conversation
body to body,
laughing over this and that
the X-ray
and what could never be said.

Love was for girls
they were
blokes

giddy for each other
lacking a vocabulary
except the one they
shaped by tongue
hand and cock
sweet music
silence and
a wariness
the unimportance
of words.

Once Harry, with his teenage son,
bumped into
Jim in the street,
chip off the old block
raw-boned and incapable of speech —
a remarkable simulacrum
of the man Jim had loved.

They had a few beers together
Jim seeing in Harry's son's eyes
the unspoken question
what are we doing with this old nance?
'You might learn a little'
Jim heard Harry tell his son
as the young man,
head hard as a new rugby ball,
leaned to get into the Holden,
slamming his door shut
as if he wanted to keep something out.

The car accelerated away,
leaving behind only Jim
who smiled to himself.
Harry confided
when the boy was outside,
kicking stones at sparrows.

His middle name was Cairo.

Jane Westaway

Available Light

SINCE 5.30 GRACE'S TABLE HAS been immaculately laid and every nerve-end quivering on the verge of joyous welcome. For the first hour she tended the organic lamb shanks and their family of baby vegetables, put numerous finishing touches to the table and tidied her desk, all as if this extra time alone were a godsend. The last hour has been spent rigid with misery. She has unbent only to top up her glass with the Alan Scott chardonnay she inadvisedly uncorked at 7.15. Every minute that fails to deliver Laurence ages her by a year. At this rate she'll be dead by Boxing Day. That being so, she spends a few moments overseeing her funeral. The day is still and overcast — rain too obvious, even for her. The flowers are understated too, and the bulk of the mourners an undifferentiated blur. Only Laurence stands out, broken-hearted, and ready, now she has gone forever, to publicly declare his love in a ringing eulogy.

She gulps more Alan Scott and, briefly immunised against mistressly forbearance, reaches for the telephone. Through its earpiece she hears the banging of her heart and, beyond it, the yawning of an abyss. She teeters on its brink like a hapless game-show victim . . .

'Laurence Cowan here. Leave a message and I'll get back to you pronto.' The delay before the beep is long enough to indicate the existence of several other messages (from whom, about what?). Then comes a gap that's all hers.

'Laurence, er, Grace . . . Earnshaw speaking. Friday evening . . . Friday. I wonder . . . would you give me a call when you get a moment. About that, er, job. Um. Great. Thanks.'

Nervous as always that her message might be intercepted by someone other than Laurence, she wonders if she would sound more genuinely businesslike if she appended a Merry Christmas. Probably. But the conviction that he will have one — and without her — is too much to bear. She hangs up.

It amazes Grace that no matter how bad she feels, she can always find a way to feel worse. She ought to know better — better than to get involved with a married man, than to organise her life around his sparing appearances and pin her hopes on a shared future. She does know better, but what difference does the knowledge make? None at all, as far as she can see. So what on earth's the point of being a social scientist? If human beings are so blindly irrational, what hope has scientific method of pinning them down? More to the point, how come the misery triggered by one man has spread its tentacles across her whole life, called her very existence into question?

She blows out the candles and, through a haze of tears, sets about clearing the table. She feeds chaste shanks to the bin, virgin garlic mash to the waste disposal. The idea of reheating them for some solitary meal is too gloomy to contemplate. But disposing of them is also, like blowing out the candles, a feint to tempt his appearance. She replaces one still-gleaming glass on the shelf, and with a deft flick of the wrist tops up her own. She remembers once, on a provincial Spanish platform, asking a man with a face wrinkled like a walnut when the next train was due. Later, she realised she had confused similar words, telling him she was hoping for a train rather than waiting for one. But peering down the line into the boiling distance she understood that it didn't make much difference: to wait for a train (or married man) was to hope for one; to hope was to wait. And wait and wait. Even Spanish trains stick to a more encouraging schedule than married men.

She reaches blindly through her tears for the olivewood salad bowl, its glassy contents dressed two hours earlier in a show of faith that he would arrive any minute. People admire her vinaigrette. But tears might add another dimension, constitute a secret ingredient for a whole new school of cooking: Cordon Extremely Bleu; Cuisine Triste. She prods the depressed greens with a server. If she were Laurence she would photograph this bowl. It is eloquent, iconic, it says everything. And actually — she gives it a shove — she wishes it would bloody well shut up.

Her weeping has attained a relentless tidal pull. Connoisseur though she is of the kind of voluptuous melancholy courted by candlelight and scented baths, Billie Holiday and Eric Satie, she knows this is despair and to be entertained at her peril. She wipes her eyes and snorts determinedly into an antique Irish linen napkin. He might still come . . .

She douses the tabletop with Spray 'n' Wipe and rubs hard. On a little crest of hope she reaches for the telephone to check that he didn't call while she was leaving the message. He didn't. She dials Anna. 'Sorry you missed us,' coos her friend. 'Leave us a message and we'll give you a call.'

Us. We.

Grace checks again for a message, then drags herself to the kitchen. Seven out of ten adults report improved feelings of well-being after washing up, so she ignores her Swedish dishwasher and waits for the sink to fill with hot water. She tips out two iron pills from the bottle on the granite bench. A majority of women — whether iron-deficient or not — are happier on an iron supplement. The precise nature of happiness remains stubbornly resistant to scientific method but, hoping that she'll know it when she sees it, she gulps the pills with the dregs of the wine bottle. Then, for good measure, crunches a vitamin C tablet. He might still come.

She ploughs through the dishes, each pot and utensil mocking her raging national holiday phobia. Mere mention of Labour Weekend and Queen's Birthday makes her heart pound and her palms sweat. These are less long weekends than existential pits, devoid of life and meaning. They prevent her being with Laurence while at the same time forcing her to imagine him in the bosom of his family. The four days of Easter and the endless Christmas/New Year/holiday season nudge her into misery, insomnia and substance abuse. Christ, what place do these religious festivals have in a society that the latest census proves is as good as godless? Water runs from the sink with a scornful slurp.

He might still come. In the bathroom she throws cold water at her blotched face . . . and, in the dark behind her hands, conjures up her favourite fantasy — the one she knows as After He's Left His Wife.

She takes her hands from the single dripping face in the mirror, smoothes her freshly cut bob and cleans her teeth. She reapplies lipstick and shapes it into a carefree smile. Ready to return to the living room, she installs Laurence on her couch and makes his face light up as she sits next to him. He kisses her cheek.

The scene becomes slightly harder to picture after this, for though she blooms in his presence, conversation with this virtual Laurence is hard to sustain. She can imagine its tenor — loving, intent — but not its substance. She reaches for the paper. *Or do you want it?* Of course he doesn't; he is rapt in her. She scans the death notices. Her own does not appear. Though Cowan does, and her heart turns over. But it's Thomas Gerald OBE, not Laurence. *Peacefully at home after a long illness bravely borne.*

Peacefully at home — a contradiction in terms if the average home life is anything to go by.

Wishing me dead, eh? teases Laurence, hand on her neck.

Absolutely. Look at the trouble you give me. She makes him flinch and hang his head so that she can kiss his hand and they can both pretend that he is the one who suffers.

You don't, of course, need to wish dead men of a certain age, they oblige readily enough. Laurence is eleven years her senior — a dangerous time for men, a demographic spike. Every year a significant number of middle-aged males suffer heart attacks on top of women who are not their wives. She wonders how she would cope with this eventuality — medically and socially. But why worry? The chances of him dying in her company are statistically negligible since he's hardly ever here, let alone with enough time for life-threatening sex. And she won't attend his funeral for the simple reason that she won't know he is dead: no one will tell her because officially she does not exist.

A non-existent Grace on the couch next to her imaginary Laurence takes refuge from an uncertain future by opting for nostalgia . . . the first time he came here, to photograph her swish new apartment for Anna's glossy lifestyle magazine. 'Oh,' she said, on opening the door, 'it's you.'

'And you!' They laughed. She let him in.

'I meant to get in touch,' he said, dumping gear on her table. 'I really enjoyed talking to you at the opening.'

'Well,' she said, as disconcerted as if he'd passed an elaborate compliment, 'your photographs were . . . are, I mean . . .'

He asked to look around. 'Lovely clean lines,' he said. And, 'I like the way you've kept it simple.' He seemed to mean more than the décor.

He read the titles of her books, flipped through her stack of *New Yorker*s and *Vanity Fair*s, even inspected the snaps on her office pinboard, while she cursed herself for not hiding them from a real photographer. There was more looking around, more admiration of her taste that she didn't know how to interpret, more awkward conversation and meaningful looks. She made coffee. He took pictures. When he peered through his viewfinder at her white bedroom she withdrew fast, inexplicably flustered.

He took his coffee to the window and gazed across her tiled terrace at the city. 'We're over there, just below the green belt,' he said and sighed. She had no idea what his sigh meant. She stood there politely and told herself it meant nothing and that nothing was happening. She could hear him breathing. He felt too close and too far away. Her knees quivered and her own breathing became unreliable. Either she wanted him to touch her or she was terrified of it. She felt that in the thirty minutes since she had let him in she had been delicately stripped, admired, and left untouched.

'None of which proves anything,' announces a newcomer to the couch. This person resembles the expert in a toothpaste ad — white coat, unfashionable spectacles, hair scraped into a scientific bun. She consults a clipboard. 'On numerous occasions you have maintained that this was the moment you fell in love' — she flips pages — 'but in doing so you ignore the latest research. When scanned, the brains of those claiming to be madly in love show activity not in the emotional centre, but in the regions associated with motivation and reward . . .'

'Yes, but . . .'

'The same regions activated by eating chocolate and snorting cocaine. Which makes you, I'm sorry to say, an addict. When a promised hit remains undelivered you immerse yourself in a fantasy future in which the stimulant is freely available. A habit which, I am sure you know, can be as destructive as heroin.' Clipboard frowns professionally. 'You need help.'

'I get help,' whines Grace. 'There's Viv.' Except on public holidays, when Grace needs her most, her counsellor is an essential prop from whose premises Grace feels able to limp away into another interminable week.

'A prop,' repeats Clipboard. 'A crutch. A support. Something without which a flimsy structure would collapse. What you really need is—'

'Another drink,' says Grace through gritted teeth.

Clipboard has dealt After He's Left His Wife a fatal blow. Grace smooths the silk cushion she is clutching and gets to her feet. On her way to the bottle of Glenfiddich in the kitchen cupboard, she casts an eye over the apartment to reassure herself that what Laurence so admired that day eighteen months ago is still intact. It is. She isn't. She's a mess, her once-simple lines cluttered by dreams and fears, furies and secrets, pains and jealousies, shames and needs. And a mammoth task it is hiding them from him, scurrying about like an anxious housewife, continually shoving out of sight this shameful detritus that's quite beyond the reach of Spray 'n' Wipe.

Scotch gurgles into the glass. She takes a slug, shudders, takes another. It's not as if she hasn't tried to snap out of it. Like the time she went to that party with Anna. Get out and meet people, Anna said. Men, she meant. And sure enough, the music and mounting hilarity banished After He's Left His Wife to the outer edges of Grace's consciousness, marooning her in a conversation pit with a bunch of raucous strangers. And she let that dreadful Bryce Tozer put his hand on her thigh because for a few minutes it felt better than nothing. Anna, though, met a divorced English lecturer that very evening, becoming overnight less a friend than a *we* who keeps promising to call back.

Then there was the time Laurence and his wife took a winter break in Fiji and Jessica said treat yourself, that's what I used to do —

and what Jessica used to do is highly significant because things worked out for her (though not, of course, for Hugh's ex, who broke into the lovers' new home, cut up various items of underwear and emptied an ironic bottle of extra-virgin olive oil into Jessica and Hugh's king-size bed). So Grace took herself off to Face It for the afternoon, to lie under the hands of a series of chirruping young women who massaged, smoothed and wrapped. But when she was finally left alone for the tint to dry on her lashes she began to weep and couldn't stop, and the girls had to sponge blue-black from her cheeks while she pretended her mother had died.

By five past eleven, Grace is seated at the sleek desk in the office off her living room, trying to turn the time to advantage by tackling work. She stares blindly at her 2002 planner, trying not to wonder what it says about her that, for Laurence, family comes first. She must try harder, that's all. She must be his refuge, his safe harbour, his oasis.

She tries to feel like an oasis. It makes her want to cry again.

She studies the planner more intently. It promises a survey of battered wives for Women's Affairs, something for an agency on responses to a new design in men's briefs (for this you need an MA in social science?), and a report on a sex education pilot for the Ministry of Education. Eighteen months of waiting for Laurence and its attendant withdrawal from normal social life have freed up so much time for work that her output, and her income, have more than trebled. She flicks pages but can summon little enthusiasm for what a control group of fourteen-year-olds believes about contraception and sexually transmitted disease. Do they warn girls of the dangers of married men? Surely a vital aspect of any sex education programme.

She keeps flicking . . . and is ambushed by non-scientific terms — kiss and stroke and cock. She slams the report shut. She will go to bed. With herself. She needs no alibi, is never claimed by prior commitments, and never has to lie to be with herself. Fantasies aren't lies; the trick is knowing the difference.

The pure cotton sheets are delicious against her limbs (ninety-seven per cent of couples report better sex on fresh bed linen). She thumbs through her mental card file: the unprofessional teacher; the strike-offable doctor and his compliant nurse; the stranger on the train? Yes, she can feel his hand on her leg. Hang on, though, not a train — too much daylight and too few people standing. Not the tube, either — too hot and smelly. And not BART — too brightly Californian. The Metro — rush hour, people pressing in on all sides, and from behind an insistent hand moving up her thigh . . . In the convenient crush no one notices her growing excitement nor his other hand on her breast (I love you, Grace. Shut up, it can't be Laurence; it won't work if it's him). She quivers with delight as the clever hand takes charge. But it's happening too fast — they haven't got to the power cut and she wants to slip her hands under his eccentrically roomy coat and into his jeans and, oh yes, this must really be the Metro because she needs an accordion player to cover her whimpers, and now the lights are out and he has both hands on her buttocks and is pushing inside her and she's groaning and gasping and so nearly there that surely it won't hurt just for a second to imagine it isn't a stranger at all but . . .

The train screeches to a halt, the lights blaze, and she gazes at Laurence with frank dismay. Even her fantasies are no longer her own, even solitary pleasure is denied her.

Some time later she flings herself naked from her tangled bed. She seems to have drunk the precise amount of alcohol guaranteed to generate a sober all-night vigil, and is screechingly, jaw-grindingly, hair-hurtingly awake. She pulls on trackpants and a sweatshirt that was her sister's bad idea ten Christmases ago — maybe fresh air will do the trick. On the terrace she discovers a rare, windless night, ten thousand stars set in a navy-blue dome, and a sliver of moon. Look at that, whispers Laurence in her ear.

With a tremor of something oddly like relief, she realises that this is one hour in twenty-four when her lover is unlikely to be anywhere near her ear. She ducks inside for the keys to the Saab, and five minutes later — having negotiated several bands of drunken revellers — she has parked beneath a fairy-lit Norfolk pine and is gazing out across the heaving harbour. But the waves are disconsolate rather than dramatic, and something is squirming in the front seat of the next parallel-parked car. When she gets out of her own, the thing splits in two and stares, before joining forces again. After a token walk to the wall — and the sight of more conjoined bodies on the sand — she returns to the car and resumes staring seaward, striving for aesthetic appreciation or sleepiness, whichever comes first.

A few minutes of this and she decides the fish on her sweatshirt is making a better job of pedalling its bike. With a muttered curse she starts the car, intending to drive straight home for a soothing cup of camomile tea and another go at unconsciousness.

A minor detour allows her to pull up at the end of Laurence's street. She peers down it in a ferment of dread and longing. She has no intention whatsoever of doing what she did a few months before. Laurence and his wife seem to have some kind of understanding about Friday evenings that allows him off the marital hook, and Grace to more or less rely on seeing him, at least for an hour or so. But that particular week he had said sorry, they were having a party because . . . well, actually, it was their anniversary. He tried, unsuccessfully, to hide the hint of pride. The initial punch to Grace's stomach yielded to aching disappointment, which, by the night in question, had curdled to something sour and poisonous. Something that, in spite of her oh-so-casual observation at the time that anniversaries were acts of God and nothing to apologise for, impelled her across town to his house. It was ablaze, guests spilling onto the veranda, jazz floating down the street. It looked to Grace, parked a few houses away, like the centre of the universe. Which made her some distant sunless planet where nothing lived and no one cared to land.

'Not thinking of doing it again, are you?' It's Clipboard, from the back seat, her cool tone suggesting that a repeat performance would be evidence of less intelligence than a lab rat, which after a few shocks learns to stop expecting rewards. 'Staking out a lover's house,' she goes on helpfully, 'isn't merely stupid, it's probably criminal if not actually deranged.'

Grace shuts her up by swiftly turning right and promising them both a quick pass only. In spite of this official permission, her mouth dries and her hands are sticky on the wheel, but, anxious to avoid incriminating dawdling, she accelerates enthusiastically towards number eighteen.

She just has time to register that the house is in uninformative darkness when there is a sickening thump. The car mounts a small but definitive hump. She executes a classic emergency stop and the brakes squeal theatrically. The car slews, hops twice and stalls.

She folds groaning over the wheel. It's a tribute to the sharpness of her mind at this ungodly hour that every aspect of her situation hits home within nanoseconds. She has had an accident requiring her to stop spectacularly and probably for some time outside the house of her married lover. She is guilty of injuring, possibly even killing someone outside the house of her married lover. She will have to telephone for an ambulance, and, since she didn't bring her mobile, she will have to knock at a nearby house sure to belong to someone who will mention the incident in a neighbourly sort of way to her married lover and include a full description of her, the perpetrator. She will have to report the accident to the police and her insurance company, fill out forms in triplicate and identify the scene of the accident as right outside etc. She will have to get out of the car and inspect the damage under a street-lamp that will illuminate her guilty presence. Even as she sits here prevaricating, someone is writhing in agony, possibly bleeding to death, centimetres from her back wheel.

Someone who might possibly be her lover's wife.

She has killed the saintly Rozalind. She is a murderer and not a jury in the land will believe it was an accident. She will get life and be sent to the prison where she saw that play a couple of years back, when a woman who had killed her children glared at Grace, seated helplessly in the front row, as if it were all Grace's fault and Grace felt pretty much as if it was (which is where an MA in social science gets you). When Grace is sent to this facility she will refuse to take part in dramatic productions. She will do a correspondence course. In Greek. Or art history. Anything but social science. Photography, perhaps.

A tap at the window prompts a ridiculously girlish shriek. The face near hers is as old and bristly and repellant as last time. She refuses to wind down the window; he's quite possibly dangerous. 'All right, then?' he barks.

'Fine,' she mouths, groping for poise and wondering about the state of his long-term memory.

'Poor bloody . . .' she hears — an entirely inappropriate way to refer to a dying woman, which only confirms his loose grip on reality. He raises a hand to tap again so that when she suddenly lowers the window he almost falls inside the car. His vast, dilapidated gabardine coat exudes tidal waves of dog-end and unhygienic age. She tries not to think how in styling if not scent it resembles the coat of the competent stranger on the Metro. He glowers — 'You again' — and waves at the road behind the car. 'You hit Henry. I was a witness,' he adds with authority.

'Henry?' repeats Grace, struggling to fit this name to the saintly wife.

'Cat.'

She falls back in her seat. Cats aren't reportable. You can just drive on if you hit a cat.

The witness has gone. She toys with the keys, thinking, go, go now — before you disturb anyone else, before lights came on in number eighteen and something much worse happens. Like Laurence discovers you outside his house, and he's on the kerb in his pyjamas, with the saintly Rozalind (who isn't dead after all) in her nightie (something foul in a fleecy floral print) and she looks at me and then at him and sees it all, and he ends it like he's always said he would if she found out.

'Oi,' calls the old bloke, far too loudly, 'he's twitching.'

She gets out of the car, hoping her proximity might encourage him to keep his voice down. He is bent low by her back wheel. 'See?' he orders. He glares into her face, causing her to recoil from a killer dose of halitosis.

Now she has taken a few steps and is inhaling the mild air she feels somewhat calmer. 'Right,' she says in a manner she hopes will persuade him to leave everything to her. She peers at the pathetic object on the road, little more than a furry bump. Someone's beloved furry bump. She doesn't like cats. She therefore has no doubt that she would prefer the bump to be dead rather than half alive. Fewer problems all round. And the owners will get another one, they always do. Its eyes are shut, which is a blessing. But Gabardine Coat is right — its paw is moving. Not much, but enough to indicate that the wretched animal has thus far cheated death. 'Shit,' she says. 'Shit, shit, shit.'

Gabardine Coat scowls at this unladylike language. 'Henry,' he says again. 'Number eighteen.'

She staggers. But when he reaches for her, the prospect of being touched — let alone supported — by this decrepit person has a salutary effect. 'You know them?' she enquires as casually as she can. 'The people at eighteen?'

'I know Henry,' he says with an emphasis intended to convey greater faith in cats than human beings. 'Talks to me. Sits on the veranda, sometimes comes down to the pavement, lets me stroke him.'

'And the er . . . people?' prompts Grace, heart in mouth.

He shrugs sagging gabardine. 'Dunno their name. Dunno what he does.' Grace has to stop herself from telling him. 'Talk to her sometimes. We talk about Henry. He's old.'

As if to underline his status Henry waves the paw again, and then suddenly, shockingly, opens his eyes. The old man bends lower still. 'There, old boy, okay, Henry? You'll be hunky-dory, won't you, poor old boy . . .' All accompanied by firm strokes down the full length of the cat's body, which, now it isn't dead, strikes Grace as outrageously obese. She can't believe this stroking is proper practice, either — the animal must be injured, possibly internally, and shouldn't be touched or moved. But before she can say anything to this effect she hears loud purring. Cat and man seem so deeply engaged that she risks a backwards step. It isn't Laurence's wife breathing her last (she registers then banishes a moment's regret), no lights have come on in eighteen nor any house nearby; no one else has appeared on the street; the cat is not only alive but, to judge from its purrs, ecstatic (cats surely don't purr on their death-beds?); it has a champion in the old man; and it can hardly have damaged her car, which probably has little more than a few tufts of ginger fur in the tyre tread.

She has started up the Saab and is about to ease away from the kerb when the old bloke, who can move with startling speed when he wants to, sticks his head in the window again. 'What's your name, then, case of emergency?'

She pretends to be deaf and engages first gear. But it occurs to her that if she refuses to part with a name he might just be compos mentis enough to note her registration number and have her hunted down. 'Roz,' she calls in the manner of someone with nothing to hide. 'Rozalind Cowan.' And she accelerates triumphantly down the road, Clipboard reminding her that families who own a pet are twenty-two per cent more likely to feel hopeful about their lives. Grace wonders if a goldfish would do the trick.

Susan Wylie

Lolly

TELL ME YOUR STORY, I say. And she does. Again. And each time doors, windows, journeys open onto scenes that become almost familiar but shift each time. There are trains, wagons, ships and long muddy roads. Rooms, houses, entire cities flash past. People with fantastic names and even stranger roles wander in and out, pursuing stories of their own. Last time she told me her story, a man in a violet coat suddenly rode through it on a bicycle — one of those old-fashioned ones with a wicker basket. He didn't walk, he cycled everywhere and when he didn't cycle he stood still.

But how did he eat? I asked her.

He only ate outside, standing. His aunt brought his meals to the window. Or he ate a roll as he cycled, his feet going round and round as he chewed. I can't remember.

So he wasn't quite right then, a bit mad?

Perhaps, although he seemed quite sensible to me. He just liked to be on the move.

Lolly admires movement. Above her kitchen bench her wall flutters with photos from magazines, catalogues and newspapers. A dancer nearly nude, magnificent in his flight, all muscle and sinew. A sprinter, head back as she crosses the line and tangles the tape at her heart. A traveller with a case and a heavy coat. A scribble of crayon by a grandchild looks like a guide's map through the forest. A snowy heron lifts from a wharf. A bicycle.

Lolly has been a beautiful child of motion herself, at times a runner, an ice skater, always a dancer. She has shown me the few photos she took when she left her home, but it's the stories that are the real measure of her life. These happen on baking day. I do her grocery shopping and then arrive at her tiny bowerbird flat to breathe in the scents: a loaf of bread, perhaps cinnamon rolls, a cake or two, a tray of biscuits.

This is how a fine Saturday is: we sit on her narrow balcony, subject only to sun and a glancing breeze, we sip strong black coffee and break open the steaming, yeasty, sweet-spice hearts of cinnamon rolls.

There is a view of windy hills and tumbling houses. If you lean out, you can see the edge of the railway yards and often a sliver of a train making its way through the tangle of lines. Her flat is in one of the older blocks, built with the sturdy pragmatism of a thrifty council. Cupboards are what the designers did best here; they do what they are designed for — a nook for the telephone, a thin space for brooms and up high, shelves for suitcases, boxes, things to keep. There's a whole wall of them in the kitchen, a surprisingly large space in such a small flat, but it was constructed in a time when it was the one place a lot of work was done. The balcony, however, is an after-thought. People didn't live outside then; they had too much to do in the kitchen. So there's barely space for us and our chairs and a couple of blossoming plants. In the neighbour's there's just a cage with a singing canary.

It started with my mother, who coerced me: Gina, take Lolly out, take her shopping, give her a hand, I'm sure you can fit it in. I had thought of arguing. I could pretend my weeks were busy so why should I be hauling some dear little old lady around? But I did it. Of course before this there was an introduction. My mother believes in doing things the right way, and that I still need help sometimes to knock on a stranger's door. I went with her for tea at Lolly's. Instead of the frail wee thing I had expected, this upright, very direct woman opened the door. Elderly but still vital, with a halo of pretty white hair, startling pink lipstick and clothes in coloured layers as if she were planning for sudden changes in the weather.

We became friends quickly. She told me later it was because I reminded her of her favourite sister, as she was then, left behind in another time and place. Lolly might have been as old as the grandmother I never knew (and maybe that was my mother's idea, too) but she treated me like that long-lost sister. I simply was drawn in. I had other places to be and — lately more often — someone to be with, but I found the time. Soon I was helping her with her shopping, finding out that her favourite Chinese greengrocer had the freshest vegetables in the neighbourhood, and learning to sniff for freshness and ripeness without bruising the fruit. That a small, shabby café has better coffee than its shiny counterpart in the mall. How I should avoid that supermarket as she found weevils in the bins once, and that I should go to this store or that because they actually carry your parcels to your car (in her case a taxi or my car).

Soon I took her dancing. Or did she take me? One day she told me, in that direct way of hers, that she would dance again, try the place out after reading about it in a free paper she'd picked up at a café. So we go dancing each Wednesday evening. After watching three sessions of her showing the young men the right way to hold a woman, I was no longer sitting on the hard benches lining the hall. I took my first dance steps with Lolly demonstrating (and flirting a little) to the boys with eager eyes but slower feet. She holds her diminished height well as she dances the steps — the salida, the ocho, the cortada — sedately, in a way that forces the young men to bend and wait. It is a gracious way to alter the world.

It is easier for Lolly being with younger people; she doesn't share many of the old days, good or otherwise, with the old people in the flats. I listen a lot and speak little, which makes a difference. Everyone seems to spend so much time talking, filling the air with themselves, whereas I am shy, one of the quiet people whom others mistake for wise or stupid. I teach mathematics in a high school. That is all of me that I need to tell people. As soon as that explanation is out of my mouth, they groan (sometimes roll their eyes) and complain about long-gone maths teachers, or how the smartest guy at maths was sad and lonely, or how they struggled with algebra but who needs it anyway? They tell me these stories about their failures with something approaching pride, as if there's a club of useless maths students they belong to, as if I should be interested, which sometimes I am if it helps me work out a problem one of my own students might be having. But I have heard it all, really, and I know algebra is hard for you in the way talking about myself is hard for me. It's not something that occurs to me. My maths does. So in my head there's a timeline I am calculating, a little faulty, of all the things Lolly tells me, the ordinary things such as birth, childhood, marriage, family. And her major sins: flirting, running away, being happy all of the days of her life.

It was the gypsy in Lolly that admired the violet man on his battered bicycle, who slept in a tent summer through winter, although in winter the tent was erected in a barn for shelter from the snow. He slept with his bike so he didn't have to walk too far before he could ride again. When he finally replaced his bicycle after the wheels buckled under the strain of one last kilometre, he set it in the garden, slightly aloft, so the wind could spin the wheels and the bike could whirl along to wherever it had to go, taking part of him with it.

She told me this on a cold wet night, after we had come back from dancing in a chilly church hall. Her father was proud of his house with its lovely tiled floor in the entrance. One day a piglet escaped and ran squealing through the hall, which made her mother angry as it skidded muddy marks all over the floor she had just polished. Everyone was laughing and trying to catch the piglet. The man dropped his bicycle in front of the animal to stop it going through the gate. Her mother had thanked him awkwardly, as no one really knew what to say to him any more.

He took his hat off and bowed before picking up his bicycle. Then he tenderly brushed it off, adjusted the seat and plucked at a spoke — just as if it were a child that had fallen. But I haven't told you about him yet, have I?

And she told me about him: a short journey into the story of his coat, why he wore it, and the love of his life whom everyone had remembered from years back, when she had died in his arms of some fever. He never spoke after that — that anyone knew.

Madness is its own planet, Lolly said. She says that about Love too. There are places you can be with their own rules, where normal rules don't apply, where the wrong thing is right, where nonsense is wisdom.

Like baking, really — love and foolishness. We can buy bread, cakes, but perhaps not in the flavours she desires. So I guess the baking is an excuse for my company, a reason to talk. I don't have many places better to be, other than in my own flat, the library. My few friends are slipping into marriage and children leaving me in an awkward, in-between place of troubled romance. Lolly said dancing would be good for me. She was right. I felt more uncomfortable sitting there watching. It's easier to move, to meet people when you have something in common. Even better as dancing requires so little talking. My brain has nothing to do but follow. I admire the way everyone's feet move, carving patterns on the floor, like geometry, algebra, equations, everything arriving at a solution. Yes, I admit: I do it because it's good for me.

So what are we dawdling for? she says, and we carry on.

She decides on the recipes, the flavours. I do the hard work, creaming butter and sugar until we can no longer hear the scratch of sugar on the bowl. She will roll out dough because she has a special technique, which she shows me each time so I can take over and she can cut out the stars, ducks, trees. And people: gingerbread men. She arranges the shapes on the trays, pushing away my efforts to have neat rows, with a flick of her bony wrist. Her hands are curling with arthritis and blotched with age. Mine look empty, unmapped territory by comparison. I bend to put trays in the oven, but she will check whether they are just the right shade of tan before getting me to bring them out to cool on the table by the window.

She gives away a lot of our baking, feeding bewildered people she acquires. I have seen her open the door of her flat into the lobby three floors up, to thrust a parcel of cake into a neighbour's hands as they leave on their way downtown. They have to go all the way back to their flats and I wonder how many miss their bus because of our baking. I know she delivers some to the city mission for the old guys to have a treat. There's enough to go around.

As we stir, blend, sift, measure, pour, shape, bake, smell and taste we talk. It is usually her story, or more of it is hers than mine. It's repeated each time with a twist. Like a cake where the basic method and ingredients are the same (cream butter and sugar) but this time lemon, last time cinnamon. Like a riff in a jazz tune, a change to steps in a dance. I forget the annoying things during the week: my students who grumble and procrastinate and approach their passions sideways like crabs. And lovers who do likewise. I can ignore all that when Lolly tells her stories.

Lolly's story goes — loosely, roughly, excluding most of the ancillary scenes, time shifts and characters — like this.

I was a girl in the far edge of Poland at a time when many women still wore skirts to the ground and horses were transport if you had money. We heard rumours of motorcars, trucks, tanks with fortified walls, but as these came from the west or the war, they were most probably lies. I walked barefoot in summer and in knitted woollen socks and clogs in winter. My mother and father had a proper house in the village, with a fence, a garden and a larch tree with a swing. I had brothers and sisters then. Not now, no longer; I am the crumb that is left from the table.

We would crowd the table at dinner time, letting the men and boys eat the most because they had been working the hardest. We grew most of our own food. I would fetch eggs from the hens with my sister, the vegetables from the garden. We would take a basket and off we'd go, across the yard, past the milk cow, the pigs and the large patch of summer vegetables.

I was quite pretty — don't believe these wrinkles and twisted knuckles. I had rosy cheeks, good teeth and long brown hair that my mother only cut once each spring to look tidy for the festival, so by the time I left it was down to my knees. I was vain about my hair. The way it curled in summer, the way I braided it in winter. I am glad I enjoyed that vanity, as look how little of it I have left. I went to school where I learned to read and write. I had many friends, girls and boys, and a few enemies, but we were babies so there was nothing very terrible in our battles — perhaps their smell, or the friends they had, or the street they lived in. And there was plenty of opportunity to fall in and out of love with children you had known forever.

The schoolroom was heated during the long winter by a tile stove in the corner; the best pupils got to sit close to it. I failed tests sometimes — not enough to disappoint my parents, but just so I could stay in the middle of the room, where the temperature was nice and I could see the fields out the window. We ran out there in summer and played our games. But in winter everything was under snow, like a white page. Then it was a harsh place. As you walked home, the wind would cut your flesh to pieces. You could get lost and die in the woods. People did, and as time went on more and more people were lost in the woods. I loved the dark-eyed boy who sat in the chilly far corner.

She pauses there, lost in a time when love was its own planet. The boy didn't have soft rosy cheeks or a smell of sweat. He was dry and lean and more interested in working the fields than learning lessons. But her parents betrothed her to Tedor, a boy who sat right next to the stove. A large, fleshy boy with a damp touch. He was kind, she said, but stupid. Tedor could not say no to anyone. In his kindness he was cruel. He slid through life as a pleasant, compliant man. He would side with the enemy, she was eventually to learn without surprise. He listened too much to his mother, then his teachers. And when his young wife didn't know what to say to him a lot of the time, he went back to listening to his mother, who of course found fault with Lolly, even though she had promoted the match. But there was always something about a bride that could and should be improved on by a caring husband. Not having babies was the most obvious error.

Babies, laundry, housework. Lolly laughs. If I have time to read, then I should be having babies; if I arrange flowers, babies. It wasn't that we didn't try, but there was no eagerness, no liveliness, and what baby would decide to come into a family like that? She laughs again: Hah!? A question mark rises from the end of it — a small part of her is going back to that house in the village to ask if she had done the right thing, an ear still tugged by the dissatisfaction of the mothers (her own mother also joined in).

So I left, she says with a little bounce in her chair. She pours more coffee and pulls another soft layer from her roll and pops it into her red-lipsticked mouth. I get up, stretch and go into the hot kitchen to put ginger biscuits into the oven. I know what's coming, but expect something new. I open a window a little to let in some breeze. It looks out onto a world that isn't really there, the hills wavering, vanishing as a snowy village appears.

I didn't leave at the first opportunity, oh no! she tells me with theatrical surprise. There was a carpet merchant, dark-eyed, prosperous, who tempted me with rose sweets. Then an artist, a portrait painter, fair as an angel, wickedness flirting around his soft mouth. She often giggles at this point. But what about her first love? Was he married? Dead in the woods? I never remember to ask.

These men passed through the village on their way from wherever to somewhere else, wooing as they went and leaving no regrets, except hers. She regretted that they could go, travel, get away from the small village where nothing changed. She had the courage to go with any of them, but she also saw in them a willingness to settle. Their mothers' words were hooked onto their ears. They wanted to stay in the pretty village by the river more than they wanted to stay with her, while she wanted to go, but not to leave. If she could parcel up all that she liked most about the place and put it on a train and take it with her, it would be easy.

    I loved my village, the forests where we would go mushrooming, the river where the boys would fish, the church with the candles and prayer. My mother would go there to pray about everything: to ask for the chickens to lay, for bigger vegetables or a good fruit crop, for work for my father and brothers, for a neighbour to stop gossiping, for a warm summer or a mild winter. She asked Mary for everything. They were like two women chatting over their shopping list. And just when I would get ready to sneer at her blind faith (the way young people do, such fools we are) it would happen: the eggs would come in such excess we would sell them at the market; likewise, vegetables and fruit, and we girls would be preserving, pickling, drying, or bartering it for buttons or cloth, or giving it to the needy. Father was never without work for long. And I heard her praying often for me (so loud I could hear, so embarrassing I blushed) to be a good wife and mother. Everyone knew what she meant. Her prayer was answered, too, only not in the way she had hoped!

    When Lolly left her home, her husband, her family, it was for a musician, a slender brown accordion player. Karol. The phrase 'my mother says . . .' never tumbled from his solemn mouth. His mother was so long dead she was a myth. He was his own person. She could tell by his eyes — sad, soft and often closed as if he were dreaming up a new tune or chord to himself. She danced with her plump, wheezing husband (of course he ate more of her cinnamon rolls than he should) and watched the musician dreaming his music.

    What did he play? I ask, and she tops up the coffee. Red, yellow and blue flowers bloom around the cup.

    Oh, the old tunes, folk songs you might call them, to help the old people remember and sing, and some new music from the cities so the young ones could be shocking. She laughs again and it's the laugh of a young woman.

    So what happened?

    The musicians stayed for the festival, for a week. I liked his music first, then his smile, then the way he looked at me, with respect. I spoke to him often. He was intelligent and adventurous. We would meet in the village square and talk, sometimes just about the weather. I was a well-thought-of wife with a solid, kind husband so there was no gossip. In just one week, we decided so much about each other. So romantic. And when I left, it was not with Karol. I waited a whole month, and then told everyone I was visiting my cousin in the city, where I went only to catch the next train out, almost doubling back, to find him. I did not return to our village until much later — when the regrets had been overtaken by another war, a famine, cruelty and many frozen years. It was strange going back: nothing was the same. It is easier to keep moving forward.

I wrote to my mother a few times but never got a reply, then I wrote to my favourite sister. She told me our mother was angry at me and would not talk to me again. My sister had made matters worse by marrying someone my mother didn't know — an engineer who worked on bridges so had to move around. We broke up the family, my sister and I; we should have stayed in the village, furnished our mother's home with more grandchildren, kept her close. She couldn't go anywhere, and was perhaps afraid of growing old alone there, of never seeing us again. The world outside doesn't really exist when you have lived in the same place forever. In some ways I wasn't leaving: I simply had somewhere else to go. I was more afraid that if I stayed, I would become rooted to that spot like some old tree.

I took trains and buses, asked about the band in many train stations and town squares, until I found them playing at another festival. His eyes were closed but I stared at him so hard he imagined I had come for him, and his eyes opened with tears of joy when he saw me standing there. Everything I owned was in one small suitcase. I had taken some pictures from home, just one or two of the family, my favourite sister, the village overlooking the river and fields. Enough to remember. Nothing of my husband or my own house, and it had been a comfortable house, I had been lucky there, but I would need to forget those quickly.

Ahh! Karol. He was like a cinnamon roll, she says. Soft outside, and warm and spicy inside with a melt of butter. He died a few years ago. Of joy, she says, of utter happiness. This strong, lively man who did not remember a single word of advice from his mother about women died quietly in his sleep next to his wife, after playing in a band for the wedding of the granddaughter of a close friend, a fisherman, in Wellington. So far from where they began.

There's a photo in the hall that she has pointed out to me many times: musicians in hand-tinted pastel, young and sombre, with a girl standing to one side holding up a tambourine dripping ribbons and sound. There I am, she tells me each time, as if she's not sure I remember. She is a tall girl, pretty, her eyes alive as if there were a cathedral of candles inside her. Her hair is short, a dark line at her neck. She has told me before, and will tell me again someday, that he cut it for her and they sold the hair to a wigmaker for a lot of money. It was a sign of their new freedom, she will say. He is seated next to her, his accordion on his lap half-opened. Despite his stiff pose, the moustache and the old-fashioned suit with the waistcoat and ribbons, he looks modern, like someone I might know. A nice young man with dark dreaming eyes, his hair slightly mussed as if she had just run a hand through it for fun.

They travelled around with the band to villages, towns and cities, playing at festivals, parties, on street corners. Anywhere to make music or money, whichever was more urgent. They had nowhere particular to be. Wandering around after playing one night, they heard a new sound. Tango. He heard it with a musician's ear, his eyes shut to memorise the lines of notes; she heard it with a dancer's body and, eyes opened, watched the steps revolving on the floor. A bittersweet sound that makes you happy, then sad; that invites you to dance or make music or simply sit still and enjoy; that helps you to remember and to forget. Karol took his accordion and learned, from anyone he could, how to play these songs from the new world, but with the old world still lingering in their walls.

The music brought a new idea for us, she says. That there was an ocean so wide that it would take weeks to cross. We had seen lakes so large they might as well be seas, and we glimpsed the Mediterranean once from a train — that surprising colour and those sun-baked islands. But we didn't know anyone who had ever left Europe, or come back. First we had to imagine an ocean, and people closed for weeks inside a boat bringing their music in instrument cases, furled like a secret national flag. This is how the music always sounds to me: in red, yellow and black. I learned to dance the steps, alone, to my lover's playing. I learned to dance with other men, always trusting that as long as Karol's eyes were closed he was with me.

She shuts her eyes sometimes and sways, still dancing with him through black, red and into a gold as bittersweet as autumn. Sometimes she will get up and put on a record, but today the breeze is enough.

This dance brought us here, strange to say. Karol hardened himself against the fear of being buried alive in a boat's hold and got a job in a ship's orchestra. I was a lady hostess, dancing with the lonely men who would try for their fortunes in South America.

When she tells me this, each time I see that space between strangers that she would cross with confidence, charm, small talk, laughter even. I admire how she does it now, picking up the steps all these years later. She had not danced since Karol died. Years of motion without grace. Until I took her to that draughty hall. It was the least I could do.

Karol fell in with the sailors, she says, and learned about ships and engines and explored the oily caverns. By the time we arrived in South America he was on his way to a trade. Ships are women; he always admired women. We stayed for a time learning the language, the food, the music. Learn a new language and gain a new soul, they say. We did. He sailed up and down the coast on freighters, picking up new tunes at each port and making rough sailors gentle with music. But it wasn't home, so it was never safe — always something, some trouble. Money, papers. People.

She holds her breath and I can only imagine a world gone mad.

So! We came here. Gypsies in a place where everyone has come from somewhere else, so it doesn't matter, it becomes home. Lolly's palms pat a rhythm, one-two one-two-three-four, on her thighs. Swirls of flour waft up from the orange marigolds on her apron. Ahhhh! She breathes again and settles to enjoy the sun. She is everywhere and in one place.

Where are you? I ask.

Here and there. Here with you, my lovely young friend. But also with him on the ship, and at our marriage, where only our landlady and a fisherman came. We were so happy in our little room. The iron bed was like a warm brown nest. And he is with me in this flat. He is my love in the village and he is the old man in here. She holds her hand over her heart. And when I see my sons, he is their fine father. A fine father. It doesn't matter where you go, you can keep it all with you.

She looks at me straight, her blue eyes clouded with age, as if everything she has ever seen sits there in layers across the cornea, able to be watched at a moment's notice like a magic lantern show. Arriving here, making their home, finally acquiring furniture, things to put into cupboards, books, children, reasons to put photographs in frames. Karol worked on ships, ferries, boats of all kinds, oiling and fixing them, making them seaworthy. Lolly worked in a bakery making cakes that to her were foreign and therefore exciting, but she has returned to the recipes she learned from her mother. Her three sons are scattered across the world, working, married with babies. Living their lives, she says. One son has gone to live near where it all began.

Like a circle — no, more like a Möbius strip, I say, then show her, as I do to entertain and amaze my students. I tear a strip of baking paper, flipping one end of the paper to close the circle. See, it's like a figure of eight, Lolly, a never-ending winding loop.

You need to get out more, Gina, she says.

I laugh and pick at a ginger biscuit, still warm, sweet, sharp. I have huddled my struggling heart inside its cracked shell for a while now. It is a familiar way to be.

There are good men out there, she instructs, wagging a thin, crooked finger at me. You need to be having adventures. But you won't find them in here, in this kitchen with me. Pat, pat. A puff of flour rises up, marigolds dance, a violet man wheels by disguised as a cloud, the wind twists washing and startles the trees. I want to argue, you're wrong, I want to say, but the oven timer shrilly interrupts and everything settles back into place.

That night I dream. I am a bird, living in a world of birds above the earth, under the open ceiling of the sky. We are part of no one's lives but our own, but they are part of ours, those land-born, gravity-fed others. We believe in air, sun, branch, nest, seeds or a scrap of bread and the sudden thrill a turn of the wing can deliver. I wake up and understand the violet man with his endless bicycle. Love and madness. I had been trying to fall in love with a man who wouldn't learn to dance with me, perhaps ideal in every way but that. I end it with him within an hour of waking up.

I don't need to tell Lolly. She knows by the way I walk in the door the next Saturday morning and say Oranges! Mr Ngan had new season's oranges in the shop today! and hold up a gleaming gold planet.

Spiro Zavos
Always Marry Up

'Bless me, Father, for I have sinned.'

'Yes, my son.'

In all of his previous confessions Stathos had paused at this opening mantra before inventing some worthwhile sins to confess. 'I have lied about four times,' he'd lie. Now the pause was real, not a fake intake of breath. He was conscious of a tightening in his throat. His palms were sticky. He could hear from outside the confessional box the murmuring of voices and the shuffling of people moving around the vast interior of St Mary's Church. How should he describe to the priest what happened two days ago with Lauren, last Saturday night in fact, at the Majestic Theatre while they were watching *To Catch A Thief*?

Sitting in the darkness that somehow isolated him from the rest of the audience he had become aroused when Grace Kelly provocatively asked Cary Grant, 'Do you want a leg, or a breast?' She held up a piece of a roast chicken and smiled in an ironic, flirty manner. Take both! Stathos wanted to shout. He dropped his arm, which had rested casually around Lauren's shoulder. He touched her breast, ever so slightly. As if the contact were accidental. Lauren did not react. Emboldened, Stathos dropped a hand onto Lauren's lap. She adjusted her glasses, which she had put on after the film started, peered at the screen and placed her hand on his. During a car chase scene along a winding road scythed into the rocky mass of the Alpes Maritime, with Grace Kelly's scarf streaming in the wind while her hair remained unruffled, Stathos moved his hand on its own exciting journey over Lauren's skirt. Ever so slowly, to prevent an ice-crackle of her petticoats, it gently jerked, like the car on the screen manoeuvring its way around the tight corners, up along her stockings — how hot and coarse they felt — to the cool, marble-smooth flesh of her thigh.

'Yes, my son. How long has it been since your last confession?'

It was just his luck to get Father Mahoney. Father was famous — infamous? — for his tough attitude to 'sins of the flesh'. Stathos could see his huge, vein-seamed nose through the gauze grille of the confessional.

On the ledge under the grille, on Father Mahoney's side, there was a copy of *Turf Digest* and a bag of mints. Father Mahoney's face contorted into a gorgon twist as he crunched down hard on a mint.

'I think, Father,' Stathos said, conscious that he was stonewalling, 'I think perhaps . . .'

'Yes, son. You think perhaps what? Get on with it, my son.'

'It's been about two months, Father.'

'Good, my son.'

Six months, actually. That was the time he had met Lauren at Tom Turner's engagement party.

'It's been two months, Father, since my last confession and in that time I've been guilty of telling lies three times using bad language I suppose ten or so times Father many times anyway using Christ's name in vain and—' There was nothing for it now but to stop the gabble and confess his real sin. 'I've kissed and pashed and touched up a girl, Father, and I've abused myself.'

Stathos paused while Father Mahoney's crunching intensified. 'A few times, Father,' he said, barely whispering out the words.

'Whart!'

'A few times, Father.'

'Pashing?'

'Fondling, Father. Sinful fondling.'

'Is that all, my son?'

'I think so, Father.'

'Tink.' Father Mahoney was inclined to lapse into an Irish brogue during awkward confessions. 'Tink? Remember, my son, your bardy is the temple of God. When you're tempted, always think of the Virgin Mary. You wouldn't want her to see you doin' somethin' sinful, now, would you. Would you?

'No, Father.'

'Now, this abuse. Did anything come out?'

'Come out where, Father?'

'Your penis, son. Not your hat! Penis, son. While you were fondling, abusing and, as you say, pashing.'

Stathos thought that if he replied in a murmur, Father Mahoney might stop his bellowing. 'Enough to make a small stain on my pants, Father.'

'Can't hear. Speak up, my son.'

'A small stain, Father. On my pants.'

'Whart! You must have been pullin' like a Clydesdale. Mortal sin, young man. Mortarl sin if anything comes out! Don't let anything come out. It's the coming out that is the sin. Spreading your seed like Onan. You understand? No? Well, if you play around down there

there's not much problem. The problem starts if something comes out. We can't have that. The precious semen is for the procreation of babies. Do you want to go to hell? Well? Weeellll?'

'No, Father.'

'No, Father, quite raight. You must never have anything to do with this slut again. She is an occasion of sin for you. I'll wager she's not Cartholick.'

'No, Father, she's not.'

Father Mahoney popped another mint into his mouth. He glanced down at his *Turf Digest*, a look Stathos thought replete with wistfulness. 'Say three Hail Marys, then,' Father Mahoney said, his voice firm but kindly, 'say three Hail Marys. Make a firm purpose of amendment. And say a little prayer for me.' Father Mahoney began to patter a rush of words of absolution in Latin.

From his Christian doctrine classes at his secondary school, St Patrick's, Stathos had learnt that loving the sin, not the sin itself, was the real evil. He loved his sinning with Lauren. There was no way he could make a vow never to sin with her again.

'I'm meeting her, Father, right after I've finished here. In the Botanic Gardens,' Stathos blurted out.

'You are what?'

'Meeting Lauren after this confession in the Botanic Gardens.'

'You understand, young man, the notion of the occasion of sin? It is a sin to go somewhere where you are likely to commit the sin.'

'I've arranged to meet her, Father, and that's what I'm going to do.'

There was an explosion of sound from the priest's side of the confessional booth. 'Out of my confessionarl, raight now!' Father Mahoney bellowed.

Stathos made a clumsy exit, tangling in the confessional curtains. The line of penitents waiting to confess to Father Mahoney — several plump women in felt hats and old tweedy coats and a couple of elderly men in suits — looked at him in a mixture of amazement and bewilderment. There was some shaking of heads. They turned and watched Stathos genuflect in rote fashion at the door of the church before pushing through the heavy wooden doors leading to the porch.

Outside the church a hard sunlight seared into Stathos's eyes, like the fires of hell, forcing him to blink and avert his head as he made his way down Manners Street towards the Cable Car and the Botanic Gardens.

Professor Wesley Blackstone swept into the lecture theatre, drew his black gown around him so that he resembled a crow and in a high-pitched voice silenced the hundred or so chattering students arrayed in front of him in tiered rows with the greeting, 'Good afternoon, lady,' and he made a slight, mocking bow to Lauren sitting in the front row with Stathos, 'and gentlemen.' He looked severely towards the back of the lecture theatre where a handful of suited recalcitrants, law clerks who needed to pass Roman Law before they could gain their Bachelor of Laws degree, were perched on the windowsills. Professor Blackstone made no secret of the fact that he regarded himself as the guardian of the integrity of the legal profession. Students whom he regarded as unworthy of the profession, several every year, were denied a pass in Roman Law, even though they had jobs as clerks with prestigious firms in the business district of Wellington city.

Professor Blackstone wrapped his black gown tighter around himself. He strolled back and forth along the podium like a captain on the quarterdeck. As if speaking to himself he said, 'Take this case and let's tease out some of the principles of Roman Law from it.' He had an intermittent lisp, which converted the pronunciation of the occasional word like 'tease' into 'teath'. There were hisses from the recalcitrant suits.

'Brutus wants to win the Wellington Cup chariot race. He needs the fastest horse in the country to do this. He is a man of ways and meanth. So he approaches the best studmaster in the district, Cassius. Anyway, our ambitious Brututh buys from Cassius the horse Leander, regarded as the fastest in the land. Unfortunately, he is given the wrong horse. Brutus accepts the horse. His payment for it is accepted by Cassius.' There was more hissing from the recalcitrants. Stathos, along with most of the class, turned to see what was happening down the back. 'Turn around, gentlemen,' Professor Blackstone said, looking directly at Stathos. 'There is more to our puzzle. As the wrong horse is leaving the stud farm of Cassius, a bolt of lightning strikes the animal dead. The horse unfortunately lands with a thump on a groom, and kills him. Is it important whether the horse falls inside or outside the gates of the stud farm? Who is responsible for the horse's death? Who is responsible for the groom's death? Has Brutus an action against Cassius for fraud?'

'We have against you, Professor Blackstone!' Stathos heard a student intone from the back of the hall.

Professor Blackstone did not respond to the insult. 'Is there a legimate contract,' he went on, 'between Cassius and Brutus, when the wrong goods, namely the wrong horse, have been exchanged? Does the signing of the contract, in other words, make it valid? Or does there have to be more than the actual signing of the contract involved? Does the selling party have to ensure that the goods being exchanged are the goods the buyer believes he is buying? Or does the buyer have to make sure that what he is buying is what he thinks he is buying? Interesting matterth for consideration, don't you think, lady and gentlemen?'

For about thirty minutes Professor Blackstone and several obviously bright and well-informed members of the class challenged one another in an erudite discussion of the facts of the case. Terms like *mens rea* and *caveat emptor* were exchanged between the men with the easy nonchalance of tennis players lobbing balls to one another before the match. Lauren clearly understood the intricacies of the arguments being bandied about for she had her head down as she took notes in a precise notation. Stathos had difficulty following the arguments and drew a series of boxes on his notepad in frustration.

There appeared to be a resolution of the case, or so it seemed to Stathos, because Professor Blackstone was nodding his approval of a summary by one of the smart students. 'There is, though, something else that has come into play,' Professor Blackstone said, interrupting the smart student. 'Before the chariot race begins, someone lets out the air in the tyres of Brutus's chariot.'

The one o'clock bell sounded, marking the end of class. Professor Blackstone unfurled his gown and swept as magisterially out of the lecture room as he had entered. 'Fair go, Prof,' a recalcitrant yelled out in frustration, 'what's the bloody answer?'

Turning towards the class at the door and in the careful enunciation of a parent to a child, he replied: 'Of course, there were no tyreth in the days of Brutus, were there? Good afternoon, lady and gentlemen.'

In the student café some minutes later Stathos told Lauren he was going to drop Roman Law. He didn't want to be a lawyer. It was something his father had insisted on. He couldn't get decent marks for his assignments from Professor Blackstone. It was clear to him, he told her, that he'd been marked out as a future recalcitrant to be kept out of the profession.

'Are you sure, Stathos?' Lauren said as she waved to a group of her friends at a nearby table. 'What will your dad say?'

'It's his ambition, not mine, for me to become a lawyer. "Of courth there were no tyreth in the days of Brututh." How stupid can you get? The law is stupid. No wonder Dickens said the law is an ass.'

'You have to learn how lawyers think, Stathos. It's a language, just like French or Latin or English. Once you understand the language of splitting hairs, you'll get it.'

'That's okay for you, Lauren. All your family have been lawyers. You live in Roseneath, Blackstone loves you. My father is a fish and chip shop owner.'

Lauren pouted. 'Having a great big log on your shoulder is most unattractive, Stathos.'

Stathos was adamant. 'I'm tossing it in, anyway. That's that.'

Lauren's voice had an anxious lift to it. 'When are you going to tell your dad? You know he'll go berserk.'

'I'll tell him when I tell him. But not right now.'

It had been six months since his mother had come back from Porirua Hospital. The electric shock treatment had aged her irrevocably. It had seemingly melted the mass of her body like wax and then compacted it into distorted, bulging layers of breasts, stomach and thighs. She was no longer angular and fine featured. Stathos saw a dumpy, squat figure with a large U downturn of the mouth and black patches under her eyes stirring the pot of soup. Her stirring action was mechanical. There was a vacant look on her face as if she were bracing herself for an unexpected shock of pain.

'Why you stare?' she said to Stathos. The wooden stirrer in her hand was turned towards him like a dagger.

'Just smelling the soup,' Stathos replied.

'Time you married a nice Greek girl. Soon you be making plenty of monies as a lawyers. You must be thinking about a wife and home. Eh?' His mother had a disconcerting habit of going to the crux of a conversation without indulging in introductory niceties. 'Nice Greek girl make you chickie and limoni soup. Make me a yaya and make Micka a papou.'

'We'll see,' Stathos replied.

'From Sydney. The nice Greek girls are best there.'

'We'll see.'

His mother cut up two lemons and squeezed the juice into a bowl. She broke three eggs and whisked the mixture with a fork for a minute or so. The pale, plasticy colour of the egg yolks turned a vivid yellow. She took chunks of chicken, poured some broth from the pot on it and carefully tipped in the egg and lemon mixture. Then she peppered the soup until its top had a coating of brown.

'For you, your favourite, every time you want.' She pushed the bowl across the table to Stathos. 'If you have a nice Greek wife to make for you. Mother and father won't be here forever.'

He took the soup downstairs to the living room of his flat. The television news showed an anti-Vietnam War march on its way down to Parliament Buildings.

He heard his father come out of the bedroom upstairs. He called out to Stathos from the upstairs landing: 'Missus and me want to find you a nice Greek girl for marry, do you hear? Lawyers must be marry. More respect for them, then. More monies. We'll do the finding if you like. Someone from Sydney, don't you think? No Kiwi girl. A nice Greek girl from Sydney, we're thinking. Okay?'

Stathos spooned the delicious soup into his mouth. He couldn't bring himself to respond. He was thinking of how unlike a nice Greek girl Lauren was.

'We are privileged today,' Professor Jack McGregor told the English II class, about forty students, with roughly equal numbers of male and female students, 'to have the first-rate treat of a wee lecture on the Romantic poets by, in my humble opinion, New Zealand's finest living poet, James K Baxter.'

In his final year at St Patrick's College his Christian doctrine teacher, Father McManus, had told Stathos's class about how this brilliant poet, James K. Baxter, was searching for God through his poetry. And how he had struggled through his arts degree at Victoria University, taking nine years to graduate. The poet was fighting the demons of drink and womanising, Father McManus told the boys. Stathos had an idea of a haggard poet, in filthy clothes, clutching a bottle of sherry that was wrapped in a brown paper bag to hide it. He used this conceit of the down-and-out poet to make several points about the poet as an outsider in his first English I class, in a critique of Baxter's 'A Clown's Cloak'. Stathos got nineteen out of twenty for his critique, a mark that encouraged him to continue into a second year of English literature studies.

But the poet standing in front of the class was nothing like the disreputable, scungy image Stathos had concocted in his mind. He was tiny in stature, with an enormous egg-shaped face. A Humpty Dumpty figure with tiny eyes that slithered along the rows of students rather than looking directly at any one of them. The poet was dressed in a dark blue velvet jacket. There was an oriental look to his appearance, like the face of a scholar in an ancient Japanese print.

Baxter took out from his jacket a packet of thin cigarillos. He put a black stick in his mouth, carefully lit the end, pulled in the smoke down his throat and, looking away from the students at something outside the window, slowly exhaled. His head tilted gently upwards in pleasure. More smoke was exhaled. Then he began talking. Stathos had never heard a more beautiful voice. The nearest equivalent in beauty he could think of was the sonorous tone of the violin played in the middle register by a master like Alfredo Campoli that time in the town hall a decade or so ago in a concert for the schoolchildren of Wellington. Stathos understood for the first time in his life the seductive power of the human voice.

He made notes in his tiny, careful script. Baxter was making a case for the Romantics being different from poets before them because they elevated the worth of the personal experience of individuals above the social experience of communities. The Romantics were freer in their verse structures than Augustans such as Pope and Dryden, he argued.

'The freer the verse structure, the freer the morals of the poet,' Baxter intoned, looking now directly at Lauren. This aphorism provoked a tittering of laughter from the young women in the class. 'I myself am very free,' Baxter went on. More nervous laughter. 'But only in my verse.' Applause and clapping of hands in delight from the young women in the class.

The lecture continued with Baxter reflecting on the rhymed couplet, how its tight closed form reflected a tight closed view of society exemplified by the rigidity of a marble-hard class system. The Romantics, though, were not restrained by class, Baxter insisted. Keats was working class. Wordsworth was middle class. Byron was upper class. Humanity and nature were their gods.

At the conclusion of the lecture, Stathos was so thrilled by what he had heard he felt like standing up to lead the applause. There was a silence, however, before Professor McGregor intervened. 'Most stimulating,' he said, nodding to the poet. He turned to face the class again, 'Time for one wee question, or two, I think.'

There was a silence. That awkward silence that comes when a group have nothing to say to one another yet are conscious of the rift their silence is creating. The silence became as loud as a beating drum. Professor McGregor searched diligently, with beseeching eyes, around the room for someone to speak up. The poet smoked his cigarillo. He stared languidly at one good-looking girl after another before resting his gaze on Lauren, again.

In the silence Stathos recalled a family legend that told how two sons way back in time escaped becoming priests by joining up to fight for Greek independence at Missilonghi with Lord Byron. This memory triggered a question. 'Could Mr Baxter tell us,' Stathos asked, 'whether he places Byron among the Augustans or the Romantics?'

'I would say,' the poet replied, 'that Byron was a Romantic Augustan.' A number of students, including Lauren, turned towards Stathos and laughed at him. They believed the answer was intended to humiliate him.

'No, it was a good question,' Baxter insisted. 'Byron had the heart of a Romantic poet and the mind of an Augustan. He was a passionate opportunist. A desirable combination. We'll leave it at that. The Blessed Virgin watch over you all.'

Baxter and Professor McGregor, heads close together in conversion, strolled out of the classroom.

'A passionate opportunist,' Lauren said to Stathos as they were pushed together by the slow-moving mass of students at the classroom doorway. 'A passionate opportunist. I reckon that's a pretty good description of you, too, Stathos.'

Then she was off striding down the corridor, skip-running to join a group of chattering female students. Was this a compliment or something of a reprimand from Lauren? For the life of him, Stathos had no idea what to make of her comment.

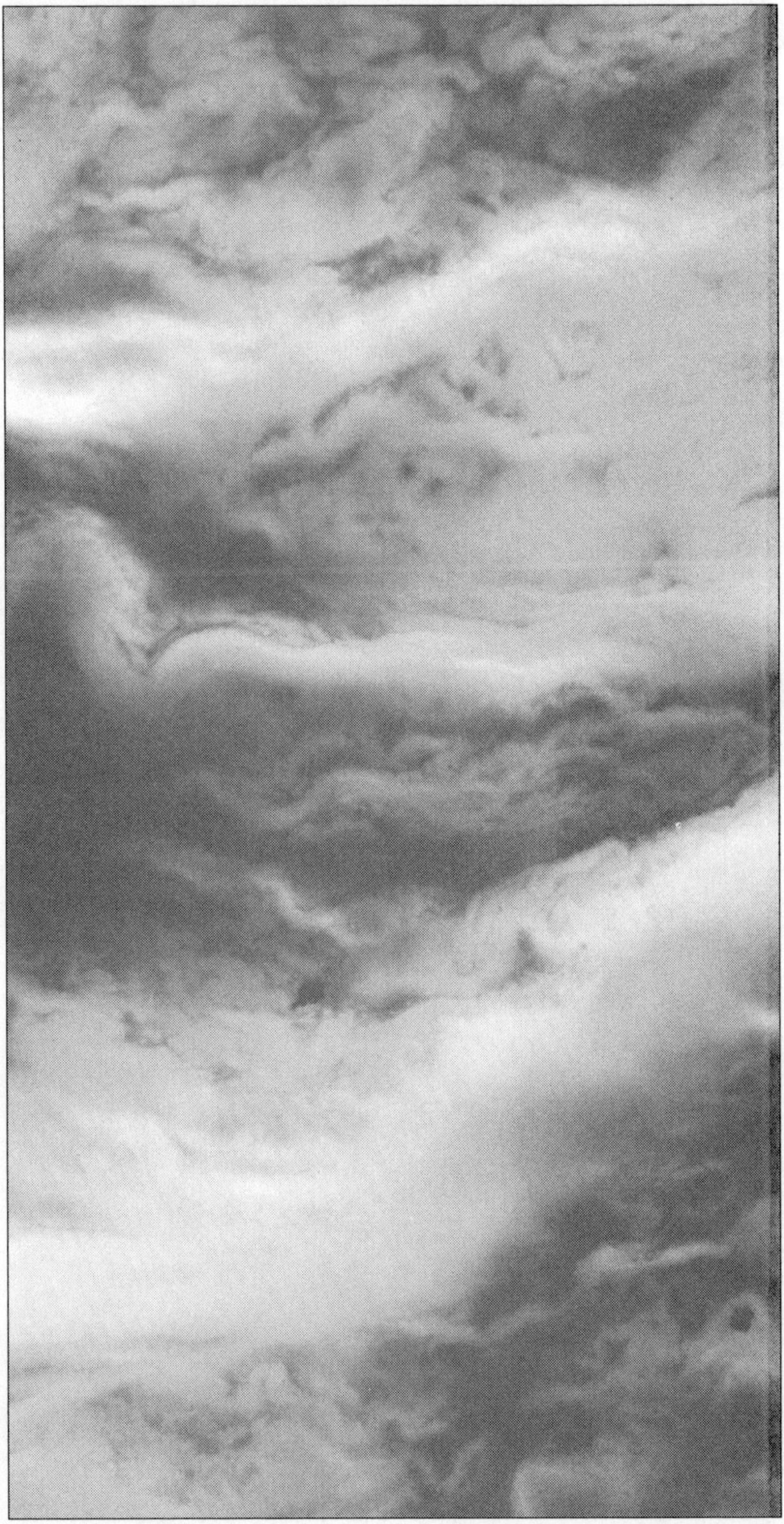

Notes on Contributors

MAXINE ALTERIO grew up in Invercargill and currently lives in Dunedin where she works full-time as a tertiary educator. She is co-author of *Learning through Storytelling in Higher Education*, an academic book published in Britain in 2003 by Kogan Page, and recently acquired by RoutledgeFalmer. Her first fiction collection, *Live News and Other Stories*, was published by Steele Roberts in 2005. Several stories in that collection have won or been placed in short story competitions while others, in slightly different forms, previously appeared in magazines such as the *New Zealand Listener*. Maxine recently completed her first novel, *Ribbons of Grace*, which is set in Orkney, China and New Zealand between 1870 and 1890. A love story between a Chinese woman masquerading as a male goldminer and an Orcadian stonemason, this work explores the themes of identity, dislocation and loss.

* The idea for 'Stories Bodies Tell', which focuses on the concept of abandonment and the notion that human beings can become lost in a variety of ways — physically, emotionally, psychologically and spiritually — arose after I read an article about embalming. The female embalmer talked about her bodies with the same reverence I have for the mountainous Central Otago landscape, which made me think about physicality in a broader sense. Writing this story enabled me to consider some of the interrelationships that exist between our physical and metaphysical journeys.

GEOFF COCHRANE lives in Wellington. He was educated at St Patrick's College, Cambridge Terrace. His books of verse include *Acetylene* (VUP, 2001), *Vanilla Wine* (VUP, 2003) and *Hypnic Jerks* (VUP, 2005). He is also the author of the novels *Tin Nimbus* (VUP, 1995) and *Blood* (VUP, 1997). Some of Cochrane's short stories were collected in the fugitive volumes *Brindle Embers* (Thumbprint Press, 2002) and *White Nights* (Thumbprint Press, 2004).

* The pieces reprinted here seem to belong together. Though

written as discrete stories, they're all the fruit of the same, excessively rich soil. An unnatural soil that dreams. Maybe I look back with too much fondness on my days of addiction to alcohol, my years of addiction to addiction, but I like to make maps of where I've been, and only I can pen them and colour them in correctly. My fanciful charts, my suspect diagrams — perhaps they allow me to drink again without really drinking.

SIÂN DALY lives in Wellington and works by day at the Office of Film and Literature Classification. She is a recent graduate of the MA course in Creative Writing at Victoria University and is currently occupied with two major projects: new motherhood and a novel begun in 2005. The novel is receiving considerably less attention than the motherhood. However, she has been working on a few short pieces, which she also hopes to have published in the near future. Her short story 'Phenomena' appears in the current issue of the online journal *Turbine 05*.

* 'Conan' was inspired by a childhood memory involving a Christmas Day picnic, although the events of the day were somewhat different from those described. While the story is narrated by a child, who describes events simplistically and primarily in the present tense, it contains much that might indicate an adult's memory. Fascination with perfection and its loss, as well as ideas of sin and guilt, forgiveness or punishment, are themes that might colour the memories of an adult recalling a tragic event, especially one for which they feel some responsibility.

SUE EMMS is a Bay of Plenty writer of fiction and poetry. Her work has appeared in literary magazines in New Zealand, England and the US. She has won or been placed in many writing competitions, including in *Takahe*, the *Sunday Star-Times*, and the Richard Webster Popular Fiction Award. Her first two novels, *Parrot Parfait* and *Come Yesterday*, were published to excellent reviews, and her third, *The Kindred Stone*, has also been accepted for publication. Sue is founding editor of *Bravado*, a literary magazine, and is Creative Writing tutor at the Waiariki Institute of Technology. In her spare time she leaps tall buildings in single bounds and catches bullets in her teeth.

* 'The Weakness of Women' came from the collision of two separate ideas. I've been musing for a long time on the army of 'good women' in this country who try so hard to be everything to everyone (in their personal circles), at a cost to themselves. Then I overheard a male friend grumbling that the 'trouble with women is they never want to fix anything. They just talk it to death'. And instantly I thought, no, no no, that's not true. We want to fix everything, for everyone.

TRACY FARR was born in Melbourne in 1962, and grew up in Perth. She has science and arts degrees from the University of Western Australia. She lived in Canada for five years before moving to Wellington in 1996. Her short stories have been published in literary journals in New Zealand and Australia, in the *New Zealand Listener*, in anthologies in print (including *The Best New Zealand Fiction 1*) and online, and broadcast on Radio New Zealand. She's been bridesmaid for short fiction awards in New Zealand and Australia, including runner up in 2001 for the BNZ Katherine Mansfield Award, and received one of the inaugural mentorship awards from the New Zealand Society of Authors in 2000, when she was mentored by the lovely and wise Elizabeth Smither. She is currently working on a novel. She lives in Wellington with her husband and son and, while working in marine research pays most of her bills, she'd really rather stay in bed all day and read.

* 'Surface Tension' is about going home, revisiting past places and times and lovers and memories, and about what's lurking under the surface of your skin and your consciousness when you do. It's set in Perth, where I grew up. Like the character in the story, I've made a home elsewhere — in Wellington. (Unlike her, I've learned to go swimming here. In a wetsuit.) I left Perth fifteen years ago and haven't lived in Australia since, but, while it's different each time I go back, in fundamental ways Perth's still home. Especially Cottesloe Beach.

The story is also about getting older, about the progress and process of life. I started writing it a few years ago now, and created a main character, Helen, older than I am — a sort of putting a toe in the water to see how getting older might feel. Perhaps the tensions I gave Helen in the story are common in middle age: reliving old dreams and past glories; envying/nurturing the lives-to-be-lived of our babies; looking for satisfaction and peace and celebration in the present.

JAMES GEORGE was born in Wellington of Ngapuhi/English/Irish descent and considers Northland his spiritual home. He has completed three novels, *Wooden Horses* (2000), *Hummingbird* (2003) and *Ocean Roads* (2006), and is progressing a fourth, *Theme from an Imaginary Western*, due for completion in early 2007.

* The idea for 'Figures in Ice' came watching young performers at a folk music concert. A speculative remark, as so often happens, set me thinking of a story.

CHARLOTTE GRIMSHAW is the author of three novels — *Provocation* and *Guilt*, published in Britain and New Zealand, and most recently *Foreign City*, published in 2005. She is a past winner of the Buddle Findlay Sargeson Fellowship, and has been named by the *New Zealand Listener* as one of the ten best writers under forty in New Zealand. The story 'Thin Earth' is part of a series of interconnected short stories, titled *Opportunity*, which she is currently working on. Her stories have appeared in the *New Zealand Listener*, the *Sunday Star-Times*, *The Best New Zealand Fiction 2* and *Stand* in the UK. Two stories from the collection were finalists in the *Sunday Star-Times* short story competition in 2005. She lives in Auckland.

* I went on a trip to Wanganui during the summer holidays. It was hot, and parts of the town were virtually deserted. There had been a murder: a young woman's body had been found floating in the river. When I wrote 'Thin Earth' I inserted into this hot, empty, slightly spooky town a character who appears in other stories in my *Opportunity* collection, a woman who leads a sheltered, middle-class life but who looks around for the experience she lacks, a woman both naïve and full of yearning, who, as a result of her solitary jaunts through the town, makes an imaginative leap: she understands what the murder means in emotional terms, and she suddenly perceives where she is vulnerable in her own life.

LLOYD JONES's *Book of Fame* won the Deutz Medal for Fiction and the Tasmanian Pacific Prize. He is also the author of a story collection, *Swimming to Australia*, recent novels *Here at the End of the World We Learn to Dance*, *Paint Your Wife* and *Mister Pip*.

* 'The Thing that Distresses Me the Most' is built around a fragment of something I heard some time ago about a middle-aged professional coming to Wellington for a conference and waking in the early hours under a bush outside the national museum. I laughed the first time I heard that story. It stayed with me I suppose because of its combination of professional honesty and human frailties. This bit of hearsay then became the foundation for the story I wrote.

SUE MCCAULEY has written four novels (*Other Halves*, *Then Again*, *Bad Music*, *A Fancy Man*), two short story collections (*It Could be You*, *Life on Earth*), a non-fiction book (*Escape from Bosnia*), two stage plays and nineteen radio plays. She has also written for film and TV. She is currently working on a fifth novel and learning to be a farmer.

* Not long before I wrote 'Disconnections' my lovely aunt-cum-mother had a smallish stroke. Watching her struggle to keep a grip on her dignity and independence was anguishing and the basis of this fictional story. I introduced the 'trust' material because I'd been hearing rather a lot of troubling stories about that ubiquitous (and iniquitous?) legal invention, the family trust. (There's a pragmatic Presbyterian part of me that feels the act of writing is more justifiable if the material has some kind of wider social relevance.)

I'm proud and delighted to say my aunt recovered and, in her ninety-eighth year, continues to live happily alone.

OWEN MARSHALL — novelist, short story writer and poet — has written, or edited, twenty books, most recently *Watch of Gryphons* (2005). Awards for his fiction include fellowships at the universities of Canterbury and Otago, and the Katherine Mansfield Memorial Fellowship in Menton, France. He received the ONZM for services to literature in the New Year Honours 2000, and his novel *Harlequin Rex* won the Deutz Medal for Fiction in the same year. In 2002 the University of Canterbury awarded him the honorary degree of Doctor of Letters, and in 2005 appointed him an adjunct professor. Marshall has spent almost all his life in South Island towns, and has an affinity with provincial New Zealand.

* 'Patrick and the Killer' is not a subtle story: the characters, language and ideas are all straightforward, and that is part of its intention. Patrick is a very ordinary New Zealander trying to cope with the vicissitudes of life as best he can. The chance involvement with violent Geoffrey Wenn brings good fortune to Patrick through media attention, and he searches for some way to acknowledge that, but is made to realise that life is not fair, but just 'the play of indifferent circumstances'.

CARL NIXON is a full-time writer of fiction. His most recent work for theatre was an adaptation of the Booker Prize-winning novel *Disgrace* by J. M. Coetzee. His new play, *The Raft*, will be produced by the Court Theatre in Christchurch in 2007. Carl's collection of short stories, *Fish 'n' Chip Shop Song*, received outstanding reviews and went to number one on the New Zealand Fiction Bestsellers list. He is the 2006 Writer in Residence at the University of Canterbury. He is working on a novel based on his story, 'Rocking Horse Road', which was joint winner of the 2005 *Christchurch Press* Summer Fiction Competition.

* 'Rocking Horse Road' began as the desire to set a story in the unusual geography of the Spit. For those of you unfamiliar with Christchurch, the Spit really is a long 'finger of bone-dry sand' between the ocean and the estuary in the eastern suburb of New Brighton. Although I didn't grow up in New Brighton, my father did. Perhaps I have sand in the blood. Several other ideas attached themselves like limpets to the Spit: the desire to write a 'literary' murder mystery; an interest in coming-of-age stories (in 1981 I was fourteen); wanting to explore how the events of our early lives impact on the rest of our lives; an interest in the concept of 'collective consciousness' (which is why the story is told in the first-person plural) and, related to that, collective memory and story-telling.

VINCENT O'SULLIVAN is a fiction writer, poet, biographer and playwright, who lives in Wellington. Until recently he taught at Victoria University. He was awarded the Creative New Zealand Michael King Writers' Fellowship in 2004.

* 'Mrs Bennett and the Bears' fell into place from 'real life' in a way that seldom happens with what I write. Several years ago I was in Hokkaido, in the far north of Japan, to speak about the Japanese prison camp at Featherston and the production of my play *Shuriken*. A former student of mine who now managed a number of retirement homes kindly took me to the mountains to see the famous bears. I was staying at a hotel rather like the one in the story, with hang-gliders poised as though in flight in the huge space of the atrium. There was a woman staying at the hotel who made me think of Mrs Bennett, although no doubt she was very different, and it wasn't too hard to think of a New Zealand civil servant visiting Hokkaido. So the pieces were pretty much there, so to speak, and the story fitted itself together.

JO RANDERSON is a Wellington-based writer and performer and author of *The Keys to Hell* (short stories), *The Knot* (an illustrated adults' story) and *The Spit Children* (short stories). Jo is also the author of numerous plays and theatre works that have been performed nationally as well as in Norway, Denmark, Australia, the Czech Republic and Britain. Jo was the Robert Burns Fellow for 2001 at Otago University and received the Bruce Mason Playwriting Award in 1997. She is the founder and artistic director of Barbarian Productions, a touring comedy/theatre company (see www.barbarian.co.nz or www.joranderson.com).

* I started writing 'The Sheep, the Shepherd' when I was

travelling. The combination of exhaustion and the dislocation of journeying thousands of kilometres plunges your psyche into some strange states. It is a similar feeling to when I try to contemplate war — I just get stuck, thinking, why, why does this happen? Why does anyone think conflict is a good way to solve disagreements? So I was thinking about all these things and I started writing this story, and then it just kept coming. Initally there were two paragraphs at the start that were introductory preambles to the philosophical concepts, but I cut those and they're still hanging around waiting to find another piece of writing to go into.

TINA SHAW is the author of five novels, the most recent being *The Black Madonna*, published by Penguin Books in 2005. Her other novels are *Paradise*, *City of Reeds*, *Dreams of America* and *Birdie*. Shaw's short stories have been published in many anthologies, literary journals and magazines, and she was first runner-up in the 2003 *Sunday Star-Times* Short Story Competition. In 1998 she edited a collection of travel essays by New Zealand writers called *A Passion for Travel*. Shaw was a 1999 recipient of the Buddle Findlay Sargeson Fellowship, and has held the Creative New Zealand Berlin Writers' Residency. She was Writer in Residence at the University of Waikato in 2005, and this year she is publishing two junior chapter books.

* 'Julia' was inspired by the 2002 murder of a young Australian woman on Norfolk Island. The description of the woman in the newspaper made her sound vulnerable, yet feisty and outspoken at the same time (it seemed to be implied that this outspoken quality might have contributed to her death) and I found the story particularly moving. I wanted to write about the incident, but in a way that wasn't specifically about the young woman's death. It took me several drafts to get the right idea on paper. I was very interested in showing a young woman who is trying to escape from both the past, and from her old destructive patterns of behaviour, so she can start again. Of course this is a hard thing to do, for anyone, but perhaps Julia will make it.

ALICE TAWHAI has written one collection of short stories, *The Festival of Miracles*, published by Huia. Another collection, *Luminous*, is awaiting publication. Currently, she is working on a third collection and a novel.

* All my stories are written to try to capture some of the images and pictures that are in my head at the time, so that I don't forget them when I think of new ones. And then a story comes to join them

together. I've written two other stories about family violence — 'Dark Jelly', (yet to be published) and 'Sex on a Hill' (published in *The Festival of Miracles*) — and I hope that each story shows the issue from a different point of view. 'Sex on a Hill' is from a man's perspective.

In 'Something Will Change' I wanted to show a relationship affected by family violence between two real and unique people, rather than between two stereotypes, and I hoped it would help explain to some women why they're still there when everyone says they should leave. Family violence is what happens when two sad people find each other.

FAY WELDON, conceived in New Zealand, was born in Britain, returning as a small baby to spend her early years in Christchurch, the Coromandel and Auckland. She went on to read Economics and Psychology at the University of St Andrews in Scotland, and worked briefly for the Foreign Office in London, then as a journalist, before beginning a successful career as an advertising copywriter and subsequently writing full time. Her first novel, *The Fat Woman's Joke*, was published in 1967. It was followed by over twenty other novels, five collections of short stories, several children's books, non-fiction books, magazine articles and a number of plays written for television, radio and the stage. Her memoir, *Auto Da Fay*, was published in 2002. She received an honorary doctorate from the University of St Andrews in 1990 and was awarded a CBE in 2001 for services to literature. She is currently Chair of Creative Writing at Brunel University in London.

* The BBC recently commissioned a group of TV writers to do updates of Shakespeare plays. They turned out most successful: lively and imaginative. Free of the dead hand of script editors, able to cite Shakespeare as their excuse, writers were able to write what was not politically correct or motivationally sound. Very little in contemporary literature or drama surprises any more. Literature is seen, as it was in Russia, and in China, and now increasingly in the West (and Australasia), as a tool for the improvement of the nation: that's why it gets so dull. The story here is much extended: I'd had to cramp it into 2000 words for fifteen-minute radio: I just got it out of its corsets so it could breathe, which it did with alacrity.

PETER WELLS is an author and film-maker. His books include the memoir *Long Loop Home*, which won the Biography Award at the Montana New Zealand Book Awards in 2002, and *Iridescence*, a novel that looks at the hidden history of early settlers in New Zealand. His films run the range from drama to documentary. His latest project has been writing the screenplay for the feature film *Firebird*, a look at the life of Freda Stark, a woman of scandal in New Zealand of the 1930s.

* 'Little Joker Sings' came about through a sense of dissatisfaction with the narrative arc of Annie Proulx's *Brokeback Mountain*. It seems a long time ago that gay men in narratives either had to die violently or end up lonely and tragic. While respecting the setting of her novella — a bleak and conformist landscape in which fundamentalist religion is powerful — I was also aware of New Zealand stories about men who met during World War II and formed strong bonds that were both comradely and erotic. I have heard of these men having relationships over a lifetime. Indeed, Frank Sargeson, one of the key figures in New Zealand literature, stands as a testament to the liveliness of these kinds of (often hidden) relationships. 'Little Joker Sings' is an attempt to write back into history one such story that otherwise might have been elided.

JANE WESTAWAY has published two novels and a short story collection. *Reliable Friendly Girls* (Longacre) won Best First Book at the New Zealand Post Children's Book Awards 1997, and *Love and Other Excuses* (Longacre) was shortlisted for the same awards in 2000. *Good at Geography* (Penguin) also appeared that year. Her short stories have been anthologised and broadcast, and she co-edited the non-fiction anthology *It Looks Better on You: New Zealand Women Writers on Their Friendships* (Longacre 2003). She is co-editor of the review journal *New Zealand Books*, and reviews for the *Dominion Post* and Radio New Zealand's *Nine to Noon*. She lives in Wellington with Norman Bilbrough, and teaches judgement writing for the Institute of Judicial Studies.

* This piece comes from a nearly completed novel, *Available Light*, which covers four days in the lives of Laurence, a middle-aged photographer, his wife Roz, and his younger lover Grace. I'm intrigued by the way people withhold vital truths from those they love in the name of 'protecting' them. All three characters are to some degree guilty of this, and suffer from it, too. And I'm mystified by time — how people handle it, how they use it to bolster up the meaning they give their lives, how it sabotages them. Grace lives in an agonising present, which she tries to escape via a fantasy future. Roz, who has raised two children, helped her husband in his business and looked after his aged mother, lives — not entirely satisfactorily — in the present. And Laurence, under pressure and always running late, has run out of hope; his consolation is the past. I wanted to see what happened to these three — apparently stock — figures, and their perceptions of time and each other, when one of them is seriously injured in a car crash and can no longer stage-manage his life.

SUSAN WYLIE has lived in Wanganui, Christchurch, Wellington and, briefly, Henley-on-Thames. She has been writing for more than twenty years as a public relations professional. She started writing fiction in 1996 after moving to Napier. She has won prizes for her short fiction in Hawke's Bay, and her story 'Lolly' won the Bank of New Zealand Katherine Mansfield Premier Award in 2005.

* This version of 'Lolly' is fuller, more well rounded, while keeping the sense of movement that drove the original story. Lolly is a character who literally followed me around the house as a few details on an index card, and when I sat down to write, she pretty much wrote herself. I have always enjoyed meeting immigrants, learning their different world views and seeing the efforts they make to balance blending in with keeping their identity. Lolly is a mix of some women I knew growing up — when the 'foreigners' were simply neighbours and my friends' mums. Tango, the dance and music she loves, has assimilated many different cultural and musical influences, and is about making a connection, and even a new reality, each time with a different partner. I also was playing with the idea of how we talk about our lives — what we choose to say, what we don't reveal, and how we skip around time and place while keeping the main thread trailing along. And how as listeners, we can never experience the same story. We stay in the present moment: we gaze out the window, wonder about the smallest of details, and image the story from our own experience. No two people hear or read a story in the same way, and we never tell our own story the same way twice.

SPIRO ZAVOS has published a dozen books of fiction, non-fiction, biography and rugby history. His latest book is the bestselling *How to Watch a Game of Rugby* (Awa Press 2005).

* I was sitting at my desk at the *Dominion* newspaper offices writing an editorial when my telephone rang. Kevin Bell, a lawyer and friend, told me I had been awarded the Katherine Mansfield Fellowship for 1978. That was in April 1977. My wife and two young children and I arrived in Menton to take up the fellowship in February 1978. I had decided not to think much about what I would write in Menton before I got there. Writers will tell you that if you go through material too much in your head before writing it down, you may well lose the magic of it. The same thing applies to talking too much about what you are hoping to write. So when I got to the writing room in Menton I decided to fill out a short story I had written for *Landfall*. The short story called 'The Shilling' became a novella called *Faith of our Fathers* which was published by the University of Queensland Press. 'Always Marry Up' is the opening section of the sequel to *Faith of our Fathers*. The setting is Victoria University of Wellington in the late 1960s. The Vietnam War provides an undertow to the main narrative, just as the 1951 waterside workers' lockout was a backdrop to *Faith of our Fathers*. In the sequel, which is now a first draft waiting to be revised and reshaped, the intention is to introduce real people, such as James K. Baxter, into a fictionalised world of the Greek community in Wellington in the 1960s.